# Life and Times in Victorian Weardale

## The Letters of Francis Vickers

Frank Sanderson

Copyright © 2012 Frank Sanderson

All rights reserved.

ISBN:1478274115
ISBN-13:978-1478274117

ACKNOWLEDGEMENTS ................................................................... v

| | | |
|---|---|---|
| 1. | **INTRODUCTION** | **1** |
| 2. | **THE EARLY YEARS** | **9** |

    The Coming of the Railways ............................................................. 10

    Schooldays ........................................................................................ 11

    Greenhead Farm ............................................................................... 12

    Emigration to Canada ...................................................................... 13

    Francis Vickers and Mary Bowman .................................................. 16

    Primitive Methodism in Weardale ................................................... 18

| | | |
|---|---|---|
| 3. | **EIGHTEEN SEVENTY-FOUR** | **21** |

    The Accident-prone Colliery-owners ............................................... 21

    Founding of Stanhope School Board ............................................... 23

    "Manly Conduct and Brilliant Exploits" .......................................... 25

    The Warm-hearted Guardians of the Poor ...................................... 25

    Victorian Criminal Justice ............................................................... 26

    The Letter to George Vickers ........................................................... 27

    The 1874 General Election .............................................................. 28

        *The Liberal Victory in South Durham ........................................ 30*

        *"A Deal of Agitation" ................................................................ 31*

    March Monday ................................................................................ 33

    News of Family and Friends ............................................................ 34

    Weardale to Australia ...................................................................... 35

    "Very Fresh considering their Ages" ................................................ 37

    The Fatal Railway Accident ............................................................. 42

    "All Sorts of Machinery in England" ............................................... 44

| | | |
|---|---|---|
| 4. | **EIGHTEEN EIGHTY-ONE** | **47** |

    Walter Beaumont's Crusade ............................................................ 47

    The Letter to George Vickers ........................................................... 50

    The Duke of Howl John .................................................................. 53

    Family News .................................................................................... 55

    Purchase of Newlandside Farm ....................................................... 56

    The Snowsfield Athlete .................................................................... 56

The Farmers' Distress ............................................................. 58
"Pity without relief is like mustard without beef" ..................... 60
Death of a Flour Miller ............................................................ 61
Liquidation by Arrangement .................................................... 62
Family Quarreling ................................................................... 64
"Your old Mrs Read" ............................................................... 64
The Weather in Weardale ........................................................ 65
   *Caught in a Snowstorm* ........................................................ 65
   *"A Pitiable Tale"* .................................................................. 66
   *The Great Weardale Flood* ................................................... 66

## 5. EIGHTEEN EIGHTY-SEVEN — 69
Queen Victoria's Jubilee .......................................................... 69
Women's Suffrage ................................................................... 71
Farmers Fighting a Losing Battle ............................................. 73
The Stolen Heifer .................................................................... 74
"Blockheads" and "un-English Radicals" ................................. 74
"Stirred with a Candle" ........................................................... 76
The Letter to Thomas Vickers ................................................. 77
"Strict adhesiveness to Truth" ................................................. 78
Radical Leadership for Tenant Farmers ................................... 78
Trade Unionism in Weardale ................................................... 83
House of Lords Reform ........................................................... 84
The Proprietor of Tow Law Auction Mart ............................... 84
Thomas Crawhall: "a Worthy Citizen" .................................... 87
"A Lover of Cattle all his Days" .............................................. 88
"One Farmer Undermining Another" ...................................... 90
The Variable Weather of 1887 ................................................. 92

## 6. EIGHTEEN EIGHTY-NINE — 95
Support for Irish Home Rule ................................................... 95
The Mayor of South Melbourne .............................................. 96
Death of a Champion Wrestler ................................................ 97
Skeeing (sic): The National Sport of the Dale ......................... 97

Opening of Eastgate Memorial Church ............................................. 99
Admiration for Primitive Methodists ............................................... 100
The Letter to Thomas Vickers ........................................................ 101
"Working up to our Promised Years" ............................................. 102
News of Family and Friends ........................................................... 103
Death and Destruction in America .................................................. 105
The Markets ................................................................................... 105
The Weather in Weardale ................................................................ 106
"Tom Tiddler's Ground for Tramps" ............................................... 107
Plight of the Elderly Poor ............................................................... 108

## 7. EIGHTEEN NINETY — 109

A Fracas and a Horse-whipping in Weardale ................................. 109
Another Crisis in the Mines ........................................................... 113
Death in the Workhouse ................................................................. 113
Broken Leg at Shaftwell Head ........................................................ 114
The Letter to Thomas Vickers ........................................................ 115
A Wedding and a Funeral ............................................................... 117
The Influenza Epidemic of 1889-90 ............................................... 118
"Few Prettier Places" ..................................................................... 119

## 8. EIGHTEEN NINETY-SIX — 121

Assaults and Threats at Sandedge .................................................. 121
Sir Joseph Whitwell Pease in Weardale ......................................... 122
The Star of Tow Law ..................................................................... 122
The Letter to Thomas Vickers ........................................................ 125
Age Taking its Toll ........................................................................ 126
"A Great Many Deaths about Stanhope" ....................................... 126
Pease Myers to Eastgate ................................................................ 129
Howl John to Ullswater ................................................................. 130
From Strength to Strength ............................................................. 133
The Weardale Extension Railway .................................................. 134

    *Postscript 1: Death of a Stationmaster* ................................................ *138*

    *Postscript 2: Richard Mews unamused* ............................................. *139*

    *Postscript 3: Sale of Horses, Cobs, and Vehicles* ............................... *139*

    *Postscript 4: The end of The Coach and Little Jimmy* ..................... *140*

    *Postscript 5: Death of Richard Mews* ................................................ *141*

The Snow Storms of 1895 ............................................................................ 142

Stanhope Transformed ................................................................................. 143

## 9.     NINETEEN HUNDRED     147

"Terrible Night on Bollihope Fell" ............................................................. 147

Opening of Institutes in Ireshopeburn and Westgate ................................ 148

An Enterprising Auctioneer ........................................................................ 149

Sensational Property Sale at Wearhead ...................................................... 153

The Letter to George Vickers ....................................................................... 154

The Workhouse Diet .................................................................................... 158

Dr Thomas Livingstone ............................................................................... 158

## 10.     NINETEEN HUNDRED AND ONE     159

The Letter to Thomas Vickers ..................................................................... 160

The Deadly Thunderstorm .......................................................................... 161

The Storm in Weardale ................................................................................ 162

New Town Hall at Stanhope ....................................................................... 162

## 11.     END OF AN ERA     165

Francis Vickers: "A Man of Characteristic Generosity" ......................... 165

A Family Difficulty ..................................................................................... 166

Joseph Vickers: "An out-and-out public man" ....................................... 171

Concluding Remarks .................................................................................. 173

*ACKNOWLEDGEMENTS*

Many people have helped with my research into family and local history over the years. In 1980, I interviewed my uncle, Francis Joseph Sanderson (1904-1993) of Vesey Farm, Great Holland, Essex. Born in Bedburn, he had an amazing memory, a strong streak of romanticism, a yearning for immortality, and was loquacious enough to provide me with over 4 hours of taped interviews without any difficulty. His frequent mention of his tenant-farming kin in Weardale caught my attention and soon led to meetings and/or correspondence with, amongst others, Minnie Farrage, nee Vickers of Durham, Ken Vickers of Greenfoot, Stanhope, his cousin Connie English of Coventry, and Edward Hands of London who had assembled an extensive Vickers family tree (much of the primary research having been completed by his mother Mavis in the 1980s) and placed it on the internet. Later, correspondence with distant cousin and family historian Eileen Perkins, neé Hankey, led me to third cousin John Ross of Castle Hill Farm, Tow Law who provided me with stories about John Walton Watson, and photographs of him and his wife Ruth Kipling Sanderson. To each of the above I am deeply grateful.

Over the last six or seven years, I began a regular correspondence with Robyn Roper of Diamond Creek, Victoria, a descendant of John Vickers of Greenhead, and Sheila Potter who is descended from Joseph Vickers of Howl John and is a niece of Minnie Farrage. Grateful thanks to both Robyn and Sheila for their support and encouragement in this venture, and for the valuable information and photographs they provided about their Vickers ancestors: Robyn filled in many gaps about members of the family who migrated from Weardale, and Sheila gave me copies of the Letters of Francis Vickers which provide the inspiration and starting point for this book. And it was through Sheila that I established contact with Steve Clendenan of Ontario, a descendant of George Vickers, one of the recipients of the letters. I am indebted to Steve for the information about the migrants Thomas and George Vickers and for the excellent photographs of his ancestor George.

When I was searching for information about Weardale many years ago, I came across June Crosby's *Weardale in Old Photographs,* first published in 1989. June's 1500-word introduction provided me with an excellent summary of the history of Weardale, and the text accompanying each of the photographs offered further illumination. And I am most grateful to June for recent access to her extensive collection of photographs, some of which are reproduced in the book. Thanks also to Sheila Hogarth of the *Weardale Gazette* for the excellent photograph of Greenhead Farm.

With some difficulty I formatted the book myself but realised that the book cover needed professional input. So many thanks to Holly Grant (Hollydesigns.co.uk) whose excellent work on the cover has enhanced the book considerably.

I owe a debt of gratitude to my brothers Tony and Richard Sanderson who have been a great help during recent visits to the North-East. I enjoyed Richard and Kath's hospitality at Whorlton, and Tony and Pat from High Etherley could not have been more helpful. Tony accompanied me on an information-gathering trip in June 2012 and his greater familiarity with Weardale proved very valuable. We visited Belle Vue Farm (now offering superior bed-and breakfast accommodation), the home of the letter-writer Francis Vickers for fifty years, and nearby Pease Myers Farm where our great great grandmother Margaret Vickers was born and raised. We also visited the Weardale

Museum, Ireshopeburn where David Heatherington and his wife Jean were very helpful in providing access to relevant items from the extensive and well-presented collection on the history of Weardale. I had previously corresponded with David and his brother Ken, and I am most grateful for all the valuable information they have freely provided, including photographs, family tree advice, and the Roddam Map of Stanhope and district, 1851.

A trip to Tow Law proved particularly valuable. There I met Harry Vickers who ran Tow Law Auction Mart until it closed in 2005. The grandson of Thomas Herbert Vickers, he was able to provide me with photographs of his great great uncle Joseph Vickers of Tow Law who founded the mart in 1882. Whilst there, I took the opportunity to revisit John Ross of Castle Hill House Farm, a retired farmer and descendant of Margaret Vickers of Pease Myers. John gave me some good stories and family photographs, including one of his grandfather John Walton Watson who features in this book.

Finally, I owe a particular debt of gratitude to Patricia who has accommodated my long hours of writing and internet searching with steadfast support and good humour. She has shown great interest in my project from the outset, always offering encouragement and more than happy to engage patiently and cheerfully in frequent discussions about the content and style of the book. She has read the drafts and given valuable advice which I have invariably followed. Without her support the task would have been impossible, and so to Patricia, my heartfelt thanks.

Watercolour of Stanhope St Thomas by Sheila Potter. It is the place where many generations of the family were christened, married, and laid to rest.

# 1. INTRODUCTION

I've always been interested in history. At school in Bishop Auckland in South-West Durham I studied history as far as 'A' Level, and learned in fascinating detail about great empires, kings and queens and wars and battles that have shaped the world. But I learned next-to-nothing about local history and about the ordinary lives of ordinary people. Alongside the great events of history, there was a parallel universe occupied by the vast majority of English people, most of whom until well into the nineteenth century, lived their lives in tightly knit rural communities. And although the history of these communities appears less glamorous and less important than the momentous events described in history books, there is nevertheless a great curiosity for many people today in discovering more about the lives of their forebears. Researching local and family history soon reveals many people of extraordinary talents and provides the local historian with the opportunity to collate and record information about kinfolk and their communities for posterity. It may even tell us something about ourselves and our origins. To take a mundane example, I knew that I was named after my grandfather Francis Sanderson, but I soon discovered that Francis was a family name used by the Sanderson and Vickers families from at least the early eighteenth century.

The interest in my Weardale forebears began after my father's death in 1974, and what started out as mild curiosity developed into a life-long fascination. In 1977, I began reading books on family history and thereafter began visiting family history archives such as the County Records Office in Durham, and the Public Records Office and Somerset House in London. I visited churchyards such as Stanhope, Wolsingham and Hamsterley in search of relevant monumental inscriptions. I also began talking to older members of the family and visiting previously unknown cousins in the North-East.

Weardale is the upper valley of the Wear, extending as far as Wolsingham the earliest capital of the Dale. It is an area where the extensive mineral wealth - lead, ironstone, limestone, and silver - has been exploited since the time of the Romans. By the late sixteenth century stock farming became a major activity, and many of the dale's farmers supplemented their income by working in the quarries or becoming miners for the London Lead Company which had been founded in 1692 with headquarters in Stanhope.

June Crosby notes that "Undoubtedly, the isolation of the Dale, the dangers of mining, the hazards of quarrying and the unpredictable fortunes of farming have helped create an independent, caring and versatile community and one with a wonderful sense of place. Life for many was hard until after the last war, yet resilience and creativity emerged, backed by the Methodist ethos."[1]

The strength of non-conformism in the dale owed much to the history of the established church in the affairs of Weardale. It was part of the remote western estates of the Bishops of Durham and the activities of hunting, stock rearing and mining were controlled by ecclesiastical officers who commanded little respect in the dale. The remoteness from the bishopric at Durham combined with the neglectful and sometimes harsh actions of the landlords, led to a population that was largely hostile to the church and very independent in spirit. It is easy to see how a mood developed amongst dales

---

[1] *Weardale in Old Photographs*, June Crosby, Stroud, Alan Sutton Publishing, 1989.

people that outsiders, not least absentee landlords, were responsible for creating problems for the area through exploitation.

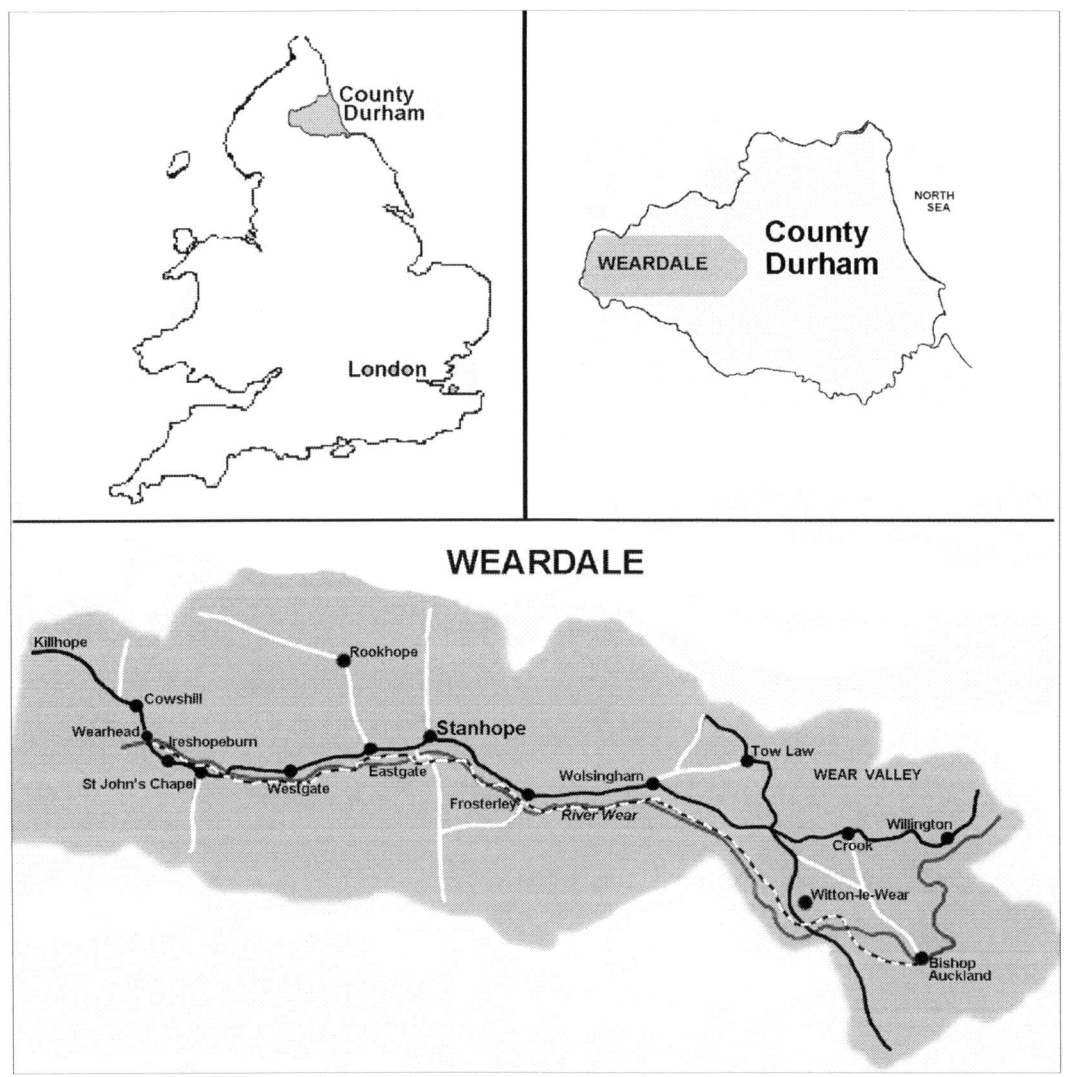

1-1 Weardale is situated in the west of County Durham

There is no doubt that life has been hard over the centuries in the Durham Dales. Before "global warming", winters were long and the weather was often harsh. Very cold weather, blizzards and deep snow, all less common recently, made winters especially difficult for the farmer, who may not have had the convenience of running water and electricity until well into the twentieth century.

One of the people I met in 1979 was Minnie Farrage née Vickers of Durham, my fourth cousin. Minnie, who was born at Belle Vue Farm, Stanhope in 1907, gave me valuable information about the connections between the tenant-farming Sanderson and Vickers families of Weardale and a number of precious photographs. Although I have no photographs of my great great grandparents John Sanderson (1782-1865) and Margaret Vickers (1785-1869), Minnie had photographs of Margaret's brother, my ggg uncle

# INTRODUCTION

Joseph Vickers of Howl John Farm (1790-1885), his wife Elizabeth Collingwood, and their first-born son Francis Vickers (1821-1903) of Belle Vue Farm with his wife Mary Bowman. The photograph of Joseph Vickers of Howl John gave me a vivid connection with my Weardale kin from the eighteenth century.

1-2 County Durham, showing many of the villages and towns mentioned in the text

These closely-related families can be traced from at least the seventeenth century as hill-farmer/miners/quarrymen on the moors of Weardale in the vicinity of Stanhope. By the end of the eighteenth century, through a mixture of ability, hard work and good fortune, they became well established and respected tenant farmers. In the nineteenth century, their fortunes largely reflected the prevailing economic conditions for North Country farmers, with more or less tough times after about 1815 which ultimately encouraged ambitious young farmers such as George and Thomas Vickers to seek opportunities in the Colonies. After a period of prosperity in the third quarter of the century, there was an extended period of economic depression from the 1870s which affected miners and farmers alike, leading to mass migration from Weardale. Some family members left the land for good, and others, inspired by the success of earlier pioneers in the Colonies and America, joined the migration abroad.

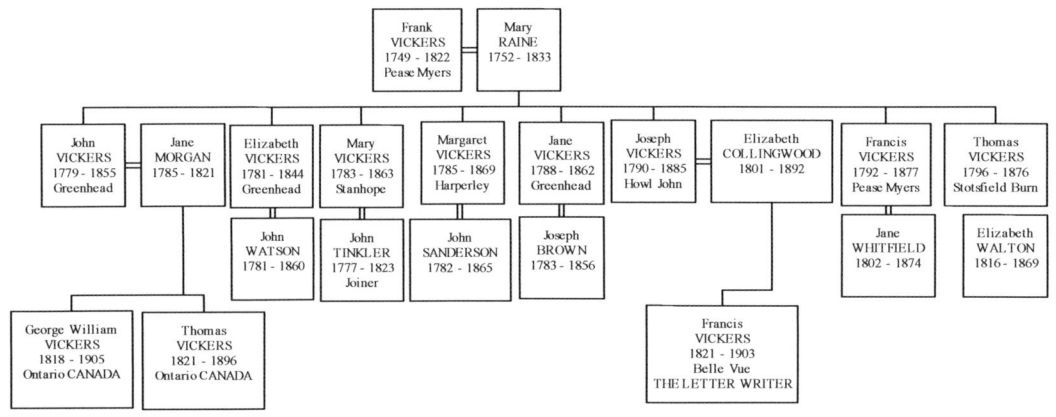

```
                    ┌─────────┬─────────┐
                    │  Frank  │  Mary   │
                    │ VICKERS │ RAINE   │
                    │1749-1822│1752-1833│
                    │Pease Myers│       │
                    └─────────┴─────────┘
```

(Family tree of Frank Vickers and Mary Raine, showing children:)
- John VICKERS 1779-1855 Greenhead = Jane MORGAN 1785-1821
- Elizabeth VICKERS 1781-1844 Greenhead = John WATSON 1781-1860
- Mary VICKERS 1783-1863 Stanhope = John TINKLER 1777-1823 Joiner
- Margaret VICKERS 1785-1869 Harperley = John SANDERSON 1782-1865
- Jane VICKERS 1788-1862 Greenhead = Joseph BROWN 1783-1856
- Joseph VICKERS 1790-1885 Howl John = Elizabeth COLLINGWOOD 1801-1892
- Francis VICKERS 1792-1877 Pease Myers = Jane WHITFIELD 1802-1874
- Thomas VICKERS 1796-1876 Stotsfield Burn = Elizabeth WALTON 1816-1869

Grandchildren shown:
- George William VICKERS 1818-1905 Ontario CANADA
- Thomas VICKERS 1821-1896 Ontario CANADA
- Francis VICKERS 1821-1903 Belle Vue THE LETTER WRITER

1-3  The family of Frank Vickers and Mary Raine. The double line between boxes indicates a marriage. Because of the repeated use of the same Christian names in the family, individuals are distinguished by a Christian name variant, and/or by principal place of residence, e.g., Frank Vickers of Pease Myers, his son Francis Vickers of Pease Myers, and his grandson, Francis Vickers of Belle Vue. Three of Frank and Mary's grandchildren are shown: George William and Thomas Vickers who migrated to Ontario, and Francis Vickers of Belle Vue who wrote the letters to his Canadian cousins. The author is the gg grandson of Margaret Vickers and John Sanderson. For more detail on:- the children of John Vickers of Greenhead, page 13; the family of Joseph Vickers of Howl John, page 9; and the family of Francis Vickers of Belle Vue, page 17.

Despite the relatively better standards of health in rural communities throughout the nineteenth century (as compared with the burgeoning towns and cities), both the Vickers and the Sanderson families had more than their fair share of premature deaths. Great great grandparents John Sanderson and Margaret Vickers were pre-deceased by four of their five daughters, including Jane who was burnt to death at Hamsterley School in 1834 aged eight years.[2] And Francis Vickers and Mary Bowman of Belle Vue lost three of their seven children during infancy, and a son and a daughter in early adulthood.

In contrast, many family members lived to a ripe old age. My ancestors John and Margaret Sanderson were 83 and 84 respectively when they died in Weardale in the 1860s, and Margaret's brother Joseph Vickers of Howl John was 95 and the oldest resident in Weardale when he died in 1885. Margaret's grandson, Frank Sanderson of Nafferton in Tynedale, died in 1934 aged 82 and was described as coming from "a long-lived family".

Arguably the greatest achievement of nineteenth century Britain was the building of the railways. Joseph Vickers of Howl John was 35 years old when George Stephenson's *Locomotion* first travelled from Stockton to nearby Darlington in 1825 and he no doubt experienced the wonder and convenience of this new form of travel. But it would have been his children and grandchildren who most benefited from the ability to travel on relatively long excursions and return within the day, to transport livestock quickly and cheaply, and to travel to the seaside and spa towns for holidays and recuperation with

---

[2] Jim McTaggart covered this story in his "Dales Diary" column in *The Northern Echo*, August 20, 2011. Also available at http://www.hamsterleyvillage.com

## INTRODUCTION

great convenience. It is likely that members of the family travelled to London in 1851 to see the Great Exhibition at Hyde Park; inexpensive excursions to the exhibition from all parts of the country were extremely popular, and six million people attended.

Having become fascinated by these able farmers from Weardale, and wishing to know more about their lives, I began to correspond with distant cousins, including Robyn Roper from Victoria, Australia, and Sheila Potter from Hartlepool, who were equally fascinated about their Weardale ancestors. Robyn is descended from Margaret Vickers' brother John (1779-1855) and his wife, Jane Morgan (1785-1821), and has meticulously researched various branches of the family in Weardale, Australia, New Zealand, and Canada. Sheila, descended from Joseph Vickers of Howl John, inherited the Vickers family photographs from her Aunt Minnie, and we were able to cross-check and confirm the names of those depicted. Through her network of family contacts, Sheila had acquired a number of letters written by Francis Vickers of Belle Vue (Sheila's great great grandfather) to his cousins George William and Thomas Vickers, the two youngest sons of John Vickers and Jane Morgan, who migrated from Stanhope to Ontario in the early Victorian period. These letters, which Sheila shared with Robyn and myself, provide a real insight into life in late Victorian Weardale and served as the inspiration for writing this book.[3]

In the letters, written between 1874 and 1901, Francis keeps his cousins informed about the fortunes of close family members, but he also includes a wealth of information about family friends and acquaintances, many of whom would have been known to his Canadian cousins before they left Weardale (and many of whom, on closer examination, turned out to have family connections). But more than that, he touches on important issues and events of local interest: for example, the triumph of the Liberals in South Durham in the 1874 General Election (See page 28), the Darlington Hiring Fairs (See page 33) and the opening of the Weardale Extension Railway in 1895 (See page 134). He had a lot to say about the effects on tenant farmers of the agricultural depression which began in the 1870s, and frequently commented on the weather, even enquiring about hurricanes in North America.

After I had transcribed the letters and produced electronic copies, I then decided to provide more detail on the people and events mentioned by adding footnotes to each of the letters. Over the last few months, the footnotes mushroomed into a book, a book inspired by the letters but which covers not only the content of the letters but also stories about life and times in late Victorian Weardale, stories gleaned largely from Victorian newspapers. I have attempted to breathe life into the characters and events to which Francis makes passing reference, placing the family members and their friends and acquaintances recorded in the letters in the local historical context. Many of these people featured in local newspapers for; their prize-winning stock at agricultural shows that brought prestige to Weardale for its stock breeding; their public service on local boards; their political leadership on issues affecting not only tenant farmers but also miners and quarrymen, and for their important contributions to the local economy. Typically, they were highly respected pillars of the community, and we can not only feel admiration for them but also take pride in their achievements.

---

[3] The Weardale Museum at Ireshopeburn has copies of the letters

What emerges in the book is a partial local history, a series of snapshots of life in Victorian Weardale, providing information which will be of interest to family historians and to all those who are interested in the history of the dale.

Chapters 3 to 10, covering the period 1874-1901, each focus on the letter written in the year corresponding with the title of the chapter. For example, Chapter 3, entitled "Eighteen Seventy-Four" includes the letter written on March 20th, 1874, together with a commentary which explains and elaborates on the contents of the letter. And by way of introduction to the chapter, contemporary and particularly local noteworthy events reported in the press are described and discussed.

One of my main newspaper sources was *The Northern Echo*, the first edition of which was published on January 1, 1870 in Darlington. The main funding came from the Pease family, prominent Quakers, Liberals, bankers, coal-owners and railway pioneers from Darlington who were intent on challenging the local conservative newspapers, the *Darlington & Stockton Times*, the *Darlington Mercury* and the *Auckland Chronicle*. The *Northern Echo*, which would have been the newspaper of choice for Francis Vickers of Belle Vue and his many fellow Liberals in Weardale, became very popular in the 1870s under the inspired editorship of WT Stead.

1-4 William Thomas Stead

William Thomas Stead contributed articles to the paper from its inception and was made editor in 1871 at the age of 22, thus becoming the youngest newspaper editor in the country. A very able man and one of the most controversial figures of the late Victorian

# INTRODUCTION

era, Stead pioneered investigative journalism and supported the Liberal cause to such effect that leading Liberals William Gladstone and Joseph Chamberlain became admirers, and the historian Edward Freeman declared the *Northern Echo* to be "the best paper in Europe". *The Northern Echo* continued to fight the cause of equality and progress after the departure of WT Stead to the *Pall Mall Gazette* in 1880, and it is still being published in Darlington to this day. Stead became an increasingly prominent national figure and in 1912, he embarked on the *Titanic* to take part in a peace congress at Carnegie Hall at the invitation of the US President, William Howard Taft. When the ship hit the iceberg, Stead helped women and children into lifeboats before retiring to the 1st Class Smoking Lounge to read a book. Last seen clinging to a raft, his body was never found.[4]

Many stories from the family have been handed down through the generations, stories which help illuminate the lives of our forebears and how they lived. Sheila Potter tells the story of Joseph Vickers and his sons at Howl John breeding a champion white bull, *The Duke of Howl John,* in 1874 which won at The Royal Show at Carlisle (See page 53). To get to the various shows, Joseph's son John used the railways and had special leather "boots" made to cover the hooves of the bull for the walk to the station.[5]

Sometimes we are provided with insights into why we look and behave the way we do. Robyn Roper, the great great great granddaughter of John and Jane Vickers of Greenhead, visited Stanhope a few years ago and recalls meeting distant cousin Ken Vickers at Greenfoot Farm:-

> To my surprise he was a shorter, lighter version of my father in old age. He summed up his father and his brothers as "Greyhounds with Roman noses who never walked anywhere if they could run". Uncle John Siddle some time before had said of my grandfather, "He never walked anywhere if he could run". To have identical words uttered by distant relatives half a world apart must say something characteristic about our Vickers family.[6]

Maybe there are genetic factors at work. Charles Vickers junior of Snowsfield Farm, a cousin of Joseph Vickers of Howl John, was a professional runner in the 1840s, competing for prize-money in the North-East of England (See page 56). My nearest Vickers' ancestor is my great great grandmother Margaret, the sister of Joseph Vickers of Howl John, so perhaps there's a genetic reason that I never walk anywhere if I can run?

---

[4] http://en.wikipedia.org/wiki/
[5] Roper, Robyn D, *Family History: Vickers of Weardale in County Durham,* 2006.
[6] Ibid, page 1

**1-5** Tenanted farms west of Stanhope: Most of the people mentioned in the letters lived between Stanhope and Eastgate, an area shown in the above map. The ancestral home of the Vickers family was Pease Myers, Francis himself farmed at Belle Vue, and his father Joseph ultimately farmed at Howl John on the banks of the Wear. Cousin Charles Vickers farmed at Snowsfield before the farm was taken over by Thomas Sanderson of Thimbleby Hill (and West Newlandside) in 1881. Francis's Canadian cousins George and Thomas Vickers were born at Greenhead which was also farmed by another cousin, Francis Brown. Francis's son William Vickers first farmed at Pease Myers before moving to Eastgate House in the 1890s. The Morleys farmed at Sweet Wells, the Reeds at Shield Ash and Ludwell, and the Stephensons at Billing Shield. The Hildyards, major landowners and landlords in Weardale, lived at Horlsey Hall for part of the year.

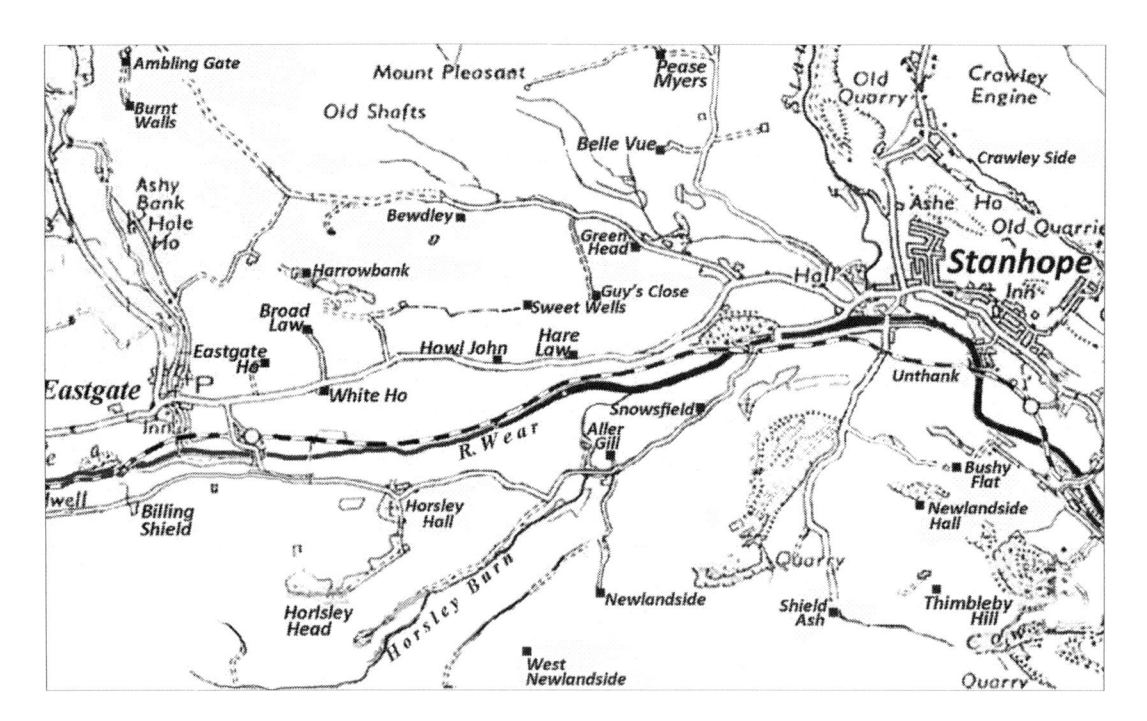

## 2. THE EARLY YEARS

Young Francis Vickers will have been sad and regretful when his cousins George and Thomas Vickers from Greenhead Farm migrated to Canada in the early Victorian period. Much of their childhood would have been spent together: they were of similar ages, they would have attended school together, and would have played and helped out on the farms together. Moreover, George and Thomas lost their mother Jane in their infancy, which makes it likely that Francis's family at nearby Pease Myers played an important role in their upbringing.

Emigration of family members at that time was a traumatic event for families. Because of the sheer distances involved, the likelihood of never seeing the migrants again, and the difficulties of communication, not least because of the prevailing illiteracy, strong bonds would inevitably weaken over time. However Francis and his Canadian cousins were literate and kept up a correspondence throughout their lives.

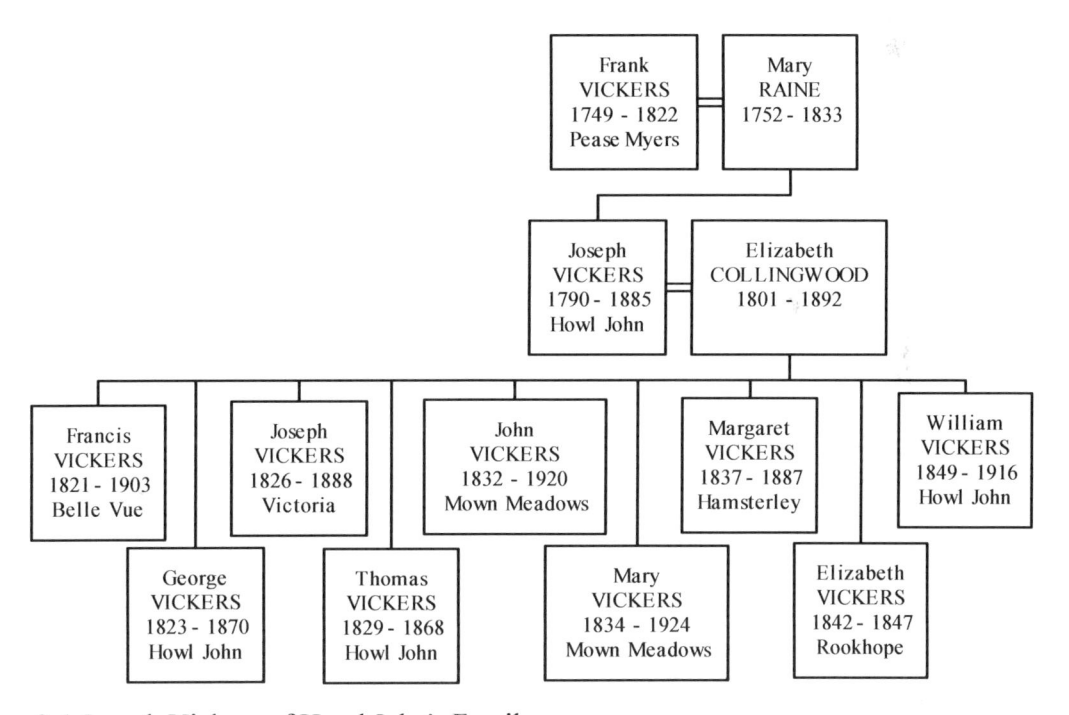

```
                    Frank VICKERS          Mary RAINE
                    1749 - 1822            1752 - 1833
                    Pease Myers
                           |
                    Joseph VICKERS         Elizabeth COLLINGWOOD
                    1790 - 1885            1801 - 1892
                    Howl John
```

| Francis VICKERS 1821-1903 Belle Vue | Joseph VICKERS 1826-1888 Victoria | John VICKERS 1832-1920 Mown Meadows | Margaret VICKERS 1837-1887 Hamsterley | William VICKERS 1849-1916 Howl John |
|---|---|---|---|---|
| George VICKERS 1823-1870 Howl John | Thomas VICKERS 1829-1868 Howl John | Mary VICKERS 1834-1924 Mown Meadows | Elizabeth VICKERS 1842-1847 Rookhope | |

2-1 Joseph Vickers of Howl John's Family
Francis Vickers of Belle Vue gives news of his surviving siblings in his letters to his cousins in Canada.

2-2 From Belle Vue, looking east towards Crawleyside

## *The Coming of the Railways*

Francis Vickers, the first son of Joseph Vickers and Elizabeth Collingwood, was born in December 1821, in the year of the Coronation of George IV and 19 months after the birth of the future Queen Victoria. He was born at Pease Myers, a farm of 116 acres situated about 2 miles North-West of Stanhope, into a family of long-established Weardale farmers. It was a time of momentous change in this part of the world, with the first rail of the Stockton and Darlington Railway laid at Stockton-on-Tees in 1822. Three years later, there were "wild scenes of enthusiasm" at the opening of George Stephenson's Stockton to Darlington line, the first railway in the world designed for steam locomotives. By 1830, there was 100 miles of track in Britain, by 1852, 6,600 miles, and by the death of Queen Victoria, the figure had risen to 19,000 miles.[7] In Weardale, the railway reached Frosterley by 1847, Stanhope by 1862 and Wearhead by 1895. This phenomenal growth spanned the lifetime of Francis Vickers of Belle Vue and had a truly revolutionary effect on British society:-

> It was only yesterday but what a gulf between now and then. Then was the old world. Stage coaches, more or less swift riding horses, packhorses, highwaymen, but your railroad starts a new era. We who lived before the railways and survive out of the ancient world, are like Father Noah and his family out of the Ark.[8]

---

[7] Freeman, M, (1999) *Railways and the Victorian Imagination*, YUP, pp. 1 and 4
[8] Quoted in Briggs, A. (1963) *Victorian Cities*, p 14.

## THE EARLY YEARS

The arrival of the railways had a stunning impact on people. In the 1850s they were mesmerised by the sight of the huge steam engine:-

> The men at work in the fields and quarries stood like statues…and women in their best gowns and bonnets fled the villages and congregated at the corner of every intersecting lane. Every horse was on the alert, viewing the huge moving body as it approached, with a mixture of fear and surprise.[9]

This development in the middle of the nineteenth century completely transformed communications and transport, thereby widening the horizons of people who had lived their lives in enclosed communities, not least in the northern dales:-

> A farmer's diary of 1872 shows that it was possible for him to leave home at Holwick, (just over two miles up the Tees from Middleton), travel to Penrith and return with some sheep, something quite impossible by public transport today. [10]

Francis's father Joseph was born in 1790 at Pease Myers. He was one of 8 children and second son of Frank Vickers and Mary Raine, which explains where Francis's Christian name originated. Since that time, there have been scores of descendants named Francis/ Frank, including the author who is the great great great grandson of Frank Vickers of Pease Myers.

### *Schooldays*

Unlike many young children in the locality and indeed the country, Francis as a young boy had had the great advantage of being sent to school. During the late 1820s, education for children had to be paid for by the family and so only those from relatively well-off backgrounds were able to attend. It was only in 1833 that the government introduced grants of money to schools, but not everyone who ran the schools was able to read, so the standard of education was still often not very good. It appears that during the Victorian era, the schoolteacher was commonly the most ridiculed person in the village. David Souden quotes the Rev Richard Cobbold of Wortham's description of Maria Jolly who ran the local Dame School:-

> She required no puffing up from others, being sufficiently puffed up within herself to think herself wonderfully clever… and in one sense she was! – because anyone may teach that they do understand, but it requires a very clever person to teach that they do not understand![11]

---

[9] Quoted in Souden, D. (1991), *The Victorian Village*. p. 120
[10] Coggins, D. (1989) *Teesdale in old photographs*. Stroud, Alan Sutton Publishing.
[11] Souden, D. Op cit, page 25

That Francis had a relatively good schooling is evident from the letters he would write in later life to his cousins in North America – well written, full of interest, and only a few errors with punctuation and spelling. In contrast, many of his contemporaries, including some of his cousins, were illiterate to the extent of not being able to write their own names, having to sign official documents with their Mark, usually an "X".

## *Greenhead Farm*

By the beginning of the nineteenth century, the Brown family were long-established tenants at Greenhead, but several other families also lived there. In 1806, John Vickers, the brother of Joseph Vickers of Howl John, was already working at Greenhead when he married farmer's daughter Jane Morgan at Stanhope St Thomas. In 1807, his sister Elizabeth married John Watson who worked at Greenhead as an agricultural labourer. And on September 16, 1809, Greenhead tenant Joseph Brown married Jane Vickers, the sister of John and Elizabeth.

2-3 Greenhead, tenanted in the Victorian period by, inter alia, the Brown, Vickers Stephenson, and Heads families, was where Thomas and George William Vickers were born and raised before migrating to Ontario. This photograph, provided by Sheila Hogarth nee Craig, shows the main farmhouse in the late Victorian period with "a French family" standing in front of the house. The Craigs bought the property in 1939, and Sheila was born there.

# THE EARLY YEARS

Over the next 15 years John Vickers and Jane Morgan had 8 children at Greenhead, including George William Vickers, born on December 29, 1818 and Thomas, born on July 16, 1821. Jane died not long after Thomas was born, possibly as a result of complications connected with the birth.

Premature death of a mother with young children was not uncommon in Victorian times and when it happened, the wider family would offer whatever support it could. So it is likely that the Watson, Brown and Vickers' families were involved in raising their young nephews, which would explain why Francis became particularly close to his cousins. George was three years and Thomas a few months older than Francis - not only would they have been at school together in Stanhope, but they would also have spent much time together at Greenhead and Pease Myers.

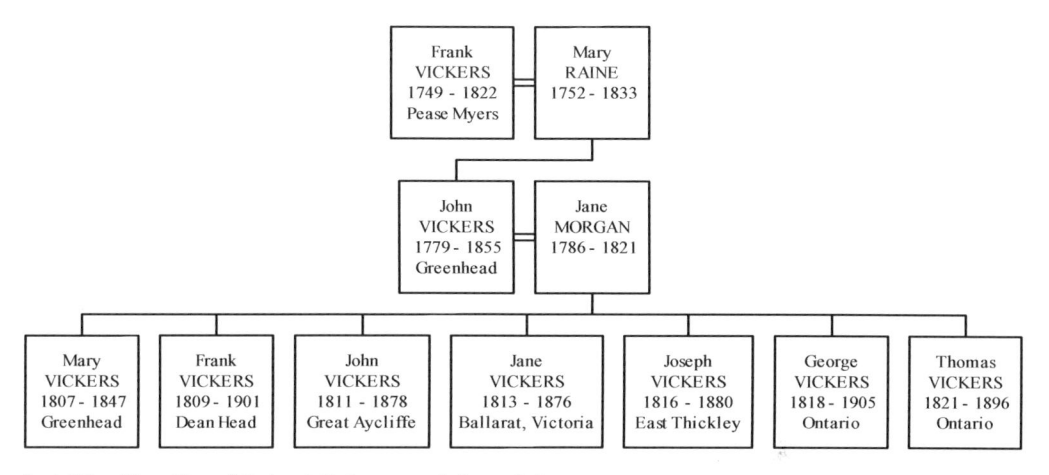

**2-4** The Family of John Vickers and Jane Morgan.

## *Emigration to Canada*

With two older brothers already established and with limited prospects of gaining productive local tenancies, migrating to North America to take advantage of the opportunities for farmers would have had an appeal to George and Thomas. The newspapers of the time had frequent company statements and advertisements about the opportunities in the New World. In 1841, The Canada Company's progress with emigration from the British Isles was published in *The Newcastle Courant*, a newspaper read in Weardale, and this or similar reports are likely to have captured the imaginations of George and Thomas Vickers. An extract follows:-

> The report of the company throughout presents, to the public eye, a prospect which, whether it is viewed with reference to the past, present or future, is equally gratifying. It is stated that a body of settlers who emigrated to Upper Canada a little more than ten years since placed themselves on the Company's lands near Guelph (Ontario). They consisted of 156 families, of which number 120 had no capital whatsoever. There were in all 436 persons. They now possess 100 houses; they have cleared and cultivated 2,830 acres; they have 488 head of cattle, 41 sheep, and 9 horses; and the aggregate value of their property…is found to be £22,653. There are many instances of an increase in capital in ten years of full

sevenfold, and other cases displaying still more striking examples of prosperity... In 1827, the town of Guelph was untenanted but by the wild beasts of the forest, without a tree having been felled; it is now a district town with four churches, numerous public buildings, possessing a large and increasing population, and is still increasing in wealth and importance.[12]

The following advertisement was placed in the *Newcastle Courant* on April 2, 1847 about the availability of land at moderate prices in the Eastern Townships of Canada:-

> **TO EMIGRANTS**
>
> **THE BRITISH AMERICAN LAND COMPANY** beg to draw the Attention of Emigrants to their Land situated in the Eastern Townships of Canada - in proximity to Montreal and Quebec.
>
> Farms with, and without partial Improvements, can be had at moderate Prices, and on easy terms of Payment.
>
> The St. Lawrence and Atlantic Railroad will pass from Montreal through the heart of the Eastern Townships to Portland, on the Atlantic Coast. Of this Railway 45 Miles are now in progress of Construction in Canada, and the Remainder will be speedily be undertaken. Emigrants will readily perceive the great Advantages to be derived from a settlement on Lands which are thus being brought into immediate and rapid connexion with markets.
>
> Further information can be had at the Company's Offices, 35, New Broad Street, London. Or on arrival at Quebec, from Mr S. M. Taylor, Government Emigration Office. And at Sherbrooke, Eastern Townships, from A. T. Galt, Esq., the Company's Commissioner in Canada.

2-5 Land at moderate prices in Canada

With interest raised about the opportunities in Canada, there were the practical considerations of how to get there. Such information could be obtained from the British American Land Company, but there were also advertisements from Shipping Companies (next page)[13].

---

[12] *Newcastle Courant*, April 23, 1841
[13] *Newcastle Courant*, January 25, 1850

# THE EARLY YEARS

> **EMIGRATION TO UPPER CANADA AND WESTERN STATES, VIA MONTREAL DIRECT,**
> WELL-KNOWN regular Traders, A 1 Brig KEEPSAKE, 500 Tons Burthen, William Buston, Master; new A 1 Barque GIFT, 550 Tons Burthen, William Gray, Master.
> Captains well acquainted in the Trade.
> These vessels are well adapted for the Convenience of Passengers, being fitted up with Ventilators, Life Boat, &c, and are not to be excelled by any Class of Vessels for Accommodation and Comfort.
> Will undertake to forward Passengers to Kingstown, Toronto, Hamilton and Buffalo, or any place on Lake Ontario, by Steamer direct from Montreal.
> Will sail the later part of March or beginning of April, 1850.
> For Freight, Passage, or Information to Emigrants, apply to      WILLIAM GRAY,
> 5, Sidney Street, North Shields.

2-6 Emigration to Canada: how to get there

George Vickers moved down the Wear Valley to Shildon with his father and family in the mid 1830s, not long before Princess Victoria's accession to the throne in 1837. A labourer in Shildon in 1841, he emigrated to Canada in 1842 and settled in Euphrasia Township, North-West of Toronto where he farmed 600 acres. He married Mary Ann Bere from Pennsylvania in 1846 at St. James Cathedral in Toronto (then known as York). They had nine children before Mary Ann died in 1869 and was buried in St. James Anglican Cemetery in Fairmount, Ontario.

2-7 George Vickers and Mary Ann Bere

George's brother Thomas followed him to Ontario in about 1850, presumably encouraged by reports of George's positive experience in Canada. He married Alice Dixon in 1853 and they had eight children. They lived on a farm in St. Vincent Township, Grey County, Ontario, outside of the village of Meaford.[14]

---

[14] Information about the brothers was provided by Steve Clendenan, one of the numerous Canadian descendants of George William Vickers.

## Francis Vickers and Mary Bowman

On December 14th, 1850, shortly before cousin Thomas Vickers followed his brother George to Ontario, Francis (pictured left) married Mary Bowman at Stanhope St Thomas. He was just turned 29 years old and Mary, recorded as 22 years old although she was only 20 (was she uncomfortable about the nine-year age gap?), was the daughter of William Bowman, a lead ore smelter from Stotsfield Burn, and his Hexham-born wife, Isabella Dawson.

After their marriage, Francis and Mary lived at 80-acre Belle Vue Farm with his parents Joseph and Elizabeth and his younger brothers and sisters. Robyn Roper notes that "Belle Vue is over 400 years old, originally a thatched roofed hunting lodge of one room used during the Bishops' wild boar and deer hunts. It became a farm during the 1800's."[15]

2-8 Francis Vickers of Belle Vue

At the time of the 1851 Census, Mary was visiting her parents at Stotsfield Burn with her 1 month-old son, Joseph. It is likely that she had gone back to her mother for the birth of the child and had stayed there to recuperate.

Joseph, Elizabeth and their unmarried children moved from Belle Vue to Howl John on the banks of the River Wear in 1852 following the departure of Richard Hutchinson, who was the young tenant of Howl John Farm in 1851. Over a decade earlier, the farm was described thus:-

> Howl John Farm, situate in the Parish of Stanhope, and laying contiguous to the Turnpike Road between the Town of Stanhope and East Gate, containing 132 Acres of Arable, Meadow, and Pasture Land, with a Right of Pasturage upon Stanhope Common; a fair proportion of the Land is in old Grass, the Arable is a rich Turnip and Barley Soil, with Limestone and Draw Kiln upon the Premises. The House and Out-buildings are large and commodious, now in the occupation of Mr Cuthbert Bainbridge Jun[16], as Tenant.[17]

---

[15] Unpublished *Family History of Vickers of Weardale in County Durham*, by Robyn Roper of Diamond Creek, Victoria, Australia – a descendant of John Vickers (1779-1855).
[16] Cuthbert Bainbridge Jun was the brother of Emerson Muschamp Bainbridge, the founder of Bainbridges Department Store in Newcastle.
[17] *Newcastle Courant*, December 11, 1840

# THE EARLY YEARS

It was at Howl John that Joseph's outstanding reputation as a stockbreeder, not only of shorthorns but also of sheep and horses, was truly consolidated. Throughout the 1850s he was prominent amongst the prizes at local shows, and by the 1860s, he had established an exceptional herd of shorthorn cattle. At the Stanhope Agricultural Show in 1864, his bull *Knight of Richard Coeur de Lion* was described as "a very fine beast, who has won nearly everything for which he has competed, both as a yearling and a two-year-old." Two weeks earlier, the aged bull he had won the premium prize at the Weardale Show which debarred him from competing at Stanhope, where he was only present for exhibition.[18]

Francis and Mary remained at Belle Vue and were to be there for the next 50 years before they retired and built a house at the West End of Stanhope – which they named "Belle Vue House". By 1861, they had five children: 10 year-old Joseph, William (7), Isabella (4), Francis (2), and 3-month-old Elizabeth who died in infancy. Another two sons died in infancy, William in 1853 and George, in 1866. In 1871, parents and children were all at Belle Vue which by then had expanded to 200 acres.

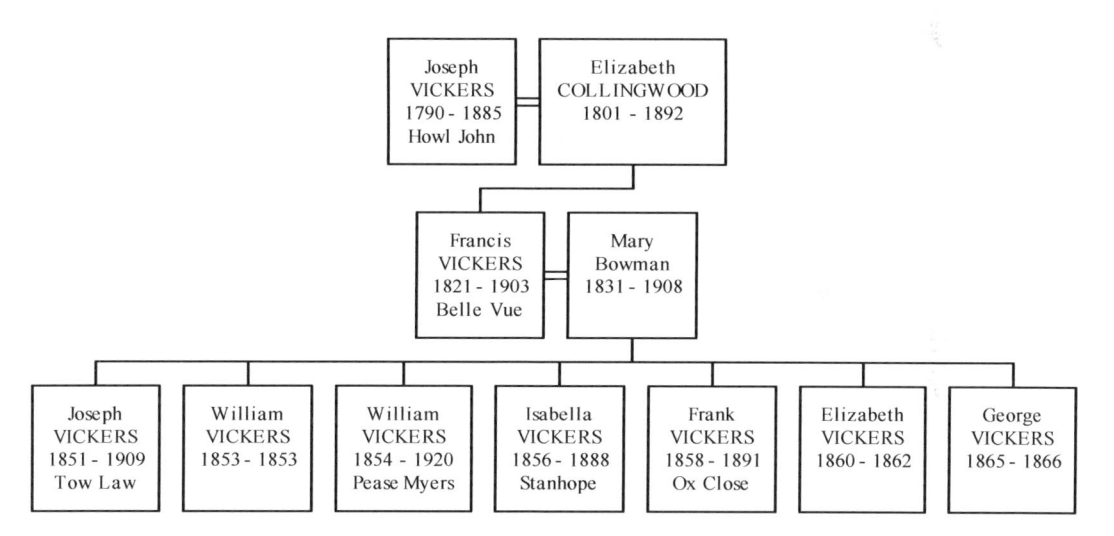

**2-9** Family of Francis Vickers of Belle Vue
Three children died in infancy and two others,
Isabella and Frank, predeceased their parents

The loss of three of their children in infancy would have been devastating and utterly bewildering for Francis and Mary. Why would God cause the death of an innocent child except to punish the parents? Some have argued that because of the high infant mortality in Victorian times, parents were less distressed by the losses than we are today. Pat Jalland's research into nineteenth century family archives causes her to reject this view. Amongst her examples is a mother's grief in the 1850s: "She had suffered too much over the deaths of her first three children to care for society. Sorrow had sapped her vitality."[19] We do not know the lasting impact of the deaths on Francis and particularly Mary, but

---

[18] *Newcastle Courant,* September 16, 1864
[19] Pat Jalland (1999) *Death in the Victorian Family.* Oxford, OUP.

their Christian faith must have been tested to the limits and might explain their conversion to Primitive Methodism where reunion of family and friends in the afterlife was keenly anticipated.

## *Primitive Methodism in Weardale*

> Primitive Methodism at the start was democratic, egalitarian, and activist. It captured whole swathes of intensely tight knit, local working class communities… It was altogether less urban and bourgeois than Wesleyanism. (It) gave whole communities a set of values, a coherent organisation and hope where a rapidly changing social order had meant dislocation and a feeling of injustice.[20]

Primitive Methodism promoted a strong Protestant work ethic and stressed the importance of personal responsibility, thrift, and the dangers of worldly pleasures. Its members were required to forsake the ungodly ways of the world, strictly observe the Sabbath, and avoid alcohol, gambling and dancing. Services were evangelical and revivalist, involving spontaneous expressions of faith, with loud and lively singing of hymns, and salvation offered to all-comers. Its "vigour and drama and colourful imagery contrasted with the decorum and the sedate hymns of the Wesleyans and the drone of the Anglican chant",[21] which undoubtedly contributed to its popularity in the dale and elsewhere. The *Primitive Methodist Magazine* describes a service in a northern village which provides an insight into what Francis Vickers might have experienced at Stanhope Primitive Methodist Chapel:-

> Never shall I forget the singing of that service. There was a little scraping and twanging of fiddle strings before all the stringed instruments – of which there were about a dozen – were brought into accord with the organ, but then such a glorious outburst of music as could not fail to help the spirit of devotion. How these North folks sing…We felt the Divine enchantment of the hour. The glory of the Lord was in his sanctuary…. After the first hymn came the prayer… These men have what the old Methodists called the 'gift of prayer', and the preacher had that gift…He carried his congregation along on the pinions of his own faith, until a low rumbling of murmured responses broke forth in loud 'Amens'. Suddenly, one man sprang to his feet, and, with a loud shout of 'Praise the Lord', jumped into the air. 'Make the place of Thy feet glorious', exclaimed the preacher, and with outcries of 'He does it', the petition came to close. The reading of the Scriptures was interspersed with a few remarks here and there more or less appropriate – generally less – and the service would not have suffered by their omission. But the Sermon… What a mixture of humour, passionate appeal, thrilling exhortations and apposite illustrations it was… Laughter and tears the preacher commanded at will, and when he closed with heart-searching appeals to the unconverted to fly to the Cross for pardon, one almost wondered that men and women did not spring to their feet and rush somewhere – anywhere, exclaiming with Bunyan's Pilgrim, 'Life, Life. Eternal Life'![22]

---

[20] Dolman, Rev R., *Rough Informal Energy: The Story of Primitive Methodism.* Speech at Castle Street Methodist Church, Cambridge, May 31, 2007
[21] Dolman, Rev R., *Op cit.*

# THE EARLY YEARS

Primitive Methodism had been introduced to the dale perhaps even earlier than October, 1821 when George Lazenby preached in a joiner's shop at Stanhope.[23] Essentially a working class movement, a Church for the poor and of the poor, in Weardale even landed proprietors numbered amongst the converts. A notable example was John Dover Muschamp, Esq (1777-1858) of Brotherlee who became a Primitive Methodist at Westgate in about 1820. The Rev William Dent remembered that "though he was quite destitute of the singing gift, yet he used to walk in the front of the processions holding up his hymn-book as if he could sing with the best of us; thus showing, at least, what side he was on"[24].

But not everyone in Weardale was enthused by the Primitives. In 1840, a sceptical Jacob Ralph Featherston of Black Dean described the emergence of "another sect of Methodists professing to be more strict in discipline, styling themselves Primitive Methodists; with what claim to this appellation it would be difficult to establish, but it is not worth the while to enquire."[25]

No doubt the enthusiasm and high moral tone of the Primitive Methodists captured the imagination of Francis Vickers when he joined their ranks in about 1860, but like John Dover Muschamp, he was also showing "what side he was on". In South Durham, the Liberal Party was very strong, and Primitive Methodism aligned itself neatly with the progressive/radical Liberal values of equality and social reform. The labouring class and many tenant farmers had common cause in seeking to reduce the power of the landowners: high rents made it difficult for farmers to make a living and to pay the agricultural workers decent wages. And miners and quarrymen were paid poor wages by the landowners who owned/leased the mines and quarries, and were too often laid off when the workings were shut down at the whim of an owner. Primitive Methodism was also bolstered by the growing awareness that the Church of England itself was a barrier to progress:-

> The parson stood in the way of any great alterations in the administration of public business. He controlled the vestry and the management of the public charities, as a guardian he administered the hated Poor Law, and his influence in the village school ensured that education should take place in an atmosphere favourable to the existing social order. He personified the impediment to reform, and upon him was concentrated the full force of the radical attack.[26]

Many of the leading Liberals in South Durham were Quakers and they felt a natural connection with the Primitive Methodists, as explained by Henry Fell Pease (nephew of Joseph Whitwell Pease and son of Henry Pease of Stanhope Castle) at a Primitive Methodist tea meeting at Rise Carr near Darlington in 1873: after both Quakers and Primitive Methodists endured persecution in the early days, they were now both recognised as "valuable agents in the work of Christianising society".[27]

---

[22] *Primitive Methodist Magazine*, 1896, p 830-1
[23] Patterson, WM, *Northern Primitive Methodism*, E. Dalton, London, 1909 - p154-170
[24] Dent, Rev William, Reminiscences of the Early History of Primitive Methodism in Weardale *The Primitive Methodist Magazine*, Vol. V / LXIII, 1882.
[25] Featherston, Jacob Ralph (1840) *Weardale Men and Manners*, Durham, Francis Humble.
[26] Quoted by Pamela Horn (1976) *Labouring Life in the Victorian Countryside*. p. 164

Francis Vickers and his wife Mary remained devout Primitive Methodists for the rest of their lives. They were actively involved in raising funds for the society, as in 1875 when the foundation stone was laid for the Primitive Methodist Chapel extension in Stanhope. Francis was one of 16 trustees overseeing the Building Fund and Mary was one of the ladies of the society who had prepared the ample refreshments enjoyed by almost 300 people. Henry Pease of Stanhope Castle laid the foundation stone and heaped praise on the "good and earnest workers" of the society. He then spoke of the people of Weardale generally, "I have travelled in many lands, but I never met with a people whose moral character stands so high as the dwellers on the banks of the Wear: and as for the children, they are kept so clean and tidy, and are so well cared for, that I must pay the parents a compliment for the great respect they have for their families".

2-10 Primitive Methodist Chapel, Stanhope. Built in 1849, it was extensively altered in the 1870s, becoming known as the Gilmore Chapel, after Rev Hugh Gilmore, the PM Minister who led the campaign for a Weardale School Board in 1873. June Crosby noted that "the demolition (of this dignified building) was a loss to the area's architectural heritage for it was in a style quite different from any other church in the dale."[28]

---

[27] *Northern Echo*, April 15, 1873
[28] *Weardale in Old Photographs: a second selection.* June Crosby, Stroud, Alan Sutton Publishing, 1993.

## 3. EIGHTEEN SEVENTY-FOUR

> we have had a general Election of late, which has caused a deal of agitation in some places and much Damage has been done as there has been an illfeeling betwixt the Liberel and Conservitive party.

**3-1** Francis tells George about the 1874 General Election. The Tories won nationally but the Liberals swept the board in South Durham

The letter of 1874 was not the first written by Francis to his Canadian cousins. George and Thomas had left Stanhope more than a quarter of a century earlier, and there would have been regular if not frequent correspondence over the years. In 1869, George had lost his wife Mary Ann and no doubt looked forward to hearing news of Old England from Francis. Incidentally, almost exactly a year before the 1874 letter, another "Mary Ann", Mary Ann Cotton from just down the valley in West Auckland, was hung at Durham Gaol after being found guilty of multiple murders. She had poisoned up to sixteen people including several of her own children and three husbands – her trial caused a sensation and much excitement in the locality.

In 1874, Francis and Mary Vickers were farming 200 acres at Belle Vue with two sons and a daughter still at home. They had just experienced a popular election result in South Durham and they had enjoyed a "very remarkably fine winter". The lambing started just as Francis put quill pen to paper on March 20th, and his words convey a great sense of optimism on the eve of the Spring Equinox.

## *The Accident-prone Colliery-owners*

On the day of the Equinox, a few miles down the Wear at Witton Park, there was a "shocking accident" to Mr William Culley Stobart, JP of Etherley Lodge, a director of the North-Eastern Railway Company and the owner of Etherley Colliery. Between Witton Park Station and the Wear Bridge, there was a siding to Messrs Bolckow and Vaughan's Ironworks where wagons filled with ironstone were shunted until needed. As soon as the afternoon train from Darlington to Stanhope had passed, shunting into the siding began, only for the engineman to observe a single engine coming up the line from Bishop Auckland at considerable speed and with two gentlemen on board. Thomas Trustlove, the signalman with the task of raising a signal-board when there was any shunting in progress, failed to notice the approaching engine until it was too late, and the engine hit the shunter with great force. The newspaper report explains:-

> As soon as the occupants of the engine saw that a collision was imminent, they all leaped off, Mr H S Stobart stumbling and rolling down the heavy embankment which is here about sixty feet, at a great rate to the bottom. Fortunately he was little the worse. Mr W C Stobart (his brother), on leaping, caught his foot in the signal wire which runs along the side of the line, and one of his legs being thrown across the rail, was run over just below the knee. The injured gentleman was immediately afterwards conveyed to the Witton Park Station, and subsequently to his house at Etherley where he was attended by Dr Canney,[29] it being found necessary to amputate the injured limb. None of the others were seriously hurt. Considerable damage was done to both engines."[30]

Railway accidents like this and the one described later (See page 42) were all too familiar in Victorian Britain, and graphically demonstrate the scant attention given to railway safety. What happened here was that the Stobart brothers had missed the Stanhope train and, having urgent business up the valley, William Stobart used his authority as a railway director to requisition an engine to pursue the departed train. Thomas Trustlove was not alert to the danger, but in mitigation, no mainline engine was expected at that time. William Stobart paid a high price for this cavalier action.

Incidentally, fifteen years earlier, William Stobart was in the Canadian city of Toronto when he heard that coal had been found on his land at Newton Cap, just north of Bishop Auckland, and two miles from where the accident happened. The village his company built for the miners and their families was consequently named "Toronto" after the Canadian city.

William's brother Henry Stobart who had escaped without injury in 1874 was not so lucky in 1880. Shortly before noon on Saturday June 26th, with a storm threatening, he and Mr GW Elliot, MP for Northallerton, set out from Witton Towers to fish in Bedburn Beck which flows into the River Wear near Witton-le-Wear:-

> Mr Stobart was standing on the south slope of the railway, and close to one of the fir trees which thereabouts are numerous, when a vivid flash of fork lightning struck the tree some five or six feet from the root. Instantaneously, the terrible fluid radiated from the tree to Mr Stobart, the rim of whose square felt hat was punctured and a metal frame inside injured. Thence the lightning seems to have traversed the length of the unhappy gentleman's body. A flask which was in the breast pocket, as well as some links on the deceased gentleman's watchguard were fused, and after passing down one of the deceased's legs, the lightning made a clean puncture through the toe of one foot. Mr Elliot immediately ran to the unfortunate gentleman's assistance, and to his inexpressible horror found him quite dead.[31]

In August 1881, seven years after losing his leg, William Stobart was involved in another railway incident near Waskerley. A party of senior staff and directors of the

---

[29] Dr George Canney of High Bondgate, Bishop Auckland
[30] *Northern Echo*, March 23, 1874
[31] *Northern Echo*, June 28, 1880

# EIGHTEEN SEVENTY-FOUR

Weardale and Shildon Water Company travelled by train on the mineral line between Tow Law and Stanhope to inspect Waskerley Reservoir. From the line, the reservoir was reached by a tramway operated by a wire rope from a stationary engine. After inspecting the reservoir, several of the party, including Henry Fell Pease, decided to walk back up to the mineral line. The rest boarded the trucks and were hauled up the incline. The newspaper report continues:-

> On reaching what the man in charge believed to be the summit, the rope was detached, and in consequence of one of the trucks not having reached level ground the trucks immediately began to descend.

With the prospect of imminent disaster as the trucks gathered speed, William Stobart, presumably having learned well from his previous escapade, jumped out and reached the ground safely, despite having only one leg. Another passenger, James Thompson from Hurworth-on-Tees, was less agile, sustaining a broken leg as he tried to leap clear - his left leg was caught on the rails by the truck, causing it to jump the line, and "under the violent oscillation of this movement", the MP for Darlington, Mr Theodore Fry, was thrown out of the truck with considerable force, experiencing concussion when he landed on his head. Having jumped the rails, the trucks then came to a halt, allowing the rest of the party to alight without injury.[32]

## *Founding of Stanhope School Board*

The most notable development in Stanhope in 1874 was the establishment of a School Board. The 1870 Education Act, which made elementary education available to all children between the ages of five and thirteen, signalled the recognition that it was the duty of the Government to see that education was provided for all children. However, how education was delivered was still at the discretion of parishes, which could either fully adopt the Act or continue to deliver public elementary education by the voluntary religious societies: the British and Foreign Schools Society (Nonconformist) and the National Society (Church of England). By 1870, they provided education for about 1.7 million of the 2.5 million children of school age, and the Education Act was intended to fill the gaps.[33]

3-2 Rev Hugh Gilmore

In December 1873, a mass meeting of ratepayers of the Parish of Stanhope was held to decide whether to establish a School Board for the district. On one side was the 'undenominational' party, led by the Reverend Hugh Gilmore, a Primitive Methodist Minister (pictured), strongly in favour of a School Board on the basis that schools were so badly managed that "more of the kind would be an evil rather than a good."[34]

---

[32] *Northern Echo*, August 8, 1881
[33] Harrison, JFC, (1990) *Late Victorian Britain 1875-1901*. London, Fontana, p. 200.
[34] *Northern Echo*, December 19, 1873

On the other side were the Religious Societies, or the denominational section, arguing for the *status quo* - the churches were funded with public money to provide education for the poor and these churches did not want to lose their influence.

The meeting voted overwhelmingly in favour of establishing a School Board, which was granted in early 1874 for Stanhope Parish. At that time, there were 1,985 children of school age in the parish, but only provision for 1065. Stanhope had sufficient schools, but additional provision was needed, particularly in Upper Weardale.[35]

On Christmas Eve 1874, Rev Gilmore was honoured at Stanhope Town Hall in the presence of a large and enthusiastic audience with an expression of gratitude for his efforts in securing a School Board for Stanhope Parish.

3-3 Thomas Burt, MP

A friend of Rev Gilmore, Thomas Burt, a leading trade unionist and one of the first working-class MPs when he was returned to parliament for Morpeth in 1874, gave a rousing speech, praising the Primitive Methodists for having done more than any other denomination to improve the lowest strata of society.

To loud cheers and applause, he spoke of "the necessity and desirability of education," …that "working men were not tools to serve other people, but were gifted with intellect and capacity, and it was…the chief business of all men here – no matter what society they belonged – to develop their God-given powers." Rather than allow education to be controlled by "Ecclesiastics", to be "effectually carried out, it must be taken in hand by the great mass of the people themselves." And this required an extension of the franchise: "no great measure for the public welfare could be carried out in the House of Commons unless the people had the power to send to the House the men who would carry out those matters."

Mr Burt, clearly ahead of his time, also advocated "womanhood suffrage", because "the men were but simply halves until they were completed by the women people" (Loud applause and laughter)[36] (See debate on Womens' Suffrage in Chapter 5).

In responding, the Rev Gilmore said that he would "rather have the sympathy of an honest man than a great deal of the world's goods". He felt that the success of the campaign for a School Board had given people of Weardale more confidence and made them more public-spirited. He said he felt strongly on the subject when he recalled the struggles which working men had to go through to obtain an ordinary education.[37]

---

[35] *Northern Echo*, March 2, 1874
[36] In the UK, Women's Suffrage became a national issue in 1872 with the formation of the National Society for Women's Suffrage.

Two years later on October 10, 1876, the first three of five new Board Schools was opened in the parish of Stanhope by the two local MPs, Mr JW Pease and Major F Beaumont. The completed schools were at Westgate, Wearhead and Lanehead, and together with uncompleted schools at St John's Chapel and Rookhope, were designed to accommodate 950 children. At Westgate School, with the chairman of Stanhope School Board Mr JC Cain presiding, Joseph Whitwell Pease gave a well-received speech. A strong advocate of a national system of education, Mr Pease recognised the difficulties faced by families in securing a good education for their children:-

> Children seem to be sent to school soon enough, but they do not attend one-half the school attendance time. Their School Board will have compulsory powers, but they must be exercised very gently and with great discretion, for in a free country like this nothing works well unless the heart and soul of the people are with the law (Applause). I know it is a great sacrifice for parents to send their children to school regularly. It is difficult, for instance, for a mother with a large family to spare a big girl who could quieten a squalling baby, rock the cradle, bring water, and help her in many ways (hear, hear, and laughter). But I would urge them to make this sacrifice in order that their children, and their children's children, might be benefitted thereby.

He concluded by announcing to loud applause that he would provide a tea-party for all children with good attendance records (fixed by the School Board).[38]

## "Manly Conduct and Brilliant Exploits"

In 1874, the Stanhope and Weardale friends of Joseph Allison presented him with a gold watch "for his manly conduct and brilliant exploits in all the principal wrestlings in England". In the Victorian period, one of the most popular sports in Weardale was wrestling, and Joseph Allison was a celebrated local wrestler. He was born in Ireshopeburn and in a relatively short wrestling career, he won 110 first prizes, fifteen cups and a belt in competitions in towns around the country, including Manchester, Liverpool, Newcastle, and London. He won many honours in Barrow-in-Furness, and in 1876 his friends in Barrow presented him with a £20 purse of gold "as a tribute of respect they entertained towards him as a man, and as an acknowledgement of the honesty and integrity he has always displayed as a wrestler".[39] (See page 97)

## The Warm-hearted Guardians of the Poor

The public-spiritedness of Weardale in 1874 was evident from the way the less fortunate were treated in the district. A newspaper report from Christmas noted that "there are few places where the cold of winter is more felt than in the district which comprises Weardale Union, and probably there are few places where the Guardians of the Poor have warmer hearts". All of the out-door paupers over sixty years of age received an extra half-crown for Christmas, and those paupers maintaining their own

---

[37] *Northern Echo*, December 26, 1874
[38] *Northern Echo*, October 11, 1876
[39] *Northern Echo*, October 22, 1889

fires were each given half a ton of coals. On Christmas Day, the inmates of the Workhouse at Stanhope had their usual Christmas Dinner paid for by the Guardians. And coal-owner Charles Attwood's generosity is highlighted: he gave twenty-seven tons to the poor of Wolsingham, and also distributed a large quantity of coal amongst the poor at Westgate.[40]

Given the prevailing tension between the ordinary folk of the dale and many of those in positions of authority, it cannot be assumed that every inmate of Stanhope Workhouse will have greeted the generosity of the Guardians with humble gratitude. Dramatist George Sims' narrative poem, *"In the Workhouse – Christmas Day"*, vividly portrayed the bitterness that some will have felt at the condescension of the Guardians:-

> It is Christmas Day in the workhouse, and the cold, bare walls are bright
> With garlands of green and holly, and the place is a pleasant sight;
> For with clean-washed hands and faces in a long and hungry line
> The paupers sit at the table, for this is the hour they dine.
>
> And the guardians and their ladies, although the wind is east,
> Have come in their furs and wrappers to watch their charges feast;
> To smile and be condescending, put pudding on pauper plates.
> To be hosts at the workhouse banquet, they've paid for - with their rates.
>
> Oh, the paupers are meek and lowly with their 'Thank'ee kindly, mums!'
> So long as they fill their stomachs what matter it whence it comes?
> But one of the old men mutters and pushes his plate aside,
> "Great God!" he cries, "but it chokes me; for this is the day she died!"

Sim goes on to explain that the elderly inmate's wife had died of starvation the previous Christmas Day because their request for outdoor relief from the parish had been refused, and his wife would not contemplate entering the workhouse. The poem concludes:-

> There, get ye gone to your dinners, don't mind me in the least,
> Think of the happy paupers eating your Christmas feast
> And when you recount their blessings in your parochial way,
> Say what you did for me too... only last Christmas Day.

## *Victorian Criminal Justice*

In July 1874 at Durham Gaol, with the Deputy Governor, the Gaol Surgeon and other officials in attendance, Peter Bray was given 20 lashes for robbery with violence in Darlington:-

> The handle of the cat was about eighteen inches long, to which was attached the nine cords, measuring in length about two feet, each cord having three knots in it. Bray having been securely fastened, one of the warders took up the cat, and the flogging was proceeded with. At the first lash the prisoner shrieked "Oh Dear", and continued to bellow forth as each fresh stroke of the 'cat' was inflicted. At the third stroke, blood was drawn, and as the strokes continued, flowed freely down

---

[40] *Newcastle Courant*, December 25, 1874

his back. At the tenth blow he was released for a short rest, before receiving the remainder of his punishment…On receiving the last blow and being released, he turned to the warder and said, "You will get your blessings for this." His back at the finish was in a bad condition. Loose cloths were at once thrown over him, and he was conveyed to his cell where he was given into the care of the doctor.[41]

Although punishment was very harsh on those days, it was not until 1948 that corporal punishment was removed from the statute book in Great Britain.

## The Letter to George Vickers

*Belle Vue, March 20<sup>th</sup> 1874*
*Dear Cousin,*

*After a long delay of writing to you for which I beg to be excused, I now write to you to give you a few particulars about Old England. We have had a General Election of late, which has caused a deal of agitation in some places and much damage has been done as there has been an ill feeling betwixt[42] the Liberal and Conservative party. The Conservatives have taken the lead though there is not one got in for South Durham.*

*You said in your last letter you wanted to hear from your Friends. I was at Darlington on March Monday and saw F(rank) and Joseph. They are all well. Joseph's oldest daughter, Jane Ann, was married 2 years since to a man named G Pearson. He was an Engine Man. On the 8<sup>th</sup> of December last, (he) was going up Barnard Castle line, soon in the morning and came in contact with a bridge that crosses the railway. He had been standing up upon his Engine and was struck off and several trucks passed over him and cut him right in two – you might see the accident in a paper I sent.*

*As for friends in Australia, I can give you very little account of either Jane or her son George, as brother Joseph has never said anything about them for a long time. As for Father and Mother, they are both very fresh considering their ages. Father is 83 years of age, and is working every day. They have only the two youngest at home, Elizabeth and William. Mary is keeping John's House at Mown Meadows. Uncle and Aunt at P(ease) Myers (are) very feeble. They keep a servant girl to wait on them.*

*We have had a great many sudden deaths about Stanhope of late. Wm Morley the Rate Collector died very suddenly a few weeks since. You perhaps would not know him but Thomas would.*

*I thank you for the portraits you sent me. Likewise the newspaper, I received one three weeks since. I gave John Read the last portrait you sent, he said I had to thank you for it and give his kind regards to you.*

*You wanted to know if we had any mowing machines. We have had one about 5 or 6 years, likewise a Hay making machine, we have all sorts of machinery in England: steam ploughs and steam thrashers and all way down to a knitting machine.*

---

[41] *Northern Echo*, July 24, 1874
[42] "Betwixt", meaning 'between' is an archaic word – its usage slowly declined through the 20<sup>th</sup> Century, surviving longest in rural areas

*We have had a very remarkably fine winter. We have had only one stormy day, it came on snow on the Saturday and went off again on the Monday and we have had very little rain, or frost. We have been very (lucky).*

*We have got the North Field and West Rigs drained which has caused us a deal of more extra work. We have only the two oldest sons at home this winter. The youngest son is at school in Darlington.*

*We are just commencing the lambing season, we have got the first this morning. We have a cow calved – she has had three times two and two times one and is only six years old.*

*Now I must conclude for the present. Hoping these few lines will find you all well as they leave us all at present.*

*With all our kind regards to you all. Likewise to Thomas and family. I remain your loving cousin.*
*F Vickers*
*Belle Vue*
*PS Please excuse the hasty scrible and bad spelling.*

## The 1874 General Election

Francis begins with news of the General Election of the previous month. The contests for seats in Parliament was between the Conservatives, who favoured royal authority, the established church, the traditional political structure, and opposed parliamentary reform, and the Liberals, who favoured social reform, individual liberty, reducing the powers of the State and the established church and (further) extension of the electoral suffrage. The 1867 Reform Act had already extended the franchise to all male householders, effectively giving the vote to the working classes, and doubling the number of voters from one to two million, out of a total adult male population of about five million.

*The Northern Echo*'s strong support for the Liberal campaign reflected the prevailing mood in South Durham, not least in Weardale. On January 27th, 1874, a meeting of the Liberal electors at the Town Hall, St John's Chapel, formed a committee to support the two Liberal candidates for South Durham, Major Frederick Beaumont and Joseph Whitwell Pease. *The Northern Echo* declared that the men of Weardale "as of old, are ready for the fight." Faced with a strong Conservative Party which expected to win the fight, the *Echo* quoted part of an "old ditty":-

> Serene on their chargers we see the two ride,
> The gallant young Beaumont with Pease at his side;
> Their plumes nod defiance as onward they go,
> And they smile with contempt at the threats of the foe.[43]

A week before the election, the newspaper published an article about the newly declared Tory Candidate for Darlington, Mr Thomas Gibson Bowles. Based on the newspaper's assessment of a speech given by Mr Bowles on the balcony of the *King's Head* in Darlington, the tone of the article is scornful:-

---

[43]*Northern Echo*, January 28, 1874

No one knows who he is, what he is, where he has come from, or what is his object in condescending to enlighten the humble electors of Darlington as to the constitution of the universe and the inner principles of all things. He warns the people of Darlington that the world is going to ruin, and it is only by taking his advice that it can escape irremediable destruction.[44]

3-4 *Vanity Fair* image of Thomas Gibson Bowles

The speech by the mysterious Mr Bowles appears to have wrong-footed the Liberals as his radical ideas made him an unlikely Tory, and therefore more of a threat to the Liberal candidate for Darlington, Mr Edmund Backhouse.

This would partly explain *The Northern Echo's* mocking treatment of Mr Bowles, but it is likely that professional rivalry and jealousy were also involved. Thomas Gibson Bowles was a journalist of substance as *Echo* Editor William Thomas Stead would have known only too well. Born in 1841 and generally known as Tommy Bowles, he became a political journalist for the *Morning Post* in 1866 and gained fame for his coverage of the 1870 Siege of Paris during the Franco-Prussian War, filing his reports by balloon and pigeon post. He founded *Vanity Fair* in 1868 and *The Lady* magazine in 1885. After his failure to win at Darlington, it was another 18 years before he entered Parliament as the Conservative member for Kings Lynn in 1892, serving until defeated in 1906.

3-5 Banner printed in *The Northern Echo* during the Election Campaign

---

[44] *Northern Echo,* January 31, 1874

## The Liberal Victory in South Durham

Benjamin Disraeli led the Conservative Party to victory over William Gladstone's Liberals, becoming prime Minister for the second time. The Liberals won a majority of the votes cast, but Conservatives won the majority of seats in the House of Commons, largely because they won a number of uncontested seats. In South Durham and in all other parts of the county, the Liberals swept to victory.

A *Northern Echo* editorial, with the unmistakeable imprint of William Thomas Stead, celebrated the victory for the Liberals in County Durham:

> Durham is Free! From Tyne to Tees not a single Tory member pollutes her soil. The Southern Division of the County completed the work by electing the Liberal candidates by immense majorities. The last link in the Tory chain has been smitten off, and the whole County, in all its constituencies, is delivered from even the small trace of Tory misrepresentation….The very fact that the rest of the country has relapsed into darkness, renders the radiant splendour of Durham's Liberalism but the more remarkable….In all the constituencies, whether the electors be lead miners in Weardale, colliers of North Durham, shipbuilders of Sunderland, ironmasters of Stockton, Quakers of Darlington, Churchmen of Durham, glassblowers of Shields, engineers of Gateshead, or merchants of the Hartlepools, the response is the same, for the electors of Durham, with one accord, declare their faith in Liberal Progress, and unanimously protest against Conservative Reaction.[45]

3-6 Disraeli and Gladstone: they loathed each other

---

[45] *Northern Echo*, February 13, 1874

# EIGHTEEN SEVENTY-FOUR

The popularity of the Liberal victory in Weardale is evident from the following report:

> REJOICING IN WEARDALE OVER
> THE SOUTH DURHAM LIBERAL VICTORY
> On Saturday afternoon last, five cannons from Mr WB Beaumont's offices at New House, were kindly lent by Mr JC Cain[46] to a number of staunch Liberals, who, having erected the ordnance on the hill behind Chapel, commenced at two o'clock to fire volley after volley, making the Weardale hills echo "true blue" and continued the firing all the afternoon, in honour of the Liberal victory in South Durham. The Weardale band played down the dale to St John's Chapel, and in the evening a public meeting was held in the Town Hall of the Liberal supporters, who expressed their thanks for their success, and were gratified to think that South Durham had been equally successful as other divisions of the county palatine in sending two Liberals to Parliament. Weardale was never more true blue than it has shown itself at the general election of 1874.[47]

## *"A Deal of Agitation"*

Francis refers to the "ill-feeling betwixt the Liberal and Conservative parties" and this was evidenced at the highest level. To say that Disraeli and Gladstone did not get on is to put it mildly, they loathed each other. Disraeli, when asked to explain the difference between a misfortune and a calamity, replied, "If Mr Gladstone were to fall into the Thames, it would be a misfortune. But if someone dragged him out, it would be a calamity."[48]

The "deal of agitation" referred to by Francis was most pronounced in other parts of the country, notably the Midlands, but there was also trouble in South Durham. For the most part, voting was conducted with "the greatest quietude and decorum", but there were election disturbances all over South Durham, including at Bishop Auckland, Spennymoor, Willington and Crook.

One incident occurred at Willington on Feb 11 1874, Polling Day for South Durham. As a band marched up the main street, a member of a crowd of Liberal supporters shouted, "It's a Tory band!" The band went into a public house, and the mob threw stones and smashed the door off its hinges before the police beat them back. They then continued along the street, smashing shop windows and shouting, "Down with the reds (Tories) and up with the blues (Liberals)."

*The Northern Echo* claimed on February 12 that riots at Crook had been provoked by "Tory roughs" insulting the Liberal voters:-

---

[46] Joseph Cowper Cain, Manager of Lead Mines, was living at Weardale House, Earnwell
[47] *Northern Echo*, February 16, 1874
[48] http://www.victorianweb.org/history

Some rowdies who had too much to drink retaliated by attacking the reds and broke in the windows of one of their houses. Window breaking once started spreads rapidly, and before long a rowdy band, whose conduct cannot be too severely censured, paraded through the streets smashing the windows of all who exhibited the Tory colours.[49]

The Tory-supporting *Auckland Chronicle* took a different view of the outcome of the election in South Durham:-

> Durham possesses the very peculiar honour of being at once almost the only county in England represented entirely by Radicals, and the only county pre-eminently notorious for outrageous crimes. Can the latter state of things have anything to do with the former?

The editorial claimed that the Tories had to fight "the enormous influence of the Pease family and their obsequious train, with a young and untried man" (Thomas Bowles). Further, the "glorious victory" by the Liberals was achieved through "falsehood, intimidation, personal jealousy, mob-rule, and money".[50]

The three local MPs were Major F E B Beaumont RE, and Joseph Whitwell Pease for South Durham, and Edmund Backhouse for Darlington.

Major Frederick Beaumont, a veteran of the Crimean War and the Indian Mutiny, was noted for his inventions, including the Beaumont-Adams revolver and the Diamond Drill for boring through rocks. He was first elected for South Durham in 1868 and served until 1880.

Joseph Whitwell Pease was a member of the Darlington Pease family, the son of railway pioneer Joseph Pease (1799-1872) who had become the first Quaker MP, representing South Durham 1832-41. Joseph junior, an owner of coal and ironstone mines in Durham and Yorkshire and a director of the North Eastern Railway Company, served as a Liberal MP for South Durham from 1865 until the seat was reorganised in 1885, whereupon he became MP for Barnard Castle until his death in 1903. He was created a baronet in 1882.

Edmund Backhouse a member of a prominent Quaker banking family from Darlington, was first elected as the Liberal MP for Darlington in 1868. He was not the greatest orator, but *The Northern Echo* was nevertheless very supportive:-

> Mr Backhouse is a genial, jovial good-hearted gentleman, who is at once a banker and a country squire. In electioneering, he believes that the innocence of the dove is better than the wisdom of the serpent. He is liberal, but not ostentatious, diligent in business, and careful in the discharge of his duties.... If (he) could but remember that a public meeting does not care for the shillings and pence, but is chiefly concerned about the round numbers, he would be more effective upon the platform than he is at present.[51]

---

[49] *Northern Echo*, February 12, 1874
[50] *Auckland Chronicle*, February 13, 1874
[51] *Northern Echo*, March 19, 1874

# EIGHTEEN SEVENTY-FOUR

## *March Monday*

Francis met his cousins on *"March Monday"* at Darlington. The first Monday in March was the date of the long-established Darlington Hiring Fair which, along with Easter Monday, was one of the great markets for human labour in South Durham.

*The Northern Echo* explained what happened on the hiring days:

> The hinds (labourers) and their women folks, according to ancient custom… come into town to be hired on these days … A hiring day is a labour market. The hinds come to sell, the farmers come to buy. The commodity sold is the labour of the hinds for the ensuing year.[52]

For tenant farmers, March Monday at Darlington was an important event in the calendar, where stock and produce would be bought and sold, and annual agreements reached between hinds and the farmers from South Durham and the North Riding. It was also a fair with all manner of entertainments and a social occasion providing the opportunity to meet up with friends and relations from far and wide.

In Darlington, men and women would stand in the market place and along High-Row, perhaps with a symbol of their trade to signify the kind of employment required, e.g., a carter with a piece of whipcord around his hat, a servant girl carrying a broom, and a shepherd carrying his crook. When a bargain was struck, the hind received the hiring shilling and was then able to enjoy the fair for the rest of the day. The yearly hiring included board and lodging for single employees for the whole year with wages being paid at the end of the years' service.

But by 1877 the farmers and Darlington Town Council had unilaterally decided that there was no longer to be a hiring fair on March Monday. The farmers argued that the hinds were not needed until mid-May and that they should not be required to hire them more than a month in advance of this date. They also complained that they were disadvantaged in bargaining with the hinds because of "the multiplicity of their transactions". The farmers also had stock and produce to buy and sell, whereas the hinds had nothing to do but get the best terms for themselves.

The hinds on the other hand objected to not being consulted about this change which had serious consequences for them. They insisted that they needed to know where they would be located by early March so that they could get their gardens in order at the best time. And they objected to the loss of the March Monday holiday which they had enjoyed "from time immemorial".

*The Northern Echo* weighed in with an unconvincing show of impartiality:-

> We abstain from entering into the merits of the case, although much might be said in favour of the contention of the hinds that their gardens would suffer from the postponement of hiring day. A poor man's garden is a valuable source of income, and in spite of what country squires and wealthy farmers may say about the ease with which gardens may be brought into good condition after May, their own gardens are not managed on that principle, and they have no right to expect that the

---

[52] *Northern Echo*, March 7, 1877

hinds will acquiesce in being compelled to adopt a mode of gardening rejected by the very men who press it upon them.[53]

March Monday continued as a horse and cattle fair until the early 1880s when Darlington Town Council appear to have had a change of policy. In 1883, the Darlington Fair again incorporated the hiring of hinds, and this practice continued for a number of years thereafter.

In 1887, it was reported that "there was a large number of hinds 'changing places' but the engagements made were unequal to the supply. The wages offered were a slight decrease upon last year's, and the men were in consequence inclined to hold out for their own terms."[54] Two years later, terms on March Monday were improved for the hinds, although supply still outstripped demand: "There was a good supply of servants, who asked and obtained in many cases about 6d per week more wages, because of trade being better and also the agricultural outlook. The wages for ordinary men was 16s to 17s per week, but foremen obtained up to 20s to 21s, all with privileges which are usually given. A good number were left over unhired."[55]

From this time there was a steady decline of hiring days which became virtually extinct by the First World War. The social climate of the late Victorian period made the hiring days increasingly unpopular, with some detractors likening them to 'slave markets'. The task of matching labourers with vacancies was increasingly undertaken by registry offices and through newspaper advertisements.

## *News of Family and Friends*

Francis met George and Thomas's brothers Frank and Joseph at Darlington Hiring Fair and writes to George that they are well. Three years earlier at the time of the 1871 Census, Frank Vickers was farming 276 acres at Humbleton a farm near the small village of Coatham Mundeville, between Aycliffe and Darlington. Frank had moved to Humbleton to make way for two of his sons, Francis and Archibald, to farm Dean Head. Frank's wife Mary had died in 1868, and present at the farm were four unmarried children, and a niece, Hannah Vickers.[56]

Just over three miles away at East Thickley, New Shildon, Joseph Vickers had a flour milling business. Present at the Bridge Street Mill in 1871 were his wife Jane, two of their children Jane Ann and Margaret, Jane's father John Furby, and Stokesley-born general servant George Pearson. Joseph's other daughter Mary had married railway stoker Edward Dunn in 1870 and they were living in Magdala Terrace, New Shildon in 1871.

A few months after the 1871 Census, Jane Ann married George Pearson, who shortly afterwards began a new career as an Engine Man on the rapidly expanding railways. The Spring of 1873 saw the birth of their son Joseph Vickers Pearson at Bridge Street Mill, but George would not live to see his son's first birthday (See page 42).

---

[53] *Northern Echo*, March 7, 1877
[54] *Northern Echo*, March 8, 1887
[55] *Northern Echo, March 5 1889*
[56] In 1861, Hannah Vickers, born 1855, is with Frank's brother John, a farmer at Great Aycliffe. She is described as John's daughter, although John is unmarried.

# EIGHTEEN SEVENTY-FOUR

## *Weardale to Australia*

In response to George's query about his sister Jane and family in Australia, Francis can give "very little account of either Jane or her son George, as brother Joseph has never said anything about them for a long time." It appears that Joseph had not mentioned the widowed and re-married Jane and her son George in recent correspondence with his brother Francis, most probably because he was no longer in contact with them.

Jane Vickers was born at Greenhead, Stanhope, in 1813. When she was seven years old her mother Jane died, leaving her and her 14 year-old sister Mary to help raise three younger brothers: Joseph 5, George 2 (the recipient of the 1874 letter), and baby Thomas. During the 1830's farming depression, the family moved to Shildon where John Vickers was a labourer and his son Frank worked as a Banksman[57], probably at Shildon Lodge Colliery which had opened in 1830.

Jane married stone mason William Siddle in 1836 at St John's Church, Shildon, with both parties signing the parish register with their marks.[58] And at the same church two years later, Frank married distant cousin Mary Scott (her mother was Stanhope-born Jane Vickers), both of them signing with their marks. It thus seems likely that George had to rely on his cousin Francis of Belle Vue for news of his sister and brothers because they were insufficiently literate to correspond directly by letter.

By the 1850s, with only George Henry of their three children surviving, Jane and William Siddle were in need of new opportunities. The Australian gold rushes started in 1851, leading to the emigration of many dalesmen throughout the decade. In 1854, Jane's cousin Isaac Vickers emigrated to the Victorian goldfields at Ballarat, and his experience will have excited the interest of other member of the family. In January 1857, under the headline "New Gold Discoveries in Australia", the *Newcastle Courant* reported the arrival at Liverpool of the White Star Line *Red Jacket* with 133,000 ounces of gold, valued at £532,000. The *Courant* quoted a letter from a Melbourne agent of the White Star Line:

> We are happy to say that the gold fields continue to turn out well...several large finds have been got, including some heavy nuggets. Emigration from England seems to have again set in pretty freely. We are glad of it; the country wants labour, and, if of the right sort, we have no doubt ready employment will be found at satisfactory wages for all who choose to come.[59]

With the possibility of fortunes to be made and at the very least "ready employment with satisfactory wages", Jane and William Siddle, their son George Henry, together with cousin Joseph Vickers (Francis of Belle Vue's brother, born in 1826) sailed for Australia from Liverpool on the *Sirocco* in 1858. The sailing between Liverpool and Melbourne was advertised in the *Newcastle Courant*, with departure scheduled for April 27th:-

---

[57] A Banksman worked at the bank or top of the pit, unhooking and emptying the laden corves (baskets of coal) into the carts or waggons.
[58] Roper, Robyn Personal communication.
[59] *Newcastle Courant*, January 2, 1857

The magnificent three-decker *Sirocco* is the handsomest ship in the port, and has made some of the fastest passages on record; her saloons are superbly furnished, and has excellent accommodation for all classes of passengers.

3-7 Jane Vickers and William Siddle in 1858

Pictured left are Jane Vickers (cousin of Francis Vickers of Belle Vue) with her husband William Siddle (1816-1863) in about 1858, not long after their move to Australia. Robyn Roper notes that the photo shows "a slim waisted, oval faced woman with her hair parted in the middle drawn straight down and tied over the ears where the ends curled. In what appears to be a pleated top taffeta gown she is seated on the right side of her husband who has a very serious demeanour."[60]

Those from the North-East seeking passage, available from £14, were invited to apply to Agents James Potts in Newcastle or Robert Sutherland in Durham City.[61] The *Sirocco* actually sailed on April 30th 1858[62] arriving at Geelong three months later.

After a brief stay in Ballarat, the Siddles returned to Geelong where William found work as a stone mason on public buildings being built with gold revenue, but unfortunately not for long - he died of a stroke and bronchitis in Geelong at the age of 47 in 1863, with Jane's cousin Joseph reporting the death. Robyn Roper notes:-

> Just short of seven months after William's death (Jane) married Henry (Harry) Weeks on 13 May 1864 at the Geelong Registry Office. She lived long enough to know about her first eight grandchildren, the first girl, Mary Jane bearing her name. The second girl, Ada, remembered her fondly. Jane did not know of the New Zealand sojourn where the thirteenth and fourteenth children were named Frank and Joseph Herbert Vickers respectively in honour of so many of her family of origin, nor that the latter inherited the Vickers family trait of "never walking anywhere if you could run".[63]

[60] Unpublished *Family History of Vickers of Weardale in County Durham*, by Robyn Roper
[61] *Newcastle Courant*, April 2, 1858
[62] *Liverpool Mercury*, Shipping Intelligence, May 1, 1858
[63] This and other information about Jane Siddle/Weeks nee Vickers, extracted from Robyn Roper's unpublished booklet, *Family History of Vickers of Weardale*, 2006.

# EIGHTEEN SEVENTY-FOUR

Jane Siddle/Weeks nee Vickers died of chronic heart disease on 3 July 1876 at Ballarat at the age of 64, and was buried in the New Cemetery, Ballarat, in an elevated, uncrowded Church of England section with some eucalyptus trees close by.

3-8 Joseph Vickers and Elizabeth Collingwood – the latter described by her great great granddaughter Minnage Farrage in 1979 as "the funny little body in the black bonnet".

## *"Very Fresh considering their Ages"*

Francis describes his father and mother, Joseph and Elizabeth Vickers of Howl John as being 'very fresh, considering their ages' - the word "fresh" has many meanings, and in this case means 'healthy', certainly apparent in the case of Joseph who was working every day on the farm at Howl John at the age of 83. Elizabeth does not look quite as fresh as Joseph, despite being about 11 years younger. Both appear to have no teeth.

Their youngest daughter Elizabeth, born in 1842, was with them in 1874, together with youngest son William who was born 7 years later when his mother was 48 years old.

Their son John Vickers married Jane Reed in 1862 and two years later they moved to Mown Meadows Farm, Crook. After Jane's death in 1870 at the age of 30, John was left to raise three young children: Matthew, Joseph, and Elizabeth (See photo on page 46). In such circumstances he would normally have been compelled to hire someone to be a housekeeper and look after the children. Fortunately, his unmarried sister Mary was able to move from Howl John to Mown Meadows to help her favourite brother – she was the closest to John in age and was bridesmaid at his wedding. Mary continued as John's housekeeper when he moved first to Catchburn (Morpeth), then to Tunstall near Carnforth, Lancs, and finally in retirement to Cleadon, near Sunderland, where he named his house "Belle Vue".

T. HEAVISIDE                    DURHAM

3-9 Mary Vickers was the childrens' surrogate mother, and housekeeper for her brother John. The photograph of Mary was taken in the late 1860s.

John Vickers was an expert cattle breeder and enjoyed great success as an exhibitor at shows for many years. After he moved to Mown Meadows, he continued to have an active involvement in his father's herd, and in April 1874 bred the champion bull *Duke of Howl John* at Howl John Farm.

The *Duke of Howl John* won numerous prizes for John Vickers at agricultural shows around the country, thereby delivering a massive boost to the reputation of Weardale for cattle breeding. It was a proud moment for the Vickers family and for the Stanhope Agricultural Society when the *Duke of Howl John* became Champion Bull at the Carlisle Royal Show in 1880.(See page 53)

# EIGHTEEN SEVENTY-FOUR

3-10 Two of Francis's brothers are not mentioned in the 1874 letter: Thomas, a farmer and draper (above left), died at Howl John in 1868, aged 39 years. George, also a farmer, died in 1870 at the age of 47.

Francis provides news of Uncle Francis Vickers and Aunt Jane at neighbouring Pease Myers. His father's brother Francis was born on Christmas Day in 1792 and continued farming at Pease Myers after his father, also Francis, died in 1822 and his brothers acquired tenancies elsewhere. In Newcastle in 1847, 54 year-old bachelor Francis married Hamsterley-born Jane Whitfield who had been a farm servant at Pease Myers. In the 1874 letter, Francis and Jane were described as 'very feeble'.

They were indeed feeble. A few months later that year, Jane died aged 73. Uncle Francis then moved to stay with brother Thomas, an innkeeper at Stotsfield Burn, Rookhope, where Thomas's unmarried daughter Margaret was able to look after him.

Uncle Thomas Vickers was born at Pease Myers in 1796. From the 1830s, he farmed Steward Shield Meadows where he gained a reputation as a horse breeder. In the 1840s, he moved to Stotsfield Burn where the Vickers family had land and became a lead-ore carrier, most probably working with lead-ore smelter William Bowman, the letter-writer's father-in-law. By the 1860s he was a farmer of 18 acres and an innkeeper at Stotsfield Burn where he died on June 18 1876 at the age of 80 years.

Eighteen months later, Uncle Francis died, 10 days short of his 85th birthday. Without children, he left all his estate of circa £1,000 to his 18 nephews and nieces including Margaret Vickers of Stotsfield Burn who had looked after him in his final years, my great grandfather Francis Sanderson of Harperley, and three other members of the Sanderson family: John Sanderson of Broomley, Margaret Hall of Hamsterley, and Mary Stephenson of Harperley.

Nineteen year-old servant Sarah Featherston was present at Pease Myers in 1871 and may have been Francis and Jane's "servant girl" mentioned by Francis of Belle Vue in the 1874 letter.

The two oldest sons of Francis Vickers and Mary Bowman were Joseph and William, born in 1851 and 1854 respectively, and they were still working the farm at Belle Vue with their father in 1874. The youngest surviving son Frank, born in 1858, was a schoolboy at Stanhope at the time of the 1871 Census but, as Francis points out, was at boarding school in Darlington by 1874. Also with the family in 1871 was Francis's daughter Isabella, but she is not mentioned in the letter.

Francis also updates his cousin with news of old friends and acquaintances. One such is William Morley senior, aged 49 when he died on February 5th, 1874 at Sweet Wells, as Francis notes, "rather suddenly". He was a Poor Rate Collector for Stanhope parish from the age of 24 and also an agricultural overseer. After marrying farmer's daughter Hannah Snowball from Byers Green in 1851, he farmed 37 acres at Sweet Wells and became a successful exhibitor of shorthorns and Leicesters. A few months after his death, his prime bull above one year old, *"British Baron"*, which had been exhibited six times and won five first prizes, won at the Weardale Agricultural Show[64]. He was also well-known in the locality because of his public service appointments and he was an active member for Stanhope of the South Durham Liberal Association. *The Northern Echo* noted that "no register (of voters) in the Southern Division was kept more correctly than that of Stanhope and St John's"[65] His death a few days before the 1874 General Election denied him the pleasure of witnessing an historic victory for the Liberals in South Durham.

Francis believes that Thomas but not George Vickers would have known William Morley, not surprising given that George migrated to Canada about a decade ahead of Thomas, and before William had assumed a high profile in the dale. William Morley senior was succeeded as the Poor Rate Collector for Stanhope Guardians and Assistant Overseer to the Overseers by his son, also called William (See page 74).

Six months after the 1874 letter, the much respected local surveyor, land and mineral agent John Joseph Roddam who had produced the "Roddam Map" of Stanhope Parish in 1851 (See page 145), died at the age of 48. In March, he had been a candidate for membership of the first School Board but narrowly failed to secure enough votes, reportedly because of over-confidence.

A popular figure nevertheless, the Roddam Memorial Fund Committee was established with Joseph Cowper Cain in the chair and William Morley junior as secretary, It was agreed that funds be raised by public subscription "for the purpose of commemorating the memory of the late J J Roddam of Stanhope, by a memorial, to show the esteem in which that gentleman was held, his kind disposition and varied abilities, appreciated by the inhabitants of Weardale and other friends". It was further agreed that the memorial should be a drinking fountain containing a suitable inscription.[66]

Contributors to the fund included Francis Vickers of Belle Vue, Francis Vickers of Pease Myers, Charles Vickers of Snowsfield[67], John Reed of Newlandside, Rev Hugh Gilmore, William Watson of White House, JRW Hildyard Esq., Richard Mews of the *Pack Horse Inn*, Henry Stephenson of Billingshield, and William Morley Egglestone.

Newspapers and less frequently photographs were exchanged in the correspondence between Francis and his cousins. In the first letter, Francis thanks George for a

---

[64] *Northern Echo*, August 31, 1874
[65] *Northern Echo*, Feb 6, 1874
[66] *Northern Echo*, December 18, 1874
[67] Sometimes referred to as 'Snowfield'.

newspaper sent three weeks earlier, and a portrait, probably of George himself. This portrait was passed to John Reed, and Francis conveys John's good wishes to George.

3-11 George Vickers, probably in 1876 at the time of his second marriage. It may have been the photograph sent to John Reed.

John Reed, a farmer at Newlandside in 1874, was born in 1827, the son of Matthew Reed and Elizabeth Blacklaw who had married in 1826. A cursory examination of Weardale genealogy reveals the unsurprising fact that farmers' sons tended to marry farmers' daughters, and that family ties remained strong over the generations. There were for example extensive marriage ties between the Vickers, Reed and Sanderson families, as seen through the marriages of five of Mathew and Elizabeth Reed's children.

- Mary Reed married Francis Brown of Greenhead[68], whose mother was Jane Vickers, the sister of Joseph Vickers of Howl John

---

[68] The first 'Francis Brown' died in infancy

- Jane Reed married John Vickers of Mown Meadows, the brother of Francis Vickers of Belle Vue
- George Reed married Margaret Vickers, the sister of Francis Vickers of Belle Vue
- Margaret Reed married Thomas Sanderson senior of Thimbleby Hill
- Matthew Reed married Jane Sanderson of Allergill

3-12 Vickers/Reed/Sanderson Links

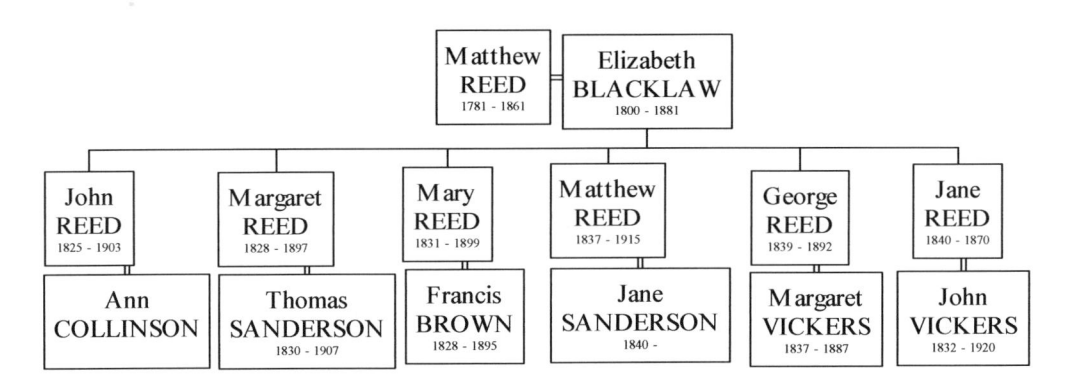

```
                    Matthew REED ══ Elizabeth BLACKLAW
                    1781 - 1861       1800 - 1881
    ┌────────────┬────────────┬────────────┬────────────┬────────────┐
   John        Margaret      Mary        Matthew       George        Jane
   REED         REED         REED         REED          REED         REED
 1825-1903   1828-1897    1831-1899    1837-1915     1839-1892    1840-1870
   ══           ══           ══           ══            ══           ══
   Ann        Thomas       Francis       Jane        Margaret       John
 COLLINSON  SANDERSON      BROWN       SANDERSON     VICKERS      VICKERS
            1830-1907    1828-1895      1840-        1837-1887    1832-1920
```

Francis Brown's mother is Jane Vickers, the sister of Joseph Vickers of Howl John. A Double Line between boxes indicates a marriage.

## The Fatal Railway Accident

George Pearson died in tragic circumstances on December 8th, 1873, a few months after the birth of his son Joseph Vickers Pearson. Francis describes the shocking news of George's death, his matter-of-fact account of the accident being based on local press reports. George was the engine driver on a heavy mineral train heading from Barnard Castle to Tebay when the accident happened. The following account appeared in *The Northern Echo*:

> FATAL RAILWAY ACCIDENT – Yesterday morning a fatal accident occurred a few miles west of Barnard Castle, at or near a place called Cat Castle Bridge, to an engine driver, called George Pearson, belonging to Shildon. It appears the accident occurred in a cut, where a water spout crosses the railway; and it is supposed that Pearson was knocked down by this spout when walking over the engine tank. When found, his head was in the five-foot way, and his body between the rails, completely cut in two. His house door key was also found near his body, which was also cut in two, and his pocket knife was found crushed quite flat. He was conveyed to Bowes to await a coroner's inquest. Seventeen laden mineral trucks and guard's van had passed over his body.[69]

---

[69] *Northern Echo*, December 9, 1873

It appears that George was standing on the tank of his engine watering his coke and as the engine passed under Cat Castle Bridge, the water spout knocked him off the tank and he fell onto the rails between the tank and the first truck. The guard only realised what had happened after the train had passed over his body. Mercifully, it was reported that his death was instantaneous.[70]

Cat Castle Bridge is less than 3 miles west of Barnard Castle. It seems that the water spout was from the Deepdale Beck which was crossed by a railway viaduct at Cat Castle (now a disused railway line). The line ran west from Barnard Castle to Partington, then south over the Deepdale Beck at Cat Castle Bridge, and then west to Bowes and Tebay.

What happened to the unfortunate George Pearson was not that unusual at the time. There were numerous railway accidents, often with multiple deaths, caused in many cases by the smallest of miscalculations – loss of concentration by a signalman, a misjudgement of speed by an engine man or as in George's case, failure to be alert to potential hazards.

> Just as the Victorian railway was a vast, dramatic, and highly visible expression of technology triumphant, so the railway accident constituted a uniquely sensational and public demonstration of the price which that triumph demanded -- violence, destruction, terror and trauma.[71]

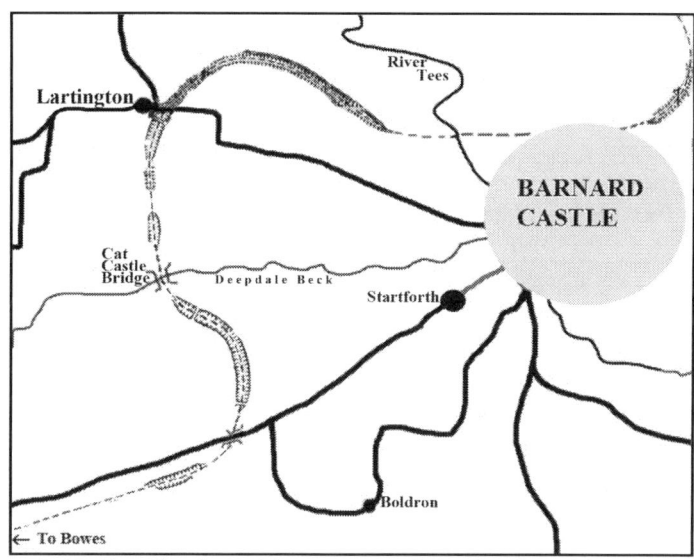

3-13 Cat Castle Bridge, scene of the fatal accident

George had been with the railway company for no more than two years when he died, so his experience as an engine man was limited, and living in Shildon, he may have been unfamiliar with the line beyond Barnard Castle. Furthermore, the railway companies were not noted for their concern for the safety of their staff or their passengers. One 1862 commentary asserted that railway accidents were not really accidents at all, but "might be

---

[70] *Auckland Chronicle*, December 13, 1874
[71] Harrington, Ralph *The railway accident: trains, trauma and technological crisis in nineteenth-century Britain.* http://www.york.ac.uk/inst/irs/irshome/papers/rlyacc.htm

more correctly described as pre-arranged homicide", given the "system of mingled recklessness and parsimony" which it accused the railways of operating[72]

By 1874, railway safety appeared to be improving but later in the year there were reminders of the dangers. In September near Thorpe on the Great Eastern railway, nineteen people were killed and fifty seriously injured in a high-speed collision between an express train and a mail train, a catastrophe "calculated to shock even the conscience of a railway director":-

> In a moment, all that remains of two fast trains is a heap of debris, intermixed with the dying and the dead. Out of this huge mass of ... window glass, of railway tires and carriage cushions, of iron springs and wooden beams, nineteen corpses are dug, and half a hundred wretches, more or less crushed and mangled, are with difficulty extricated....This time it seems as if somebody was to blame. The night inspector at Norwich gave wrong instructions to the station master at Brundall, and nineteen persons paid for his mistake with their lives. [73]

## "All Sorts of Machinery in England"

Francis proudly describes the use of machinery in "Old England", no doubt in response to George's enthusiastic observations about farming developments in North America. North Americans, known at the time for their hyperbole, were described in one Victorian newspaper report as "exaggerated Englishmen". The fact was that cheap imports from North America where agriculture was more mechanised, in combination with higher labour costs at home, were beginning to have a serious impact on British farmers.

A report in *The Newcastle Courant* a day before this letter was written summarises the problem and suggests the solution:-

> It is of course a very simple process to the labourer to put in a demand for an increase of wage, when a widespread Union is at his back, with ample funds for removal to a British colony; but the next process by which to recoup the increased outlay, is not quite so simple for the farmer, with imported corn keeping down home prices....What then is the farmer to do? The labourer must have more money, or else he takes himself off; the farmer then must effectually economise, as American farmers economise by the use of additional mechanical power. It is nothing less than a revolution that is in progress.... A tendency to get remuneration out of machinery instead of out of men, and when the result is fully achieved there will be much satisfaction (amongst farmers). [74]

Many agricultural labourers regarded threshing machines as a threat to their livelihoods and there were frequent outbreaks of agitation and civil disorder in which the machines were broken in protest.

---

[72] Harrington, Op Cit
[73] *Northern Echo*, September 12, 1874
[74] *Newcastle Courant*, March 19, 1874

# EIGHTEEN SEVENTY-FOUR

**RICHARD GARRETT AND SONS,**
LEISTON WORKS, SUFFOLK,
(Established 1778)

**PORTABLE STEAM ENGINES AND COMBINED THRASHING AND DRESSING MACHINES**
For finishing the Corn for market in one operation. They are greatly improved for home use, and are efficient, economical, simple, powerful, and durable.
**STRAW ELEVATORS AND SELF-MOVING AGRICULTURAL ENGINES.**

3-14 Advertisement in *Newcastle Courant*, 1874.

Francis speaks of a "remarkably fine winter" with very little snow, frost and rain, highly unusual in Weardale in those days. The fine weather augured well for the lambing season and enabled the draining of the North Field and West Rigs, an important process because, as Mingay notes, "only a well-drained, fertile soil would enable the heavy investment of material and labour to yield profitable results." The cost of drainage was between £4 and £8 per acre, and an agreed proportion of the cost would be placed on the tenant in the form of a drainage charge. It is likely however that this was the last significant drainage work at Belle Vue for many years, as the agricultural depression brought such expensive operations to an abrupt end in the mid-1870s.[75]

By the end of the year, Weardale and the rest of the country was in the grip of a hard winter, a situation not to the liking of *Northern Echo* Editor WT Stead:-

> With the nation, as with nature, it is winter. A snow-fall, like a death shroud, conceals all things from sight; a fog, dense almost as Egyptian darkness, broods over the land. For a time, vegetation seems to have ceased to exist. All sounds are deadened by the snow, the world speaks in whispers as if in the presence of a corpse. The murmur of the running river is hushed beneath the ice. The very ink with which this article is written is frozen into a solid mass, and needs to be thawed pen-full by pen-full in front of a roasting fire before a single word can be traced on the paper.

This gloomy editorial notes that 1874 had been a sad and dismal year but ends with an optimistic political prediction:-

---

[75] Mingay, GE (1998) *Rural Life in Victorian England*. Sutton Publishing, Stroud.

Just as the wise agriculturalist recognises the importance of this inclement season as a preparation for next year's harvest, so the sagacious politician accepts with equanimity the stern rigour of a Conservative regime, knowing that it will play an important part in rendering possible the Liberal triumphs of the future. As certainly as the snow will disappear, will the bleak season of the reaction be succeeded by the happy springtime and harvest of Liberal progress.[76]

3-15 The surviving children of John Vickers of Mown Meadows and Jane Morgan: Joseph, b 1865, Elizabeth, b 1867, and Matthew, b 1863. After their mother died in 1870, they were looked after by John's sister Mary.

---

[76] *Northern Echo*, December 31, 1874

## 4.   EIGHTEEN EIGHTY-ONE

> you say you pity us People in England. well perhaps so. but pity without relief is like Mustard without Beef if you want to show us any simp-athy you will be kind enough to keep your Beast & Sheep at home and not send them to England to under sell us.

4-1 Francis leaves George in no doubt about the plight of British farmers

Eighteen Eighty-One was notable in Weardale for the unusual severity of the weather, unprecedented even in the lifetime of 90 year-old Joseph Vickers of Howl John. *The Newcastle Courant* reported that on Wednesday, January 5th, the day before Francis wrote his letter to George Vickers, snow fell in Weardale almost incessantly, continuing throughout the night and with the wind whirling the snow into massive snowdrifts, "underneath which numberless sheep were buried".[77]   Francis often mentions the local weather in his letters, so why does he not do so on this occasion? (See page 65).

## *Walter Beaumont's Crusade*

Eighteen Eighty-One was also notable for the distress of the leadminers during the depressed state of the mining industry. Mr Wentworth Blacket Beaumont, MP for South Northumberland and with a family seat at Bretton Hall, Wakefield, the absentee lessee of the lead mines was in dispute with the Ecclesiastical Commissioners concerning the royalties they demanded, and in the absence of an agreement, many leadminers were laid off.  In the midst of the crisis, Mr Walter Beaumont, the younger brother of the lessee, travelled the dale making thunderous speeches about the unjust and unnecessary threat of closure of the mines, and printing placards with defamatory statements about his brother and his agents, Mr Joseph Cowper Cain and Mr Thomas Rumney.  One of the placards focusing on JC Cain stated:

> Immediate!  Final !  Important!  In the sight, and at this very moment, of God, the judge of each, Walter Beaumont of Eastgate, Weardale (sic), and J.C. Cain of Weardale House, agent to W.B. Beaumont, MP, who has been duly warned of your crimes, misdemeanours, &c., do when, and when only, all other reasonable

---

[77] *Newcastle Courant* , Jan 7 1881

means fail, and under the most strong necessity, and dire need, hereby solemnly and soberly on proven evidence, and after a full examination of many witnesses of tried character, accuse the aforesaid Cain of misappropriating sundry and important moneys, of gross inhumanity, &c., also of cruel intimidation, detailed injustice, and together with Thomas Rumney (of New House, Weardale, sub-agent for W.B. Beaumont, MP), of outrage against women. [78]

The accused gentlemen did not take kindly to these damning accusations. In November 1881, JC Cain sought through the Queen's Bench Division in London to have a criminal charge for libel brought against Walter Beaumont. Sir Hardinge Giffard, QC, for JC Cain, stated in court that Mr Beaumont "had taken into his head that Mr Cain, in the conduct of the management of the estates confided to his care, has been guilty of gross inhumanity and impropriety, and what not. Mr Cain says there is nothing whatever in the charges." In response, Mr Justice Field sympathised with Mr Cain but failed to see why he was seeking redress through the High Court. He refused the application and advised that Mr JC Cain should follow the same remedy as other people, namely to go to the nearest petty sessions where he lives.[79] On hearing this news, Walter Beamont declared that the judge had effectively said, "Go back, dogs, to your kennels, and bite boldly where you are known, instead of barking from afar off."[80]

The unrestrained rhetoric from a man who believed he was on a mission from God went down well with the miners, even if they were less sure than Walter Beaumont about who was to blame for the crisis. An anonymous letter writer from St John's Chapel spoke of the "painful proofs of the sufferings of the people":-

> The tradesmen who travel the dale, the medical gentlemen, the Methodist ministers, the clergymen resident in the valley, and others, in their professional visits to the homes of the people, witness cases that are heartrending. Butcher meat is as rare in many a family as tea was to our forefathers….The questions are often asked, "Why is the dale in such distress?" and "Who is to blame?" Some say the Ecclesiastical Commissioners, others say Mr WB Beaumont, MP, and his agents, Mr JC Cain and Mr Thomas Rumney, are responsible for the partial stoppage of the leadmines. There is blame attaching to some party. Whatever may be the result of the agitation promoted by Mr Walter Beaumont, it is beyond question that a change is required in the management of the industries of the dale. The sympathy of the people is with Mr Walter Beaumont, and they wish him success in his undertaking.[81]

The stakes were raised even further when mine safety made the headlines following the death at Quarry Level Leadmine in November 1881 of Joseph Robinson of Huntshieldford. Walter Beaumont queried the Coroner's verdict of "Accidental Death", arguing that managers should not have allowed Robinson to work in a shaft with such poor ventilation and foul gas. At a mass meeting in December at St John's Chapel, Walter Beaumont exclaimed:-

---

[78] *Newcastle Courant,* November 18, 1881
[79] *Northern Echo,* December 18, 1881
[80] *Northern Echo,* December 19, 1881
[81] *Northern Echo,* November 26, 1881

A free vote? A mockery in Weardale. Free work. A lie in Weardale – it does not exist here. Free air? Yes, there is free air, but it is not in the mines.[82]

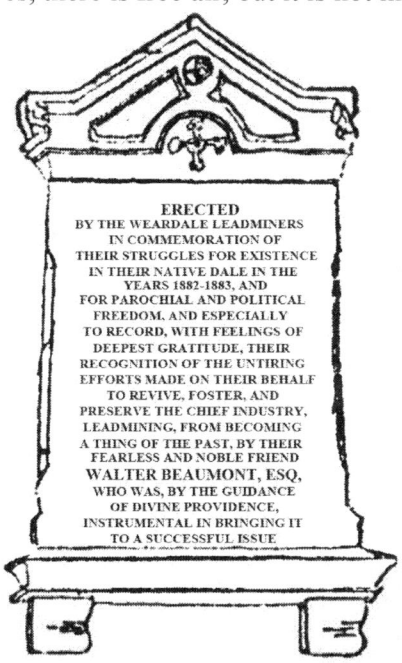

> ERECTED
> BY THE WEARDALE LEADMINERS
> IN COMMEMORATION OF
> THEIR STRUGGLES FOR EXISTENCE
> IN THEIR NATIVE DALE IN THE
> YEARS 1882-1883, AND
> FOR PAROCHIAL AND POLITICAL
> FREEDOM, AND ESPECIALLY
> TO RECORD, WITH FEELINGS OF
> DEEPEST GRATITUDE, THEIR
> RECOGNITION OF THE UNTIRING
> EFFORTS MADE ON THEIR BEHALF
> TO REVIVE, FOSTER, AND
> PRESERVE THE CHIEF INDUSTRY,
> LEADMINING, FROM BECOMING
> A THING OF THE PAST, BY THEIR
> FEARLESS AND NOBLE FRIEND
> WALTER BEAUMONT, ESQ,
> WHO WAS, BY THE GUIDANCE
> OF DIVINE PROVIDENCE,
> INSTRUMENTAL IN BRINGING IT
> TO A SUCCESSFUL ISSUE

4-2 Tablet at St John's Chapel expressing the gratitude of the miners for the support from Walter Beaumont

*The Northern Echo* commented on his 'Crusade':-

> His words have not been measured. His feelings, rather than his judgement, on the harrowing situation of the dalesmen have been expressed with great freedom.... They may not understand the object and aims of "the Squire's Brother", but they are ready to take both for granted, in view of the novel and unexpected proffer of sympathy he brings with him....There is at least this degree of method in Mr Walter Beaumont's madness, that he has managed to link the family name to the sentiments of gratitude and love at a time when it was being closely associated with passions of quite another character …(Now) the Weardale miners believe that their only trust is in Providence and Mr Walter Beaumont to avert a dreaded and dire calamity.[83]

In December 1881, with no resolution of his dispute with the commissioners, WB Beaumont closed the mines. *The Northern Echo* summarised the unhappy situation:

> That which the gradual depopulation of the valley had not been able to do, the total stoppage of Weardale mining effected. The Commissioners capitulated, and offered Mr Beaumont terms which he probably would have accepted earlier. We cannot but think that the Commissioners…do not come out of this affair with clean hands. They should never in the face of a dying industry and a district rapidly becoming depopulated have driven matters to extremities only to desert the

---

[82] *Northern Echo*, December 19, 1881
[83] *Northern Echo,* December 26, 1881

position they had maintained so obstinately for so long. If the concessions they now offer are necessitated by the present state of the lead market now, they have been equally necessary any time during the last three or four years…We do charge (the Commissioners) with having endeavoured to make their Weardale property more remunerative than was consistent with an equitable consideration for either the lessee or his much-suffering workmen…They insisted on their 'pound of flesh' till they had filled many a once happy home with misery and wretchedness. Running no risk themselves as lessors, and being called upon to cooperate with the lessee in no outlay, their share of the business has been solely the pocketing of the dues.[84]

In a sign of the 'gradual depopulation of the valley', it was reported in October 1881 that 25 people left Stanhope Station for America, with the prospect of more families about to emigrate.[85] In 1871, the population of Weardale had been 19,155 and at the 1881 census was down to 17,542.[86]

The Commissioners capitulated in early 1882, with *The Northern Echo* proclaiming, "The mines will be opened. Work and wages will again gladden many homes."[87] But continuing dissatisfaction on the part of the miners with WB Beaumont's agents was only resolved when his mining monopoly was bought out and leased to the Weardale Lead Company in 1883. The miners' leader Walter Beaumont then disappeared from the dale, but the miners showed their gratitude for his labours on their behalf by placing a tablet in his honour on the north wall of the Town Hall at St John's Chapel.[88] Sadly, the tablet (see previous page) is no longer in place.

The Liberal Party won with an overwhelming majority in the 1880 General Election, and William Thomas Stead, Editor of the *Northern Echo*, received much credit for enabling Gladstone to become Prime Minister for the second time. Benjamin Disraeli, subsequently Lord Beaconsfield, the man who had triumphed in the 1874 election and who was defeated in 1880, died on April 19th 1881 after a long illness.

## *The Letter to George Vickers*

*Belle Vue            January 6th 1881*
*Dear Cousin,*
*Yours to hand dated November 18th. I was glad to hear from you once more, and to hear of the success of you and your family in farming. Our stock consists of 11 cows, 28 young ones of different ages, from 6 weeks old to 2½ years, betwixt 400 and 500 sheep. We have only one horse rising 3 years old. We sold a mare rising 4 a fortnight since for 40 guineas.*

*Son Joseph is farming Tunstall House, 600 acres. He has about 30 beasts, about 300 sheep, and 8 horses, mostly young. Wm is at Pease Myers. Frank the*

---

[84] *Northern Echo*, February 9, 1882
[85] *Northern Echo*, October 6, 1881
[86] *Northern Echo*, April 18, 1891
[87] *Northern Echo*, January 9, 1882
[88] *Northern Echo*, September 27, 1884

*youngest was married on Christmas Day, to the oldest daughter of Thomas Sanderson of Thimbleby Hill – he (Thomas Sanderson) bought Newlandside, the farm that John Wilson lived at. Some of the family have been there since last Mayday. He has now taken Snows Field. Charles Vickers died last February, his son Joseph died June 1879. Jonathan left home some years since and married a young woman at Corbridge where he was working. There is only Wm and two sisters at home. He has had the offer of it at an advance of £24 rent. It is let for £38 more, so they will have to leave after being in the family a hundred years or more.*

*You say you pity us people in England. Well, perhaps so, but pity without relief is like mustard without beef. If you want to show us any sympathy, you will be kind enough to keep your beef and sheep at home and not send them to England to undersell us. Farmers, no doubt but it will be a benefit to the working class, but we farmers will either have to come to America or have our rents down............................*

*I am much oblige(d) to you for the papers you have sent. If you have sent one every week, I have not got them all. There is some things in them that is interesting, but I cannot follow suit as we do not get the papers every week.*

*You wanted to know how your friends are getting on. Well, I am sorry to say your brother Joseph departed this life November 27th, aged 64. I think he had died rather suddenly. He was very stout and often ailing. One of his daughters oftens went with him when he went from home, but I have not seen any of them for a long while. I should most likely have been at the funeral but we did not get the card till that night he was interred.*

*As for Frank and family, they have been disagreeing very much, as I have heard. Frank has married again - which you would see in a paper I sent to Thomas – which has caused much quarreling. He has married a young woman that has been keeping house for him. I think he will be her uncle by marriage. Joseph's Mill has been in the papers to either sell or let, which perhaps you will have seen.*

*You say you perhaps might come over to England. We should be very glad to see you or any of your family. Your old Mrs Read is still living, no doubt she would be glad to see you. If you come soon, you perhaps might see my father – I think the only uncle you have living. He is over 90 years of age.*

*Now I must conclude with kind regards to you all. Wishing you all a Happy New Year.*

*PS be kind enough to let Thomas see this letter and tell him about Joseph. I intend to write him soon.*

*So no more at present*
*from your loving Cousin*
*Francis Vickers*

---

We do not have a copy of the letter George Vickers of Ontario wrote to Francis in November 1880 but it may have conveyed the news about his marriage to Mary Anne Bell in 1876.

George's letter certainly contained news that he and his family were making a success of farming in Ontario, and at a time when British farmers were finding it hard to make ends meet. Not wanting to be outdone, Francis responds proudly with a list of the stock at Belle Vue. He also reveals that a four-year-old mare was sold for the substantial sum of 40 guineas in December 1880 – using the Retail Price Index, it would be equivalent to over £3,000 today, and using average earnings, today's equivalent amount would be over £17,000.

We learn from Francis that sheep farming was a major element of the business at Belle Vue, so despite the dramatic changes in agriculture during his lifetime and there being "all manner of machinery in England", much of the time and effort on the farm was devoted to tending sheep just as his farming ancestors had always done:-

> The life of the shepherd has a strange fascination. It is older than agriculture; in it we seem to join hands with the patriarchal days. The advance of science has done much to upset the whole system of the old-fashioned farmer, with its patent manures, steam ploughs, and reaping-machines, but science does not seem to have much to say regarding so old an occupation as this. In essentials it is what it was in the dawning of history. Lambs continue to be born in just the same way, and to require just the same care. The March storms are just as destructive as they were three hundred years ago, or a thousand years ago, and as much beyond human control. The shepherd now perhaps does not look the picturesque figure he once did, but at heart he is much the same. He is a lonely man, with the far-away look in his eyes that men have who see few of their kind, and is glad to talk when he descends for a little into the more populous lowlands.[89]

4-3 George Vickers of Ontario and Mary Ann Bell, possibly at the time of their marriage.

---

[89] Stewart Dick and Helen Allingham, (1909) *The Cottage Homes of England*.

Francis does not mention his brothers and sisters in the 1881 letter. His sister Elizabeth and auctioneer/grocer Joseph Walton had married in 1876 and were living in Stanhope in 1881. His sister Mary continued as housekeeper for brother John of Mown Meadows who, together with brother William Vickers senior of Howl John was enjoying outstanding success in stock breeding. Francis, his father Joseph, his brothers and eventually his sons were prominent members of the Stanhope Agricultural Society which had begun its annual show in conjunction with Stanhope Fair in 1834 with a competition involving a few black-faced sheep and a few cattle. From the 1850s, Joseph Vickers and sons were frequent prize-winners for sheep and short-horned cattle, competing with the likes of William Morley and sons of Sweet Wells, George Little of Eastgate, and John Wilson of Newlandside. The coming of the railway in 1862 led to the expansion of the show as exhibitors from more distant places were able to bring their livestock to Stanhope, and day-trippers from Middlesbrough and Sunderland came in special trains. The success of Joseph and sons continued throughout the 1860s, by which time John Vickers had moved to Mown Meadows, Crook.

## *The Duke of Howl John*

The reputation of Messrs Vickers of Howl John for stock breeding was sealed with the emergence in 1875 of the celebrated bull, *Duke of Howl John* (33674) which won top prizes at a number of shows throughout Durham that year. From Joseph Vickers of Howl John's herd but brought from his parental home to Mown Meadows by John Vickers, the white bull again won first prize in a strong field of shorthorns at the 1876 Beamish, Pontop and Consett Agricultural Show at Whickham. The *Duke of Howl John*, the son of the Mantalini bull, *White Duke* and descended from *Red Rosette* by Mr (John) Booth's *Royal Buck*[90], won again the following year at the Northumberland Show in August. A month later, the *Duke* won at the Stanhope Agricultural Show where William Cooke of Hexham, described as 'no mean judge' of shorthorns, stated that in the open class for bulls, the *Duke of Howl John* was worthy to be in equal competition with the very best shorthorns in the country.

In his chairman's speech, the equally impressed Mr JRW Hildyard suggested that the owners should send their stock to the Royal Show, and also to the County, such as Yorkshire, and he was convinced they would win the prizes.[91]

The *Duke of Howl John* thereafter appeared at numerous agricultural shows throughout England and the Scottish Borders, achieving a "highly commended" rating at the Bristol Royal Show in 1878. Sheila Potter, the great granddaughter of William Vickers of Pease Myers, notes that the task of getting the *Duke* from the farm to the railway station was made easier by the custom-made leather boots which fitted over the hooves – at first, for the 3 mile walk from Howl John to Stanhope Station, and then, when John Vickers took sole ownership of the bull, for the much shorter walk to Crook Station from Mown Meadows Farm.

The 'finely formed white bull' enjoyed great success at the shows at Stanhope (1879), Durham (1877, 1879), Cleveland (1879), and Gateshead (1879 Beamish, Pontop & Consett Show). Reporting on the latter, the *Newcastle Courant* observed:-

---

[90] Ashburner, Robert William, *The Shorthorn Herds of England*, 1885-6-7.
[91] *Northern Echo*, September 15, 1877

There was no difficulty on fixing upon *'Duke of Howl John'* as the first winner. Mr Vickers' large and fine white has done good service, and many of his sons and daughters have competed successfully at various shows. He is a little lumpy about the top of the shoulders, but otherwise his wealth of flesh is evenly proportioned. His formidable size, especially in the quarters, attracted great attention both in the ring and in the stall, and there was not a dissenting voice from the decision which placed him first. He has not been shown frequently this season, but wherever he has competed he has done so with credit.[92]

Further success followed in 1880 at the Northumberland Show, Crook Show, and Shotley Bridge Show, and then the jewell in the crown, the Prize Bull above three years old at the Royal Agricultural Society's Show at Carlisle on July 12, 1880. One observer recounted, "He has wonderfully good quarters, loins, ribs, and flanks, and handles well; while his head is shapely, and his countenance pleasant."[93] Another described the Duke thus: "…an immense white bull with red-tipped ears. He is a massive shorthorn, with wide loin, deep brisket, good flesh and quality."

After the Royal Show, in an early example of product endorsement, the *Northern Echo* commented:-

It will be of interest to our agricultural readers to know that Mr Vickers' bull has been fed on food seasoned with Roger Errington's cattle spice"[94]

Roger Errington was a cattle food manufacturer and town councillor in Sunderland who on March 2, 1882 at Windsor Railway Station, witnessed Roderick Maclean attempt to shoot Queen Victoria. He was a key witness at Maclean's trial for High Treason. Maclean was found "not guilty but insane.

---

UNDER ROYAL PATRONAGE OF           HER MAJESTY THE QUEEN

## FARMERS SPICE YOUR HAY
## ERRINGTONS CELEBRATED SPICE

Is the PUREST AND MOST DELICIOUS in the market for SPICING HAY that has been exposed to the weather has been largely used, and is highly recommended by those who have tested its value,

For REARING CALVES cannot be excelled. It is first-class substitute for milk,

PRICE 34s. per cwt., or in quantities of 2½ cwt. and upwards in Barrels at 30s. per cwt., carriage paid.

ROGER ERRINGTON, VICTORIA STEAM MILLS, SUNDERLAND

---

[92] *Newcastle Courant*, August 22, 1879
[93] *Preston Guardian*, July 17, 1880
[94] *Northern Echo*, July 13, 1880

Two weeks after the Royal Show, the *Duke* won again at the Highland and Agricultural Society Show at Kelso. Incidentally, this victory was reported almost three months later in the *Brisbane Courier*, alongside news of the commencement of the trial of Ned Kelly in Melbourne[95].

On September 10th 1880, John Vickers of Mown Meadows returned in triumph to the Stanhope Show in Stanhope Castle grounds where the *Duke of Howl John* was again champion prize bull of the day. Mr Hildyard was especially pleased, his advice to exhibit at the Royal Show having been followed and, as he proudly pointed out, the bull was born and bred in the dale.[96] John Vickers also won several other prizes, including 1st prize for a cow named *Rose of the Meadows* and 1st and 2nd prizes for yearling heifers *Duchess* and *Lady Manfred*, daughters of the *Duke of Howl John*.

At the luncheon, the chairman in proposing the loyal toast referred 'with a shade of sadness' to the Seaham Colliery catastrophe and to the 'arduous campaign our soldiers were following in the remote hills of Afghanistan'. Two days earlier, there had been a terrible explosion at Seaham Colliery resulting in the loss of 164 lives. And British troops, as now, were in Afghanistan, and on September 1st, 1880, had secured a decisive victory over the Afghans at the Battle of Kandahar, but this good news had not yet reached home.

Further success for John Vickers was to come with *Prince of Howl John* (2nd prize and expected to greatly improve with age) and *Duchess of Howl John* (1st prize) at the Wolsingham Show in 1883.[97]

In the late 1880s, John moved his prize herd, originally established at Howl John, from Crook to Catchburn House, Morpeth and in the mid-1890s, to Churchfield Farm, near Carnforth, Lancs. James Sinclair in his *History of Shorthorn Cattle*, notes that "the herd was always kept for the dairy purposes of the country, butter making and calf rearing. Many of the cows gave upwards of twenty-four quarts daily, and had as good a reputation in Westmorland as they had originally in Durham."[98] In 1905, John Vickers sold the herd and retired to Cleadon near Sunderland.

## *Family News*

Francis's son Joseph Vickers is recorded at the time of the 1881 Census (three months after this letter was written) as farming 580 acres at Tunstall House, a farm 3 miles north of Wolsingham on the Waskerley Beck, by Weardale standards a large farm, and Francis was naturally proud of his son's achievements. The letter does not record that on October 7th 1875 at Stanhope St Thomas, Joseph had married second cousin Jane Sanderson, with the Best Man being Joseph's younger brother, William Vickers of Pease Myers.

William was farming at Pease Myers where his father and grandfather were born. In 1878, he had married Sarah Petty in Bishop Auckland, and had a baby daughter Elizabeth Eleanor by 1881.

Youngest son Frank Vickers was married at Stanhope on 25th December 1880 to Elizabeth Sanderson of Thimbleby Hill, and in 1881 was farming with his father at Belle Vue. The marriage showed the close connection between the Vickers and Sanderson

---

[95] *Brisbane Courier*, October 19, 1880
[96] *Northern Echo*, September 11, 1880
[97] *Newcastle Courant*, September 14, 1883
[98] Sinclair, James (1907) *History of Shorthorn Cattle*

families. Francis of Belle Vue had an Uncle John Sanderson, several Sanderson first cousins, and two of his children married Sandersons. The Sanderson family were located mainly near Bollihope Burn from the early 18th Century, and moved further West to such farms as Thimbleby Hill, Horsley Head, Newlandside and Aller Gill as the century progressed.

Francis's daughter Isabella had married bank-clerk John Crawhall in 1878 and they had a son, Charles Edward, by 1881.

## *Purchase of Newlandside Farm*

In 1841, 54 year-old John Wilson senior was a farmer and lead smelter at Newlandside with his wife Mary Lowes and five children, including John Wilson junior aged 11 years. Thomas Sanderson, then 12 years old, was at Thimbleby Hill, the son of Thomas Sanderson and Margaret Atkinson. Thomas Sanderson junior, a limestone quarryman in his youth, took over the tenancy of Thimbleby Hill when his father died in 1857, and also ran a butchering business. The Sanderson family remained at Thimbleby Hill until the 1880s: at the time of the 1881 Census (3/4 April), Thomas Sanderson was still farming 41 acres at Thimbleby Hill, but as Francis indicates, some of his family had moved to Newlandside – his wife Margaret and son Thomas were farming 60 acres at West Newlandside, having moved there 'last May-Day', i.e., 11 months previously, on May 1st, 1880. Thomas had bought the farm at a time when most farmers were content to be tenants, preferring to use their capital to develop the business rather than for purchasing the land.

Thomas Sanderson junior enjoyed some good fortune during the Great Flood of 1881 which caused such havoc in Weardale.(See page 66) As a butcher, he had cattle byred in Stanhope near the river, and as the river rose at the Butts and Bond Eale grounds, Thomas removed his cattle to safety before dark on March 9th, 1881.[99]

## *The Snowsfield Athlete*

As well as buying West Newlandside, Francis reveals that Thomas Sanderson had assumed the tenancy of Snowsfield, a farm about a mile north of West Newlandside and close to the River Wear – a farm that had been in the Vickers family "for a hundred years or more". Charles Vickers of Snowsfield was the son of Charles Vickers Senior (1757-1834) who was the brother of Frank Vickers of Pease Myers (See Fig 4-4, page 58). After his father's death, Charles farmed Snowsfield with his brother William who died in 1874.

The family reputation for being "greyhounds" was long established. Charles junior was an outstanding athlete in his time, competing in the popular sport of Pedestrianism (race-walking and foot-racing) in the early Victorian period. He is likely to have raced locally before coming to national attention in 1846 at the age of 39. In July 1846, the London newspaper *The Era*, whose Editor had never heard of Charles, recorded his recent victory over the *Flying Tailor of Allendale Town*:

---

[99] *Newcastle Courant*, April 1, 1881

# EIGHTEEN EIGHTY-ONE

Charles Vickers of Stanhope and *The Flying Tailor of Allendale Town* met at Mineshead on Monday last to run their race of 120 yards for £10 a side. The competitors appeared at the mark at two o'clock and on the signal being given got away. Vickers, with a yard advantage which he maintained to the end, doing the distance in 13½ seconds (Who is Vickers? Ed).

*The Era* also gave notice that:

Articles have been entered into between William Rudd of Middlesbrough and Charles Vickers of Stanhope, Weardale. Vickers agreeing to give four yards start in 150 at the coming-in end, for £20 a side; to be run at Middlesbrough on 21st July, 1846, and to start by the report of a pistol; Rudd to allow Vickers £1 to run at Middlesbrough. The Editor of *Bell's Life* is appointed final stakeholder, and the next deposit of £10 is to be forwarded on the 15th inst. The Middlesbrough party is to find ropes and stakes, and the money not to be given up until fairly won or lost by a race.
Young Ruddick of Staindrop will run John Coulthard (alias *Black Jack*) of Bedlington 120 yards; or he will take two yards start of Sutton of Kenton, in 200 yards; or two yards of Vickers of Stanhope, the same distance, for £10 or £15 a side.
Articles have been entered into between Samuel Coulthard of Middlebrough and Charles Vickers of Stanhope-in-Weardale. Vickers agrees to give Coulthard five yards start in the last end of 200 yards, for £20 a side; to be run at Middlesbrough, on 20th July, and to start by the report of a pistol. Coulthard to give Vickers £1 for the race to come off at Middlesbrough, and the editor of *Bell's Life* to be the final stakeholder…[100]

The *Flying Tailor of Allendale Town*, James Glendinning, was a middle-distance runner as well as a sprinter. In August, 1845, he won a race over 1¼ miles at the *Hare & Hounds Inn*, Catton, near Allendale Town, in a time of 6 minutes and 13 seconds (equivalent to a mile in just under five minutes), with John Robson, the *Weardale Champion*, finishing in third place. The Catton Sports also featured a wrestling competition which was won by Brown Hodgson of Weardale when he threw William Johnson of Catton after a fierce struggle.[101]

Charles Vickers junior died on 4 February 1880 at Snowsfield and left a personal estate of circa £1,500. As Francis notes, Charles' son Joseph had died eight months earlier in June 1879 aged 42 years and his son Jonathan had left home, leaving only son William and two unmarried daughters, Mary and Margaret at Snowsfield in 1880.

---

[100] *The Era*, July 5, 1846
[101] *Newcastle Courant*, August 8, 1845

```
                    ┌─────────────┬─────────────┐
                    │   Joseph    │  Margaret   │
                    │   VICKERS   │   LITTLE    │
                    └─────────────┴─────────────┘
```

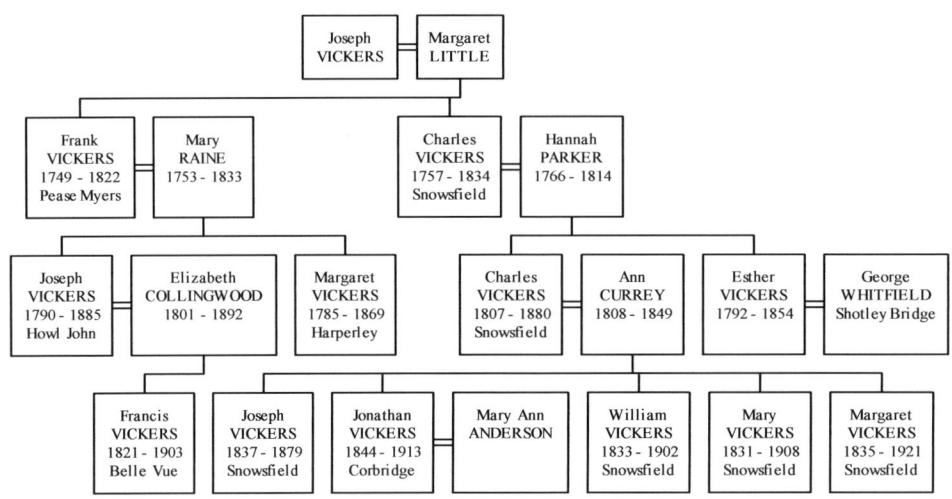

**4-4** The families of Francis of Pease Myers and Charles of Snowsfield
They remained close over several generations. Esther Vickers was the bridesmaid at the marriage of cousin Margaret to John Sanderson in 1812 at Stanhope.

Family tree showing:
- Joseph VICKERS — Margaret LITTLE
  - Frank VICKERS 1749-1822 Pease Myers — Mary RAINE 1753-1833
    - Joseph VICKERS 1790-1885 Howl John — Elizabeth COLLINGWOOD 1801-1892
    - Margaret VICKERS 1785-1869 Harperley
      - Francis VICKERS 1821-1903 Belle Vue
      - Joseph VICKERS 1837-1879 Snowsfield
      - Jonathan VICKERS 1844-1913 Corbridge
  - Charles VICKERS 1757-1834 Snowsfield — Hannah PARKER 1766-1814
    - Charles VICKERS 1807-1880 Snowsfield — Ann CURREY 1808-1849
    - Esther VICKERS 1792-1854 — George WHITFIELD Shotley Bridge
      - Mary Ann ANDERSON
      - William VICKERS 1833-1902 Snowsfield
      - Mary VICKERS 1831-1908 Snowsfield
      - Margaret VICKERS 1835-1921 Snowsfield

## *The Farmers' Distress*

At this time, the agricultural depression was hitting Weardale farmers hard. Local tenant farmers campaigned for reductions in rent and were supported by a generally sympathetic press. In 1879, Finlay Dun wrote of the "unexampled distress" faced by farmers and that "immediate substantial help" was needed from their landlords:

> The tenant's labour and his money have been expended on the landlord's heritage; tenants' capital in many instances has largely contributed to the high rents which for some years have been regularly paid. Now that these rents cannot be earned from the land, occupiers naturally desire to make fresh arrangements with their landlords....It is surely better to make reductions to the present tenants than drive them to bankruptcy, impoverish the holding as well as the holders, and ultimately to make concessions to strangers.[102]

But some landlords, and their agents, were unsympathetic. For example, a deputation of farmers met a representative of the Duke of Cleveland at Barnard Castle in September 1881 and was told that "His Grace did not see his way to give any relief in their rents."[103]

The *Northern Echo* continued to urge farmers to work in combination:-

> Agriculture has not yet been able to recover its footing. Bad weather interfered with the harvest, and afforded proof that in fixing the rents landlords do not take into account the vicissitudes of the seasons. It has been proved that farmers cannot profitably continue their pursuit under present conditions. The unfair burden of rates, the restrictions as to cropping, and the want of security for invested capital and of compensation for improvements combine to heavily handicap English

---

[102] *Newcastle Courant*, April 11, 1879
[103] *Northern Echo*, September 10, 1881

agriculture.....Farmers are slow to act, but the activity and increasing strength of the Farmers' Alliance shows that action is to be delayed no longer.[104]

At Wolsingham Town Hall on March 20, 1882, Charles J Backhouse presided at a lecture by Mr William Trotter of South Acomb on "The cause and remedy of agricultural depression". Mr Trotter argued that farmers, in contrast to those in commerce and industry, were "somewhat homespun and blunt in their manners" which he attributed to their isolated position. Speaking bluntly himself, he maintained that farmers were so fearful of antagonising their landlords, they were apt to be deferential if not cowardly in expressing their opinions, and "their individuality was sapped in consequence". He concluded that it was imperative that farmers act in combination. At the end of the lecture, William Love moved that the agriculturalists of the district form a society, to be called "The Wear Valley Farmers' Club." Seconded by Joseph Vickers of Tow Law, the motion was carried unanimously, and large numbers of farmers present enrolled themselves as members.[105]

The frustration and anger of tenant farmers was compounded by the fact that landlords overwhelmingly represented farming interests in the House of Commons. A small step in the right direction was taken when prominent tenant farmer Samuel Rowlandson of Newton Morrell, near Darlington, was adopted as a Liberal candidate for the North Riding at a meeting in York in January 1882. Reporting this news, *The Northern Echo* presented the Liberal case for fairer representation for farmers:

> That the Liberals are setting class against class is a convenient accusation...but why should not the farmers, who form so large and so important a part of the population of the country, have a voice in the country's government? On what just ground can they be refused a hearing? The grievances which they have borne so patiently, have of late been so aggravated and have become so heavy that they cannot much longer be borne.....Surely it is not 'the eternal fitness of things' that landlords should legislate for tenants...Let the landlords lay their side of the case before Parliament. But let the tenants have the same liberty, the same right....With one-hundred-and-seventy-three landowners in the Commons, there are only four tenant farmers – the men who invest their capital and employ their skill in the cultivation of the soil are excluded from the House of Commons.[106]

The problem of high rents, together with deaths in the family led William Vickers to surrender the tenancy of Snowsfield on May-Day, 1881, just over a year after his father's death. Even though he was not a poor man, he would not have relished the prospect of sinking his own capital into a loss-making business. By 1891, William Vickers was "living on his own means" with his sisters at West Terrace, Stanhope. And Thomas Sanderson was a butcher and farmer at Snowsfield whilst his son, also Thomas, had married and was farming 60 acres at the West Newlandside farm.

---

[104] *Northern Echo,* December 31, 1881
[105] *Northern Echo,* March 21, 1882
[106] *Northern Echo,* January 9, 1882

## *"Pity without relief is like mustard without beef"*

Francis quotes the old saying, using the word "pity" rather than the more common "sympathy", thus indicating the anger and frustration felt by farmers during the agricultural depression. Not only did they have to contend with high rents and a series of poor seasons but also with severe competition from cheap imports of stock and produce. And a month after the 1881 letter, the Canadian Pacific Railway was founded, which would facilitate even cheaper imports to Britain in future. In summary, the message to his cousin George is: "If you really sympathise with the English farmer, then don't send us your cheap produce."

This powerful adage was used widely throughout the 19th Century, but the origin of the phrase is uncertain. Perhaps Shakespeare inspired it when Grumio spoke of "mustard without the beef" in *The Taming of the Shrew*:-

| | |
|---|---|
| *Grumio:* | What say you to a piece of beef and mustard? |
| *Katherine:* | A dish that I do love to feed upon. |
| *Grumio:* | Ay, but the mustard is too hot a little. |
| *Katherine:* | Why, then the beef, and let the mustard rest. |
| *Grumio:* | Nay, then, I will not; you shall have the mustard, Or else you get no beef of Grumio. |
| *Katherine:* | Then both, or none, or anything thou wilt. |
| *Grumio:* | Why, then, the mustard without the beef. |

In 1816, Sir Francis Burdett at a constituency meeting in Westminster spoke of the corruption of the House of Commons, and argued that "a Constitution, without the people having any share in it, was the mustard without the beef"[107]

At a meeting of the friends of the cause of Hungary in Westminster on 16 August 1849, Liberal MP James Wyld seconded a resolution in support of Hungary in their fight against Russia for self-governance. He asked the meeting whether they would wish to support Hungary by something stronger than words, exclaiming to loud cheers, "As was said by *Hudibras*: 'Sympathy without relief is like mustard without beef'". The cited author is the poet Samuel Butler (1613-1680) who wrote the celebrated poem, *Hudibras*. In the following month, the phrase, again attributed to Samuel Butler, is used in a letter to the editor of London weekly newspaper *The ERA* complaining about the decline of drama: "….there are a select few who still cherish a taste for productions of our immortal bard, and sympathise deeply with the distressed state of the stage; but that is all they do, and, as Butler tells us, 'Sympathy without relief is like mustard without beef'"[108]

In November 1861, in a debate about the American Civil War, John George Dodson, the Liberal MP for East Sussex, cites *Hudibras* as the source when he expressed not only sympathy for the English cotton districts badly affected by the conflict but urged that there should be support for opening new markets and fresh sources of supply for raw materials. And it was not the last time that Mr Dodson, later Lord Monk-Bretton, would use the phrase. In 1882, at a meeting in Scarborough in support of Mr Samuel Rowlandson, a tenant farmer and the Liberal candidate for the North Riding, it was acknowledged that as a large number of voters were tenant farmers, then it was only fair

---

[107] *Morning Chronicle,* Sept 12, 1816
[108] *The ERA*, September 9, 1849

that a tenant farmer should represent them. Mr Dodson accepted that Liberals had treated the farmers 'somewhat coldly', but that the Tories approach had been characterised by "Sympathy without relief" which was like mustard without beef.[109]

Scrutiny of the lengthy poem *Hudibras* reveals that the adage is not to be found there, but another possible author emerged in 1862. *The Liverpool Mercury* in an editorial under the heading *"Table Talk"*, lamented the Government 'standing idly by', offering 'empty sympathy' to the people and not taking action on financial reform, concluding the point thus: "Bishop Butler is reputed to have wittily and truly said: 'Sympathy without relief is like mustard without beef.'"[110]

What are the merits of *The Liverpool Mercury's* claims for Bishop Butler? Is it a coincidence that Joseph Butler had been not only Bishop of Durham but also Rector of Stanhope? Professor David McNaughton from Florida State University, a specialist on the writings of Bishop Butler, commented on the claim: "It would be nice if Joseph Butler had written it, but I am fairly confident he did not. It's a most un-Butler like sentence."[111]

The citing of Bishop Butler appears to be a mistake by *The Liverpool Mercury*, a confusion between the two 'Butlers'. Samuel Butler still appears to be the most likely author, although the belief that the phrase was from *Hudibras* was clearly wrong, and yet was perpetuated throughout the 19th Century.

## *Death of a Flour Miller*

Francis waits until the fifth paragraph of the letter before mentioning the death of George's brother, the flour miller from East Thickley, on November 27 1880 at the age of 64 (almost *"Oh, by the way..."*).

Was it too painful a subject, or is it an example of how the Victorians were more accustomed to and matter-of-fact about death, bearing each loss "not without regret but without great sorrow"? People were sustained by strong religious beliefs and, with the exception of deaths of infants and children, would tend to accept death stoically as "God's will". By mentioning in the letter that Joseph was very stout and often ailing, he is effectively offering Joseph's brothers some explanation for his untimely death.

News didn't travel very fast in those days: It is likely that Joseph would have been buried within 3 days, so Francis, 22 miles away in Stanhope, appears not to have received word of the funeral until over 3 days after Joseph's death.

The daughter Francis mentions as accompanying Joseph when he went from home was the widow Jane Ann Pearson whose husband George had had such an horrific death in a railway accident in 1873 at Cat Castle Bridge near Barnard Castle (See page 42). Jane Ann was the only daughter living at the Flour Mill at East Thickley when Joseph died.

At the 1881 Census, three months after this letter was written, Jane Ann, her son Francis Vickers Pearson, and her widowed mother Jane, a Miller, were living at the mill on Mill Street, East Thickley. Francis mentions that Joseph's Flour Mill had been advertised for sale or rent, most probably before Joseph's death. It was still being advertised the month after the letter was written: *The Northern Echo* records:-

---

[109] *The Bristol Mercury*, January 12, 1882.
[110] *The Liverpool Mercury*, May 10, 1862
[111] Personal communication by email, December 30, 2011

> **BUSINESS FOR SALE**
> **THE NEW SHILDON STEAM FLOUR MILLS**
>
> 12 h.p. ENGINE, seven-roomed HOUSE, every convenience and large accommodation, TO BE SOLD. Apply on the Premises at New Shildon to Mrs VICKERS; or to Mr PARKER, Solicitor, Bishop Auckland.[112]

## *Liquidation by Arrangement*

It is no surprise that the mill was for sale. It would have been difficult for the widowed Jane Vickers to run a successful milling business at the best of times, but Joseph had experienced financial difficulties not long before he died. By Francis's account, Joseph was often ailing, and he was also faced with the economic difficulties stemming from the agricultural depression. A year before his death, the following notice appeared:-

> **LIQUIDATION BY ARRANGEMENT**
>
> Joseph Vickers of New Shildon, Durham, miller, First meeting at the office of Mr G Maw jun, solicitor, Bishop Auckland, on Nov 12, at 2 pm.[113]

Liquidation by Arrangement was explained by the Lord Chancellor, Lord Cairns, in a House of Lords debate in 1879:

> The Bankruptcy Statute of 1869 provided a code for the administration of the Bankruptcy Law; but then it was naturally supposed that there might be cases where a debtor might arrange with his creditors without bankruptcy, and two sections were put into the Statute to meet those eases. One of these sections provided for the case where a debtor could agree with his creditors to hand over his property to them without going to the Bankruptcy Court at all, so that they might make the most they could of it. The other related to the case where the debtor offered his creditors a composition, by himself or by some of his friends, of so much in the pound on his debts. These two processes were what was called "liquidation by arrangement."[114]

In 1879, Joseph Vickers could not pay his debts, and rather than face full bankruptcy, he opted for liquidation by arrangement, inviting his creditors to a meeting at the office of his solicitors in Bishop Auckland in order to negotiate with them a repayment of so much in the pound on his debts.

In the 1879 debate, The Lord Chancellor pointed out the potential problems with this process:

> Clearly nothing could be more desirable than that a man should meet his creditors face to face, tell them the whole truth about his affairs, and make the best proposal he could in the circumstances…(but) the practice has worked very differently from the theory. A debtor can now file a petition for liquidation by arrangement, and convene a meeting of his creditors at any time within a month, and almost at any place he pleases, and if at such meeting a majority in number, representing three-

---
[112] *Northern Echo*, February 21, 1881
[113] *Newcastle Courant*, November 7, 1879
[114] *Hansard*, HL Debate on Bankruptcy Law Amendment Bill, February 17, 1879

fourths in value of the creditors there present, or represented by proxy, pass a resolution agreeing to a composition, and such resolution is afterwards confirmed at a second meeting by a bare majority in number and value of the creditors present or represented, such arrangement is binding on all the creditors. As a rule, the chief creditors rarely attend such meetings, and the result is that the debtor, by the aid of proxies of friendly, bribed, oftentimes of fully-secured, and sometimes of fictitious creditors, can get released from his debts upon almost any terms he thinks fit. My Lords, it appears by the statistics given in the Report that actually 75 per cent of the several thousands of compositions which have been made in the year have been under 5s in the pound, and a very large proportion were even of 1s.or 2s.[115]

It appears that many debtors used liquidation by arrangement as a means of minimising their repayments to creditors. Joseph Vickers only gave his creditors five days' notice of the first meeting – and those who couldn't read or did not read the newspapers that week would only have known about the meeting by word of mouth. The outcome of the process is not known, but it appears that Joseph was able to discharge his debts, despite failing to sell or let the mill before he died. He was still living at the mill at the time of his death a year after his insolvency was declared. He left an estate of "Under £600" (£600 was the equivalent of more than a quarter of a million pounds today in terms of average earnings), and his widow Jane was at the mill at least until April 1881.

After the failure to make a sale, the property was advertised for auction in *The Northern Echo* on May 9, 1882.

---

**New Shildon**
**TO BE SOLD BY AUCTION**
at the Commercial Hotel, Bishop Auckland, on Thursday, the 11th day of May, 1882, at Four o'Clock p.m. precisely, subject to conditions to be then read.
**Mr DAVID ARMSTRONG, Auctioneer,**
**The NEW SHILDON STEAM FLOUR MILLS,**
Formerly occupied by Mr Joseph Vickers, deceased. The Mill premises contain two pairs of French Stones and a pair of Grey Stones, Silks, Elevators, and all the necessary appliances for the business. There is also a nearly new engine of 12 horse-power, built by Lourn of Stockton, about six years since.

The **DWELLING HOUSE** adjoining has Seven good Rooms, and there is a three-stall stable, with Hay Loft, Cowhouse for Six Cows, Two Piggeries, large Yard, and abundant accommodation of every kind.

The Property is Freehold, and the whole extent is about 730 Square yards.

The Premises have a frontage to Mill Street, Strand Street, and Alma-row, and are well situate, being close to the Goods Station, and in the centre of New Shildon.

The premises can be viewed on application to Mr PEVERELL, Innkeeper, Mill Street, New Shildon; or to Mr JONATHAN WARD, South Church Mill, Bishop Auckland; and further particulars can be obtained of Mr THOMAS MARLEY, Alexandra Terrace, Beverley; of Mr THOM*AS CRAWHALL, Stanhope; of Mr WILLIAM RIPPON, Stanhope; of the AUCTIONEER*, Belvedere Terrace, Bishop Auckland; or of Mr THOMPSON, Solicitor, Stanhope. April 1882

---

[115] *Hansard* Ibid.

## Family Quarreling

When widower Frank Vickers of Dean Head married a girl a third of his age, his children were not pleased. Frank's first married Mary Scott at St John's Church Shildon in 1838, and they had ten children. Mary died in 1868 at the age of 50, and with his sons taking up their own tenancies and his daughters of marriageable age, Frank may have had concerns about who would care for him in his old age.

But about 10 years after his wife's death, he employed as a housekeeper Jane Davison, described by the letter-writer as "his niece through marriage". Jane had married coal-miner David Sterling at Wolsingham Methodist Chapel in April 1876, but on October 11, 1880, Jane, using her maiden name and described as "Spinster" (not Widow), married Frank Vickers at Darlington Register Office. Frank's age is recorded as 60, more than ten years less than his real age, and Jane is described as 'of full age'.

A few months later at the time of the 1881 Census, the 71 year-old Frank was at Dean Head with his 24 year-old wife Jane. Also present was their baby daughter Frances, aged 3 months – which means that Frank and Jane had a 'shotgun wedding'. This, together with the 47 year age-gap, make it a highly unusual marriage. The children of his first marriage, all of whom were older than Jane, would not have welcomed the marriage, and so it is unsurprising that there was disagreement in the family and "much quarreling".

What happened to David Sterling is a mystery. There is no record of his death in the late 1870s, no obvious record of his existence in subsequent Census returns, and no acknowledgement of Jane's short-lived marriage on the Marriage Certificate of 1880. However, in his Last Will and Testament made in 1887, Frank bequeaths all his property "whatsoever and wheresoever unto his wife Jane Vickers otherwise Jane Stirling (sic) absolutely and I appoint her as the sole Executrix of this my will". This provides confirmation of Jane's first marriage and also, implicitly, confirmation of the continuing and now consolidated rift with Frank's first family.

Concerning David Sterling, it is most likely that he died soon after his marriage to Jane, perhaps in a mining accident. The widowed Jane, in need of employment, was able to find work through family connections: Frank would have been able to provide work for Jane as a housekeeper and also, as seems likely, a source of comfort for his recently widowed niece.

## "Your old Mrs Read"

Mrs Read (sic) is Elizabeth Blacklaw born in Brough in 1801, widow of Matthew Reed, a farmer at Shield Ash, Newlandside. There are several strong links between the Vickers and Reed families which, given Francis's description of her as "Your old Mrs Read", makes it quite possible that Elizabeth, who married Matthew in 1827, was the nursemaid who looked after the young family of John Vickers of Greenhead, including George, the recipient of this letter, and his brother Thomas when their mother Jane died in 1821 (See Fig 3-12, page 42).

Matthew Reed died in 1864, and by 1871, Elizabeth, described as an annuitant and land owner, was living with her daughter Margaret and her husband Thomas Sanderson at Thimbleby Hill. By 1881, she was living with another daughter, Mary, and son-in-law Francis Brown, a farmer at Greenhead. Francis Brown was the son of Joseph Brown of Greenhead who had married Jane Vickers (1788-1862) in 1809, and was the cousin of Francis Vickers of Belle Vue.

# EIGHTEEN EIGHTY-ONE

For George to have returned to England to see Mrs Reed, he would have had to move quickly: nine months after the 1881 letter, Elizabeth Reed died at Greenhead aged 80 on 27th October 1881. Son-in-law Francis Brown was one of the Executors of her Will of £1115, a substantial sum in those days.

But there was a little more time left for George to see his only living uncle, Joseph Vickers of Howl John. Francis reveals that his father is over 90 years of age, which would have made him one of the oldest, if not the oldest, resident of the dale. But he had some way to go to emulate Jane Sanderson of Blanchland who died in February 1881 in her 106th year. It was reported that Jane, who was born in Weardale on January 18th, 1776, had "a remarkable memory for texts of Scripture, and until a few months ago took great interest in all passing events of the day."[116]

## *The Weather in Weardale*

The weather was a constant preoccupation of the Weardale farmer. The day before Francis wrote the letter, snow storms heralded the beginning of a very severe winter in Weardale, but he makes no mention of this. Was it because he was seeking to portray a rosy picture of farming life in Stanhope in response to George's upbeat reports from Canada, and his expression of pity for the English farmer? Perhaps Francis was not prepared to provide his cousin with any cause for more feelings of pity.

### *Caught in a Snowstorm*

There had been severe weather in October 1880 on the Weardale moors, with thousands of sheep buried in unprecedented snowdrifts and large numbers of them perished. There were further storms in November, but the really severe weather began in early January 1881 just at the time that Francis was writing to George Vickers. On January 5th, there were snowstorms and gales in Weardale, signalling the start of a long winter "of Arctic severity". At about six o'clock that evening, two cartmen, John Watson and Richard Slater from Earnwell, each with two horses set out from Allenheads over the fell to Cowshill and thence home to Earnwell. The snow was falling incessantly with the wind "whirling the snow into massive ridges, under which numberless sheep were buried". When they reached the top of the pass, conditions were so bad that the carts were abandoned and they continued as best they could with the horses. With "an endless sea of blinding snow on every side", their situation became impossible when they lost the road. At this stage, John Watson, "a strong hale young man", gave his overcoat to Richard Slater, left him with the horses, and set off to Cowshill for help. Crawling on his hands and knees along stone fences for part of the way, he had little idea of the direction he was taking but somehow reached Richard Bright's inn at Cowshill at five o'clock in the morning, eleven hours after he had left Allenheads. The opinion was that John Watson's strength saved him, as "none but a strong, hale man could have withstood the many hours of exposure and exertion". A hastily assembled search party of miners and others eventually found Richard Slater surrounded by the horses on the Weardale side of the hill a considerable distance from the road. The party reached Richard Bright's inn at nine o'clock, a full fifteen hours after the cartmen had left Allenheads.[117]

---

[116] *The Times*, February 10, 1881
[117] *The Newcastle Courant*, January 7, 1881

John Watson's strength did not entirely save him from harm 9 years later in another blinding snowstorm. He was returning from Alston to Weardale in a gig with a friend when the horse got too near the edge of the track. The occupants were thrown out of the gig and John sustained a fractured shoulder and fractured ribs.[118]

In July, *The Northern Echo* recalled "the nose-nipping, finger-freezing, toe-torturing wintry days of the early months of 1881, where snow was on hillsides when flowers should have been blooming. But fate had prepared a new plague. Saved from the snowy Scylla, we were in danger from the Charybdis of floods."[119]

### *"A Pitiable Tale"*

The winter weather was equally severe the following year, with blinding snow storms, blocked roads and railways, and countless lost sheep. Tramps would suffer more than most in these conditions, as was clear from a "pitiable tale" recounted to the Weardale Guardians by the Relieving Officer in December, 1882:-

> A labourer named Peter Brown, with his wife and two children, had tramped over the bleak moor from Alston on their way to Stanhope Workhouse, the next "stage". The poor wife's condition made imperative a stop at Wearhead, and next afternoon the journey was resumed, darkness soon overtaking them. The wife became exhausted near St John's Chapel, and in the emergency her husband put her on his back and carried her, in the darkness and rain, some few miles down the valley, and five or six from Stanhope, the shivering children tottering behind. Below Westgate, at a lonely place, the husband's strength failed, but providentially a belated cartman came up. The helpless wife and her children were lifted into the cart and taken down to the Workhouse. There they remained some days, when the weary tramp was resumed, only to terminate finally at Wolsingham, where the wife and mother died in a common lodging house.[120]

### *The Great Weardale Flood*

On Friday 4th March, 1881, heavy snowfalls had blocked railways, and parcels from Stanhope had to be delivered to the villages of the upper dale by sledge. By the following Wednesday, heavy rains caused the worst floods since the great floods of 1771, with "the flood being vastly augmented by the rapid wasting away of the great accumulations of snow which yet remain in the valley". At Stanhope, low lying fields were covered with water "whilst ever and anon trees, beams of wood, wooden pillars, and sometimes pigs were carried down the mighty rushing flood". Half a mile below Stanhope Station, the Shittlehopeburn iron bridge was washed away. In Stanhope on March 10th at about eight o'clock in the evening, a large crowd of people saw the south half of the Stanhope railway bridge disappear in the flood. The gas main which crossed the bridge was fractured and Stanhope was plunged into darkness, causing "considerable excitement in the town".[121]

---

[118] *The Newcastle Courant*, February 22, 1890
[119] *The Northern Echo*, July 7, 1881
[120] *The Northern Echo*, December 9, 1882
[121] *Northern Echo*, March 11, 1881

# EIGHTEEN EIGHTY-ONE

The following month, local writer, antiquary, historian, printer, publisher and public servant William Morley Egglestone described the Great Flood of 1881and placed it in an historical context:-

> This extraordinary flood brings to memory those of 1822, 1846 and 1852, and the particulars of the damage and results of these floods are retold by those of the inhabitants who remember the events. The flood of 1822 is said to have been one of considerable size, but few people are old enough to remember it. The flood of 1846 appears to have been greater than that in 1852, but the former flood being caused by a thunderstorm, was local and of brief duration. The one under notice upon the whole appears to have been the greatest flood in Weardale in the memory of man. Several elderly gentlemen in different parts of the dale have asserted to the writer that they have never witnessed in all their lives a flood of such magnitude in the Wear as that of Wednesday, March 9th, 1881. The long and hard winter of 1880-81 seemed to culminate in the terrible snowstorm of March 3rd, 4th, and 5th of the present year. At the outlying districts in Weardale snow had not been off some parts of the ground for about nineteen weeks when the above storm occurred. A strong eastern wind had set in, and on Friday, March 4th, the blasting snow was drifted into curling wreaths even in Stanhope six feet high. At the first lamp-post, west of the station road at Stanhope, the footpath was blocked with a snow wreath the height of the north wall. Crawleyside Lane was filled in some places to a depth of eight feet, and at Fourlane Ends, near St John's Chapel, an extensive drift or wreath was found by measurement to be at one place ten feet deep. Lanes and hollows were filled, railways blocked, several cuttings being in some places, probably twenty feet deep. Following upon this snowstorm came a thaw, and on Wednesday March 9th, rain fell during the whole of the day, and a strong fresh breeze blew from the west. The descending rain and the rapidly melting snow on the great mountains, which were enveloped in a rain mist, augmented the streams to such an extent that by mid-day torrents of water rushed down the dikes, cleughs, and burns with great impetuosity, swelling the river Wear which increased in volume up to five o'clock; onward to eight it increased more rapidly and from this time to about eleven or twelve o'clock, the Wear presented a scene alarmingly grand in its terrific sublimity, such was the magnitude of the flood. Considering that, from Wearhead to the town of Wolsingham a distance of fourteen miles, the river falls some six hundred and sixty feet, or about forty-seven feet in a mile, some idea may be formed of the velocity of such a volume of water as that which rushed down the valley.....

> At Stanhope the flood was so great at mid-day that it attracted numbers of people to the river side at the Butts, and at other places notwithstanding the descending rain. At five o'clock, the water had risen at the Butts nine inches since mid-day, and a large broad plank was placed at the Butts gate to keep out the flood. At this time many people visited the stone bridge, or Briggen Winch, which place, from the character of the river bed, rendered the mighty flood a scene, which, though grand in its giant wildness, sent a thrill through the spectators. The flood rushed with its silvery crested surface down through the narrow gulfs of green stone or whin with considerable force; then, after

forming a few gigantic swelling waves below the rocky channel, the flood spread its waters over the more expanded river bed onward to Unthank. The water entered the residence of Mr JW Roddam (Son of John Joseph Roddam, 1826-1874) of Newtown, and it completely surrounded Unthank Mill.... The Bond Eale grounds lying between the Butts and the railway, were covered next to the Wear with a sea of water. The cattle belonging to Mr Sanderson were fortunately removed before dark from the byre near the river. At the railway station, the scene was terribly grand. .."[122]

After the floods, there were heavy frosts in the month of June, and then a few days of tropical heat culminating in an extraordinary storm with "such thunder and lightning as we have just been visited with were probably never heard or seen in this country this century"[123].

If that was not enough for one year, there were floods in the lower dale in October, with one Wearhead resident claiming he did not remember "such a storm of wind and rain these five years."[124]

**4-5** Belle Vue Farm in the 1920s. Alice Vickers, great granddaughter of Francis Vickers of Belle Vue and mother of Sheila Potter, stands at the gate.

---

[122] *Newcastle Courant*, April 1, 1881
[123] *Northern Echo*, July 7, 1881
[124] *Northern Echo*, October 15, 1881

## 5. EIGHTEEN EIGHTY-SEVEN

*I suppose you will be tottering down the hill a little by this time. I think you are a little older than I am. I am not as strong by far as I was when you left.*

5-1 Looking on the bright side: Francis Vickers writes to cousin Thomas who is five months older.

Six years have passed since the last surviving letter to Ontario, although Francis reminds Thomas that he had written to him on March 4th, 1884, the day after "March Monday" of that year (See page 33). Francis points out that "I have never heard anything from either you or George since."

## *Queen Victoria's Jubilee*

The year of Eighteen Eighty-Seven marked fifty years since Queen Victoria's accession to the throne. William Gladstone, in comparing the England of 1887 with that of fifty years before, saw many reasons for optimism. He praised the public press which had cast its "fierce light" on "all the dark corners of the social system till reformation and progress have become the order of the day". And the Legislature, which formerly ignored the plight of the poor, now legislated for them.

> Slavery has been abolished; the criminal code has been reformed; labour has been set free; the worst abuses of the Poor Law have been swept away; employers have been made responsible for their negligence; the flagrant evils of our factory system have been abolished; our seamen's lives have been made more secure; schools and savings banks have been brought within reach of the thrifty poor; and the post, the telegraph, the cheap press have revolutionised our communications with the world, and have spread the light of knowledge throughout the vast British Empire. The working class are now better fed and better housed and their position as wage earners is fifty percent better than it was when Queen Victoria came to the throne.... The whole condition of the people is better, higher, nobler than it was fifty years ago...(Let us) continue until we reach that ideal state when each man's welfare shall be the care of his fellow-men, and all shall move forward into that fuller happiness and content of which poets have sung, and for which statesmen and philanthropists have laboured.[125]

---

[125] *Lloyd's Weekly Newspaper*, January 2, 1887

The condition of Ireland was a major political issue of the 1880s. Gladstone became an active proponent of Irish Home Rule in 1885, thereby winning the support of the Irish Nationalists under Charles Parnell. They held the balance of power in Parliament, and their support of the Liberals led to the fall of the Lord Salisbury's Conservative Government and Gladstone's third term as Prime Minister in 1886. During this administration, Gladstone introduced the first Irish Home Rule Bill which split the Liberal Party. The result was that the bill was defeated, Gladstone's government toppled and Lord Salisbury's Conservatives returned to power within months. Nevertheless, Home Rule remained a live issue and enjoyed popular support, not least in Weardale. It is interesting to reflect that when Sir Joseph Pease visited St John's Chapel in October 1886 not long after the fall of the Liberal Government, he devoted 90 per cent of a lengthy speech to the question of Home Rule for Ireland. He described Gladstone's plans for Home Rule, an Irish Parliament for exclusively Irish affairs and the conditions on which it was based:

1. It must be consistent with Imperial unity
2. It must be founded on the political equality of the three nations
3. It should bear an equitable distribution of Imperial burdens
4. There should be safeguards for the minority
5. There should be a settlement and not a mere provocation for the renewal of fresh agitation for further demands of the people of Ireland.

Sir Joseph declared that what was required was that Ireland should no longer be coerced, but governed in accordance with the wishes of the Irish people. He agreed with Gladstone's principles but questioned the practicalities:-

> The difficulty of Ireland is in my opinion the land question (Hear, hear). Where you have a great number of small tenants on very small holdings – holdings that they could not possibly pay the rent out of the produce that they grow – you have a very great difficulty at the beginning of your legislation (Cheers). The introduction of machinery, the very low price that cereal crops produce in this country, and other causes, have prevented that demand for Irish labour which at one time existed. And those people are absolutely starving upon those allotments. Now I objected to Mr Gladstone's bill because it incorporated with the Home Rule Bill another bill for making England practically the non-resident landlord of Ireland. First of all, I think we have taxes enough at home without bearing the responsibility of the Irish landowners' burdens; and then, I think, if Ireland has to pay England during a period of thirty or forty years the interest and redemption for the capital employed in purchasing their land, I say it would add very much to one of the greatest evils under which Ireland labours, and that is the non-resident landowners.

He then turned to the difficulties with a property qualification being used for one class of representatives:

> We find the days of property qualification have gone out of the English House of Commons... Electors should not be called upon to vote for men because they have

property qualifications, but because they are men of intelligence and understand the questions which they have to legislate upon (Renewed cheers).

Addressing the concern of those who were reluctant to give authority to subversive Irish politicians who had caused trouble in the House of Commons, Sir Joseph said:-

> These men who have given so much trouble in the House of Commons, and some of who are thought to be mixed up with things that they ought not to touch – those men are the offspring of a great state of discontent in Ireland. If however the people of Ireland were placed upon their mettle, and given the charge of a great many local matters in their country, would they not undoubtedly select the wisest men in Ireland to conduct the affairs of their country?[126] (See page 95).

## *Women's Suffrage*

Great strides had been made in extending the suffrage, but women's suffrage, which had become a national issue as early as 1872 (See page 24), was still a long way off. An insight into the prevailing attitudes to this question at the time of the Queen's Jubilee is provided by a public debate convened by the Mechanics' Institute Debating Society and held at the Temperance Hall, Guisborough in November, 1886.

For the motion, "Is it desirable to extend the political franchise to women?", Arthur Buchannan, a Guisborough solicitor, argued that education was key to the right to vote, and now that everyone in the course of time would have a good education, what applied to men had equal strength for women. He pointed out that woman often took equal honours with men at university and that in term of mental capacity, "they were equally fitted to exercise Imperial rights". He contrasted the rights of the unmarried lady or widow occupying a house of her own and paying rates and income tax with those of the married woman: when a woman marries, why should she be deprived of the local franchise when in a great many cases, "the wife contributes quite as much to the expense of the household, and should have equal rights with the husband". To those who said that women did not want the vote, he reminded them that the same argument was used about agricultural labourers who, once they understood the power it gave them, soon became interested in the subject. His concluding argument was that now was the time to introduce women's suffrage since they had been for fifty years "under the dominion of a lady whom they all loved", and whose diligent attention and general business-like knowledge were unquestioned by anyone.

Mr Arthur Pease, JP and former MP for Whitby, spoke against the motion. He acknowledged that in the House of Commons, members now treated this subject seriously rather than facetiously as in the past. But he pointed to America where there was "a model of complete democracy" and where women had no voice in politics, except in Utah (he didn't need to spell out his contempt for the Mormon State with its polygamous practices). He did not question women's mental capacity, but:-

> A woman is no more fitted to be a member of Parliament, or Speaker of the House of Commons, or a magistrate than she is fit to be a stonebreaker, or to undertake the duties of a hard-working man (Cheers). I will not give way to any man in praising Her Majesty for the wonderful events of her reign, but I do not think that

---

[126] *Northern Echo*, November 1, 1886

because we had a remarkable example of a woman trained from infancy being such a great success, that it is a reason why women should be introduced into public life. I think the finer edge of a woman would be blunted and not improved for the better if she took a public part, and it would undermine too to a very great extent the respect that men have for women (Cheers). I cannot think that it would add to the comfort of home life and the general harmony of living. ...If they once pass the line, women would say that they have a right to represent as well as vote, and we would have to admit them to every public post until, in course of time, as there are about 700,000 more women than men, we would naturally find ourselves under a petticoat government (Laughter and cheers). Whether that would be a desirable thing each man should judge for himself. Women representatives would not be the most womanly of the sex, but the most strong-minded and masculine. There is sufficient bitterness in political discussion at present, without bringing into play the strong feelings and great sensitiveness of women. Generally speaking, they would be found to be uncompromising and violent Tories, or else revolutionary Radicals. I do not think that the right of ladies to sit on boards of guardians and school boards has been attended with good results. I was told by an MP recently that at the London School Board, women conducted the debateable questions there with bitterness and violent feelings, and had an uncompromising and unbusiness-like way of discussing business....and should not be MPs. History shows that no country yet has held itself up to ridicule by introducing such a measure as this. The desire should be for men to be as manly as possible and women to be as womanly as possible.

Mr Pease's views were endorsed by a very large majority.[127]

Arthur Pease, a prominent member of a progressive family of Liberals (he was the brother of Sir Joseph Whitwell Pease), had no difficulty in winning a one-sided debate. Arthur Buchannan no doubt did his best but it is evident from this debate that those advocating women's suffrage were, in the social context of the time, swimming against the tide. An accompanying *Northern Echo* editorial in response to the debate put the case for women much more forcefully and effectively than Mr Buchannan, suggesting that there was insufficient 'energy' in the movement, and too much lip-service:-

> (The movement) has more professed supporters than any other definitive proposal before the country. The great majority of Northern representatives are pledged in its favour. More than half the members of the existing House of Commons are, in theory at least, friends to the equality of women. But the question has not taken hold of their minds with the strength necessary to make the movement a success.

The editorial offers the obvious reason why the question had not been given a high priority by politicians: "among the subjects of legislation deemed likely by Governments to repay trouble by winning popularity, that of the relief of women finds no place." The injustice of this situation is well expressed:-

> ...if there is any validity in the principle of equality before the law or the community of rights of all citizens, the deprivation of women of the elementary

---

[127] *Northern Echo*, November 25, 1886

privileges of citizenship is the most striking anomaly of the time…If they break the law they are not permitted to plead their sex as a defence. They may be fined, imprisoned, or even hanged, precisely as other delinquents are. It is only when instead of breaking it is a question of making law that sex becomes a factor in the case.

The reference to mental and physical capacity in the debate is addressed:

> We have to deal with women not as women but as British subjects, and the political rights of a British subject do not depend on capacity. Were it otherwise there are men in all classes of life who would be excluded from the franchise. There are foolish males as well as females. The influence of women in politics would probably be good….The friends of peace, striving as they are with so little success to secure the triumph of reason in international affairs, would find an active ally in every woman. The advocates of temperance would be strengthened by the aid of the wives and daughters of the poor.

In 1928, over three decades later, all women over the age of 21 were given voting rights, but some of the attitudes articulated by Arthur Pease persisted well into the twentieth century.

## *Farmers Fighting a Losing Battle*

Throughout the 1880s, the tenant farmer faced a "shifting chain of circumstance", a series of challenges that permanently changed the conditions of British agriculture. In the recent past, given manageable rent levels, the weather together with health and disease amongst his stock determined whether the farmer made a profit or loss, Now other factors emerged which were well beyond his control –an expanding rail network in America and ocean-going steamers enabled cheap transportation of produce to market. In 1870, the US had about 53,000 miles of railway which had expanded to 94,000 miles by 1880. And steamers had reduced the cost of sending a ton of grain from Chicago to Liverpool from £3.7s.in 1873 to £1.4s. in 1884.[128] But no sooner had the farmers adjusted to this threat, they were then faced with imports of cheap Indian wheat and New Zealand mutton. As the *Newcastle Courant* put it, "Farmers know what they have to compete with this year; they do not know what they may have to compete with next."[129]

To mark the Jubilee Year, the *Newcastle Courant* reviewed changes in agriculture during Victoria's fifty-year reign, and succinctly described the challenges facing the British farmer:

> While our population has increased by a third, that of the United States and the Colonies has more than doubled, their industrial and agricultural productive powers having grown in still greater proportion. The consequence is they are not only able to supply themselves with most things which they require, but they are able to supply us, and this under the condition of cheap land, favourable climate, and light taxation, advantages which combined more than neutralise the disadvantage of distance and the cost of carriage. Again, during these fifty years

---

[128] Wilson, A.N., (2002), *The Victorians*. Hutchinson, London. Page 427.
[129] *Newcastle Courant,* December 12, 1884

the mother country has been, so to say, at the expense of educating these colonies and rival competitors, so that we can hardly wonder that, notwithstanding the marvellous improvements of modern agriculture, our scientific farming, and our vastly improved livestock, our agriculturalists have enough to do to hold their own in a prolonged time of depression like the present.[130]

The Jubilee celebrations on June 20th, 1887 in Stanhope began with a special thanksgiving service in the Parish Church, followed by various entertainments throughout the day: a knife and fork tea for all the elderly and poor of the district, children provided with tea and a commemorative medal, an afternoon parade from Station Road end to the Market Place where the National Anthem was sung, and then on to the Castle Grounds where sports and games were provided, and completing the day with a bonfire and fireworks in the evening. It was reported that some elderly inmates at Stanhope Workhouse remembered the Jubilee of George III in 1810.[131]

## *The Stolen Heifer*

In February 1887, *The Northern Echo* ran a story headlined "STOLEN HEIFER FOUND IN WEARDALE". The heifer was stolen on February 6th from James Atkinson's farm at Mordon, near Sedgefield, driven to Joseph Vickers' cattle mart at Tow Law, and sold to John Walton Watson, a local farmer and cattle dealer. He then took the heifer to Short Thorns Farm, Newhouse, Ireshopeburn. In what appears to have been an impressive piece of detective work, the aggrieved farmer, accompanied by Superintendent Bell of Stockton Police, tracked the heifer down to Short Thorns Farm. John Walton Watson promptly handed over the heifer and he was told that the thief had been apprehended and that his money would be returned after conviction.

It transpired that 59 year-old Robert Copeland a general labourer from South Bank, described as 'an elderly man', had stolen the heifer and, using the assumed name 'James Clark' of Bishopton, entered it at Tow Law Mart. At Durham Quarter Sessions on 4th April, Copeland pleaded guilty to the theft of the heifer, valued at £10, and was sentenced to five months hard labour.

This story has particular interest not only because of the involvement of Joseph Vickers and Tow Law Mart, but also because John Walton Watson was Joseph's brother-in-law: Joseph's wife Jane Sanderson was the sister of Ruth Kipling Sanderson, the wife of John Walton Watson (See page 109).

## *"Blockheads" and "un-English Radicals"*

William Morley junior is not mentioned in the letter but he was in the news in Stanhope in 1887. After his father died in 1874 (See page 40), the talented William junior continued farming at Sweet Wells, was secretary to the Stanhope Agricultural Society and was, along with his brother Henry, a successful exhibitor at local agricultural shows. However, by the mid-1880s, it appears that he was finding his workload increasingly onerous. In 1884, he resigned as secretary of Stanhope Agricultural Society which led to William Vickers of Howl John and John Henry Stephenson of Billing Shield

---

[130] *Newcastle Courant*, June 24, 1887
[131] *Northern Echo*, June 23 and 24, 1887

becoming joint secretaries. As Assistant Overseer and Rate Collector, Mr Morley was also causing concern amongst the Parish Overseers and the Weardale Guardians because rates were not being collected. The August 1884 meeting of the Board of Guardians received a letter from Overseer Thomas Crawhall advising the Board that William Morley had given assurances that the rates would be collected and paid into the bank within a matter of days. He also expressed his frustration at the overseers' apparent lack of authority:-

> The Parish Vestry appoints the Assistant Overseer, and your Board appoints the (Rate) Collector, and the overseers appear to have no real control over either, but appear to be responsible for any neglect. If this be so, the sooner such a state of affairs is altered the better. Yet it may be pointed out that there is a remedy which rests with the Guardians of the Union.[132]

Despite Mr Crawhall's prompting, the Guardians were still wrestling with the same problem three years later. In July 1887, William Morley was summoned before the Guardians to be questioned about the 'dilatory rate collection'. The Guardians asked why Horace Butcher, a local draper, had been made a temporary assistant rate collector - was the appointment made because Mr Morley was 'prevented by sickness, accident, or other sufficient cause' from doing his duty? The Clerk replied that the appointment was because 'the rates were so far in arrears as to render assistance absolutely necessary'. Mr Morley admitted some neglect, and it was alleged that some ratepayers had not been asked for payment for two years, and that others would only pay under extreme pressure. When Mr Butcher was questioned, he confirmed that Mr Morley had walked past houses and failed to ask for payment.[133] Perhaps William Morley lacked the necessary assertiveness to demand payments from rate-payers reluctant to part with their money.

At a meeting of the Weardale Guardians the following month, it was reported that the Local Government Board (to which the Weardale Guardians were accountable) could not accept William Morley Junior's explanations of his 'continued negligence of duty', and that he had been asked to resign his positions of Rate Collector and Assistant Overseer to the Overseers. It was recorded that Mr Morley had not yet submitted his resignation.[134]

It is not known whether Mr Morley formally resigned, but when the Weardale Guardians met in October to appoint a new rate collector for Stanhope Parish, it was announced that Mr Morley was among the 25 applicants for the post. Discussion ensued as to whether Mr Morley should be allowed to compete for the post. William Ridley, a builder from Tow law, argued that to re-elect Mr Morley would "just be to make him master of the Board and of everybody else, and to make a lot of blockheads of us all". Others shared this view, and Dr Charles Arnison JP, an ex-officio member, believed that the Local Government Board would not endorse his appointment. George Curry from Wolsingham was strongly against Mr Morley's reappointment because, even though Mr Morley was the most able candidate, he was not doing his job. However, Mr James Blenkiron, Chief Agent of the Weardale Mining Company, thought that the Local Government Board and the Auditor were not without blame, concluding that "I don't think that there is a gentleman on the board who would kick Morley when he's down".

---

[132] *Northern Echo,* August 30, 1884
[133] *Northern Echo,* July 16, 1887
[134] *Northern Echo,* August 27, 1887

This clever reference to what a 'gentleman' would not do seems to have had its effect. With large numbers of ratepayers awaiting the outcome 'with the keenest interest', William Morley was declared elected after four rounds of voting. Those who ran him closest were William Vickers of Howl John, local draper and grocer Thomas Philipson, George Bowman (Pelton Fell), Joseph Maddison (Hill End), William Morley's brother Henry, Thomas Sanderson Jun, formerly of Thimbleby Hill and now of Newlandside, and Robert Thompson of Ferryfield. The *Northern Echo* reported that "Mr Curry marked his impatience of the ballot vote, which took nearly two hours, by precipitately leaving the room, describing his colleagues as 'a lot of un-English Radicals'".[135] To Tories like George Curry, Liberal Party supporters were easily dismissed as un-English Radicals.

But this was not the end of the matter. Dr Arnison's prediction that the Local Government Board would not support the appointment proved correct. They insisted on the withdrawal of William Morley junior and a re-run of the appointment process. This time there were eighteen candidates, including four who did not seek election the last time, and all, save one from Shields, being locally resident. After five rounds of ballot voting, Robert Thompson of Ferryfield, a 24 year-old bankrider and former clerk, was elected with thirteen votes. His closest rival, John Wren of Wolsingham, the Headmaster of a Board School in Frosterley, received nine votes. Others who attracted support were John Ridley, Joseph Maddison, and Henry Morley. Some surprise was expressed in the newspaper report that the "first favourites with the Board and the public...disappeared one by one".

Horace Butcher's temporary appointment as assistant overseer was not extended. In another sign of the mood of dissension in Weardale, the post was held in abeyance until there was "definite assurance from the Home Office that the Guardians alone, and not the Vestry, have plenary powers of appointment".[136]

When the School Board met on December 16, it was stated that because the rates had not been promptly collected, there was only about £50 available to pay salaries totalling £98. William Vickers of Howl John pointed out the hardship that this situation was causing ratepayers. Schoolmasters also faced hardship in that some wished to go away for the holidays, but could not do so because their salaries had not been paid. A resolution to withhold cheques from those best placed to wait for their salaries, i.e., unmarried gentlemen, was judged to be unfair, leading to a resolution to ask Messrs Backhouse, Bankers, to honour cheques for £98.[137]

The rejected William Morley obtained another public appointment shortly afterwards. By 1891 he was "Inspector of Nuisances" in Houghton-le-Spring, with his wife and family continuing to run the farm in Eastgate. By 1901, he and the family had moved to Edwin Street in Houghton-le-Spring. William's job had not changed but by then his job title was far less prosaic: he was a "Surveyor and Sanitary Inspector".

## *"Stirred with a Candle"*

In October 1887, Mr Jonathan Hodgson, the Weardale Workhouse Master, wrote to the local paper to correct a damaging claim that had been made by Mr William Waistell at a meeting of the Teesdale Guardians earlier in the week. Mr Waistell provoked much

---

[135] *Northern Echo*, October 22, 1887
[136] *Northern Echo*, December 3, 1887
[137] *Northern Echo*, December 17, 1887

laughter when he stated that the Government Inspector had said that the soup at the Weardale Workhouse tasted "as if it had been stirred with a candle". Mr Hodgson was at pains to point out that a vagrant, not the inspector, had made the comment, and that the inspector had actually remarked that it was a good vegetable soup.[138]

## *The Letter to Thomas Vickers*

*Belle Vue,     March 19th 1887*

*Dear Cousin,*

*It is now 3 years since I had a letter from you dated January 2nd. I wrote you on the 4th of March 1884 and have never heard anything from either George or you since. I many a time wonder how you are all getting on. I suppose your family will be like ours, which have left us, except William which is living at Pease Myers. He has six children. Joseph is an Auctioneer and has a Mart at Tow Law, and a sale every week, which you will see in the newspapers which I sometimes send you. He has no children. Frank the youngest has a farm 176 acres, 6 miles South East of Durham called Ox Close House. He has 3 children. Daughter Isabella married to John Crawhall, son of Thomas Crawhall's. They have 3 children. Thomas Crawhall married his second wife about 2 years since. He is now very poorly, he had a stroke about a year since and he has never been able to walk about without help since.*

*I have had a letter from brother Joseph in Australia, his wife died last August, he has had inflammation since, but was getting better when he wrote. He says he intends starting off for home the latter end of this month, and will arrive here in May, all being well, to stay 2 or 3 months with us and then return. I had a letter from George some time since which said he intended coming over to England to see his friends but he has never arrived. Have you not thought of coming to see your old Country and friends? If you were to come you would see many changes since you left, and many that you were acquainted with have gone to their last resting place[139]. Sorry to inform you of my father's death which took place on the 24th of October 1885, just a week turned of 95 years. Also of the death of sister Margaret Read which took place on the 10th of last month. She has left 2 boys and one girl: Thomas Matthew 17, Lizzie Jane 14, and Joseph Henry 7 years.*

*Well you see it is a debt we all have to pay. I suppose you will be tottering down the hill[140] a little by this time. I think you are a little older than I am. I am not as strong by far as I was when you left. What prospect is there for farming in America? It is very bad in England. There are a few changes going to take place this May-day. One Thomas Patrick has had Steward Shield Meadows for some*

---

[138] *Northern Echo*, October 29, 1887
[139] "Last resting place": this expression occurs many times in The Bible, including in Genesis: *Then Isaac came to his end and was put to rest with his father's people, an old man after a long life: and Jacob and Esau, his sons, put him in his last resting-place.*

*years, gave it up for a reduction of rent, and John Collingwood has taken it. Wm Watson gave White House up the same way, and Wm Rippon has stept in and taken it. As bad as farming is, there is no chance of getting the rents down, as long as one is undermining another. Featherstone Collingwood is going to leave East Gate, it is too little for him and 3 grown up sons. He has taken a farm joining our Frank under the same landlord. It is 200 acres.*

*Please write and let us know how you and family, likewise George and family, are all getting on as I am anxious of hearing from you all. What sort of winter have you had in America? We have had both rough and fine. January was a very severe month, big storm with hard frost. February quite the extreme, fine weather and a hot sun, now a fortnight with the ground covered with snow, frosty nights and sunny days. Now I must conclude with best wishes from all to all Friends.*

*Your affectionate Cousin*
*Francis Vickers*

## "Strict adhesiveness to Truth"

The plain-speaking Francis Vickers is straight to the point in the 1887 letter, mildly rebuking Thomas and George for their failure to respond to a letter he had sent three years earlier. And it was not the first time that had taken George and Thomas to task (See 'Pity without relief is like mustard without beef', page 60). What seems to us like bluntness is explained by Victorian writer Stewart Dick:-

> Life in the village is full of a beautiful broad simplicity and directness. It deals more with essentials than refinements. One finds the genuinely human there, with less disguise than in the cities, where men conceal their individualities under a mask of uniformity. In the village, people are frankly natural. This simplicity is far removed from the ignoble, for its sincerity gives it dignity. The world is so small there that everyone has his distinct place in it, and the result is not a narrowing one on the individual. Rather he is impressed with a serious sense of his responsibilities, of the awful importance of the part he plays.[141]

More particularly, his directness is an example the "admirable traits in the Weardale character" described by J.R. Featherston almost half a century earlier:-

> The openness of disposition – the undisguised expression of friendship – the practical proofs of hospitality – the straight forwardness of purpose – the manly declaration of opinion – and the strict adhesiveness to truth under any circumstances.[142]

## Radical Leadership for Tenant Farmers

Francis reports that his son William Vickers junior is still at Pease Myers and had six children. One of the children was Mary Annie who was to be adopted by William's childless brother Joseph (See page 134). In June 1887 William and Sarah had a seventh

---

[141] Dick, Stewart, The Cottage Homes of England
[142] Featherston, Jacob Ralph (1840) *Op. cit.*

child, Alice. As well as raising a large family, Sarah also managed the farm dairy and was noted for her prize-winning butter at the annual Stanhope Shows.

During the 1880s, William Vickers of Pease Myers emerged as one of the leading farmers in Weardale. In 1883, at a meeting of the Wear Valley Farmers' Club in which "a very numerous muster of farmers from all parts of the dale" came together at the Assembly Room of the Stanhope Savings Bank, William delivered one of two papers on the breeding and rearing of cattle. Thomas Robinson of Shield Ash read a practical paper on *"The Rearing of Young Cattle"*, and 29 year-old William presented some *"Notes on Live Stock keeping"*. The *Northern Echo* reported that "both papers were characterised by much care and thought, and were conspicuous in the high and exceptional literary merit which distinguished them". William's paper was much more about the politics of the land laws and the need for rent reductions than about stock rearing, and whereas it would have unsettled many landowners, it went down extremely well with the tenant farmers. The speech demonstrated how radical and progressive he was at a time when tenant farmers were often deeply conservative in both politics and farming practice. And it demonstrated that the depression was breaking down the political subordination of farmers to the landowners. This is an extract from William's speech:-

> Unfortunately we can sometimes find laws of a very unnatural kind pressing heavily upon a man's honest industry. These we want entirely swept out of existence, and every encouragement afforded that a man may deserve. (Applause) If we had some of the money which now helps to swell the rent rolls applied to the further improvement of our land and stock kept upon it, our estimates would soon be increased with more food for an increasing population. A tenant should be allowed, on renting a farm, sufficient margin to keep both himself and the land he holds in a continual state of improvement. Were this the rule rather than the exception, agriculture would soon be in a much better condition than it now is. What is the reason so much land can be found now going out of cultivation? I suspect in most instances there is far too little of the owners' capital found applied to such soil. The loss arising is not a personal but a national one. I am disposed to think…that it is the sporting element which so many of our aristocrats who are entrusted with power that keeps these things where they are, and have always been. The day may possibly come when it might be asked whether it is right in the interests of a nation that game should exist at the expense of food for the people. With the extension of the franchise, which I venture to say we will all hail with applause, a little more power will be invested in the hands of a very large portion of the population who have up to the present time been mute. I do not know of a constituency with this privilege that would be better able and more likely to send a tenant farmer representative to St Stephen's (House of Commons) than South Durham. And if there be any influential and practical farmer in the division, or out of it either, whose aspirations reach so high, and who can spare the time and money which is a necessity, I trust he may give us a turn round next opportunity there may be.[143]

---

[143] *Northern Echo*, Dec 3, 1883

William Vickers of Pease Myers was among friends and with a sympathetic press in attendance, but nevertheless he articulated long-standing concerns of the local population impressively, demonstrating political awareness and courage beyond his years.

His reference to game existing at the expense of food for the people exposed a continuing source of friction in the dale. For generations, Weardale men had been accustomed to taking game off the land to support their families, and bitterly resented the game laws which criminalised this activity: the harshest punishment was for night poaching, which resulted in imprisonment or transportation without the option of a fine. The resentment was coupled with widespread disrespect amongst the population towards their so-called 'betters'. Victorian labourer James Hawker observed:-

> If I had been born an idiot and unfit to carry a gun – though with plenty of cash – they would have called me a grand sportsman. Being born poor, I am called a poacher.[144]

Even those holding public office saw nothing wrong in taking game, as was the case with Frosterley School Board member Joseph Maddison in December, 1890. At Stanhope, he and George Davison were charged with trespassing in pursuit of game on the moor near Bolts Walls Farm, over which a wealthy landowner had the right of shooting. Another pillar of the community, William Morley, stated that they had been on his farm with permission, but PC Robinson alleged that he had seen Maddison shooting and Davison driving the birds towards him. Each of the defendants was fine £1, and costs.[145]

William and his uncle William Vickers of Howl John were both Liberals cut from the same political cloth and they made an excellent double act. They were well-known as public speakers and their political views on the land question were similar, and they felt strongly that farmers should work collectively in their common interest, an idea no doubt inspired by the success of the trade union movement. But William of Howl John in particular recognised his radical ideas would not necessarily appeal to the typical landlord, and consequently expressed himself in public with care. In February 1884, they both attended the Wear Valley Farmers Club annual meeting at Stanhope Bank Buildings. With Matthew Ridley of Peakfield in the chair, William Vickers of Howl John gave a well-received speech to a "large and representative gathering" on *"The English Farmer and his Farming"*:-

> I never heard or read of any authorities who were able to write or speak from personal knowledge on all the departments of agriculture - which I rank as an art. In respect to capital invested by the farmer, it is startling to think of the insecurity of that capital. The farmer is also insecure against the ravages of the elements, and, worst of all, he has been, and is now to a great extent, insecure from the laws of the land. Farming could never be profitable where a man has to pay two years' expenses for one years' crop; and as to wheat-growing, it is a thing of the past in England. It has been proposed by one statesman to rescue the arable farmer from his unenviable position by the levy of a five shilling duty upon corn; but I believe we are further from a return to corn duty than we are from the millennium.

---

[144] Horn, Pamela (1976) *Labouring Life in the Victorian Countryside*. Dublin, Gill & Macmillan.
[145] *Northern Echo*, December 20, 1890

Assuming such a duty, the owner of the wheat-growing farm would naturally demand a share of the farmer's extra profit. Rent would be raised *pari passu* with the duty, after which, possibly, might come a season in which the tenant had no marketable corn. The corn duty would also raise very considerably the price of bread – our staple food – of which the labouring classes would still be bound to have their quantity, with the result that there would be less money to spend on beef and mutton, whilst the grazier would very materially suffer. Such a proposal is neither more nor less than claptrap, and its result would entail untold suffering upon the thousands who not even now have the necessities of life. I don't like the tall talk of the self-styled "farmers' friends", who are almost always found blocking every sensible and useful reform proposed in the House of Commons. The farmers are a power in the land, and by well-conducted agitation could promote good laws. The Corrupt Practices Act now makes it possible to send to Parliament men of less wealth and more worth (Applause). I have no sympathy with the land nationalisation scheme, but I would modify the laws to prohibit a landowner from the abuses of his privileges. The new Land Act is a step in the right direction, but no such legislation would be complete which did not provide for payment by the landlord of half of the rates, taxes, &c., chargeable on land. Between Cornwall and Berwick there are thousands of acres of land but half manured, and thousands of acres not manured at all, which is a waste of available resources, and responsible in some measure for the tide of emigration. There is more elbow room in this country than some people imagine. What is needed is a Tenant Right Act giving security to the farmer for his labour and capital, and until that is realised the land will never yield its full increase. It is not the loafer, but the enterprising and energetic man that emigrates, and hence there is a gradual depreciation in the standard of physical excellence. With regard to cattle disease, I would slaughter at the port of embarkation, which, whilst not limiting food supply, would diminish the probabilities of contagion. I quite disapprove of the official methods employed to check disease, and hold that in many instances the restrictions have proved as bad as the disease. In conclusion, I urge the combination of farmers in the clubs, especially valuable in a district where farmers have no weekly market which brings them together. The too prevalent fear that landlords regarded with suspicion and distrust their tenants who joined clubs is visionary and a mistake. No landowner will look down upon or victimise by evicting tenantry who, as sensible men, simply meet to become more sensible. It is inconceivable that in this nineteenth century any educated gentleman could or would hold such feudal views. The interest of landowner and tenant is identical, and ever will be (Applause).

During the general discussion after the speech, William Vickers of Pease Myers, throwing caution to the wind, passionately advocated the 'disintegration' of the larger farms which he held accountable for 'much evil', arguing that "Big farms required capital in proportion, and without that capital, land was liable to neglect and impoverishment." He maintained that such disintegration would be advantageous to the landlord and the tenant, but there is no doubt that many landlords would have perceived such sentiments as a great threat to their interests. Another farmer present, William Watson of White House, recognised this and tactfully declared that "it would be scarcely judicious to advance that theory with any pertinacity at present".[146]

5-2 "Farmers are a power in the land". William Vickers of Howl John

At the end of the meeting, members gave their unanimous assent to the following resolution, moved by William Morley junior and seconded by William Vickers of Howl

---

[146] *Northern Echo,* February 11, 1884

John: "That this club respectfully requests the members for the division to support the Government measure for stopping the importation of live animals from countries where the foot and mouth disease is known to exist."

In demand as a speaker, and with his reputation and influence extending well beyond the tenant farming community, William Vickers of Howl John was invited to preside at the fifth annual demonstration of the Weardale Quarrymen's Association in the Barrington Schoolyard at Stanhope in June 1885. In his speech, he acknowledged that he felt "a little out of latitude" at the meeting but was happy to address the land question which was on the programme. He regarded the past and present land laws as "amongst the greatest evils", and far too complicated and impractical. Arguing for a Radical Land Act, he regretted that there was so much land not under cultivation, "There are thousands of acres of good land on which there was room for thousands of men, land which would enrich the occupier, enrich the nations, and make us better in every sense of the word." However, he stated that there were too many men in the House of Commons who influenced the land laws (i.e., too many large landowners). He appealed to the newly-enfranchised working men to do their duty and agitate for more Radical reform, to get good laws. They needed to "bestir themselves" so that those who had been driven from the land would be able to return to it. This sentiment was loudly cheered at a meeting which stressed the importance of trade unionism, the necessity for unity among working men to enable them to achieve "the social and political positions to which they were fairly entitled". Mr Rowland, secretary of the Cleveland Miners' Association, summarised what they wanted from Radical reform of the land laws: security of tenure, fair rent fixed by an impartial tribunal, absolute security for money invested in a holding, and the abolition of all legal restrictions to the proper cultivation of the soil, and he concluded by saying, to loud cheers, how glad he was that his views "had been corroborated by such an authority as their Chairman, William Vickers." [147]

## *Trade Unionism in Weardale*

At the fourth annual demonstration of the Weardale Quarrymen's Association the previous year at Frosterley, with Dr Thomas Livingstone in the chair, the theme was trade unionism, "one of the most powerful agencies for the elevation of the working classes".[148] Mr Joseph Toyn, President of the Cleveland Miners' Association, reminded the meeting that when trades unions were first formed, they were under the guise of friendly societies, e.g., the Ironfounders' Friendly Society, formed in 1810, had to hold its meetings on the moors and waste lands of the Midlands under cover of darkness. It was not until 1824 that the law allowed them to meet to talk about wage increases or the reduction of working hours.

Mr Toyn suggested that working men had as much common sense and brain power as any other class, and with the same education and opportunities, "they would be not a whit behind the cleverest in the land". This was endorsed by the Rev Andrew Lattimer, a Primitive Methodist minister, who asked the crowd "to ever remember that intelligence is nobler and higher than position, and wisdom mightier than wealth".

---

[147] *Northern Echo*, June 15, 1885
[148] *Northern Echo*, July 14, 1884

The fact the some people believed that working men should not receive an education put Joseph Toyn in mind of a verse about Old Opinions:-

> Once we thought that Education
> Was a luxury for the few;
> That to give it to the many
> Was to give it scope undue;
> Thought it foolish to imagine
> It could be as free as air.
> Common as the glorious sunshine
> To the child of want and care;
> That the poor man educated
> Quarrelled with his toil! Anon,
> Old opinions, rags and tatters,
> Get you gone! Get you gone![149]

## *House of Lords Reform*

Touching on the blocking of franchise extension by the Lords, Joseph Toyn said that the country could do better without them than without the franchise. Mr Rowland, the secretary, ventured that "the country which had taught kings their duty when they forgot it would not hesitate to teach the House of Lords the same lesson if necessary". The House of Lords had become "an anachronism" and "out of harmony with the spirit of the age". It was intolerable that the Cabinet always had to bear in mind "not what justice demanded, but what the Lords would allow". A *Northern Echo* editorial on the same day declared that the House of Lords must be reformed "not because it is obstinate and obstructive, but because it is unrepresentative and irresponsible." William Vickers of Howl John had observed, to cries of 'Hear, hear', at a packed Liberal Meeting in Stanhope to support the Third Reform Act, that he was radical enough to believe that the country could do without the House of Lords.[150] After the Act was blocked by the Lords, Gladstone persisted and pushed the legislation through, resulting in over two million additional voters from rural areas

The process of reform of the Lords was initiated by the Liberal Government's Parliament Act 1911, but it was another 86 years before much progress was made when Labour came to power in 1997. Today, reform of the House of Lords remains a live political issue, just as it was well over a century ago.

## *The Proprietor of Tow Law Auction Mart*

Francis's son Joseph Vickers was prospering as a farmer and auctioneer. Francis mentions the weekly sale at Tow Law Mart founded by his son Joseph in 1882. Joseph had held several successful auction marts in the Market Place, Stanhope, in the early summer of 1882, and had gained a good reputation. His first auction at Tow Law took place on August 26th, 1882 at the request of Mr William Smith, the owner of the site at

---

[149] By Scottish poet Charles Mackay (1814-89)
[150] *Northern Echo,* March 24, 1884

Dan's Castle, and involved the sale of horses, cattle, sheep and pigs, as well as a quantity of cart harnesses, fifty chimney pots and half a ton of rock salt for cattle. Encouraged by local farmers and stockmen, Joseph then held the first of a series of special sales at Dan's Castle on September 9th, 1882. The event was advertised in the local newspaper:-

> The Premises are replete with all the modern arrangements of a Stock Auction Mart, and being close to railway station and easy of access from all parts by rail, will be found a very convenient place for buyers and sellers to meet. The sales will be conducted monthly, or as may be arranged in future.[151]

5-3 Tow Law Auction Mart and the *Cattle Mart Inn* in circa 1950

Joseph, 30 years old at the time, had taken the opportunity when others had hesitated to establish the mart in Tow Law to meet the needs of the many local farmers who had been faced with the expense of transporting stock to more distant markets. There was easy access to Tow Law by road and he had the great advantage of being able to build the mart right next to Tow Law Railway Station. The Cattle Mart Hotel was built at about the same time, and railway sidings were adapted to allow animals to be carried to and from the sales. And the mart proved so successful that within a few years, the catchment area extended well beyond Tow Law and district.

By becoming an auctioneer, Joseph Vickers became a 'professional' man, putting himself more on a level with the solicitor, doctor, veterinary surgeon and land agent. Mingay (1998) describes the role of the Victorian auctioneer:-

> The country auctioneer and valuer…had to have the confidence of the farmers, and this could be acquired only by showing a competent knowledge of the various branches of agriculture. Auctioneers, consequently, were often farmers or farmers' sons. In addition to presiding at the weekly markets, they were called in to sell off

---

[151] [151] *Northern Echo,* August 30, 1882

farm stock when a farmer retired or bankrupted; and they were consulted by owners and farmers anxious to buy stock or have valuations made for purposes of tenant-right, or for probate and legacy duties.[152]

Below is a typical advertisement published on the same day that Francis wrote the 1887 letter[153]:-

## BY MR JOSEPH VICKERS

### Tow Law Auction Mart

THE Second SPECIAL SALE for STORE CATTLE and SHEEP will be held on Saturday First, March 19th, 1887. Present Entries:- 130 Steers and Heifers, 1 to 3 years old; 3 S.H. Bull Stirks; 60 Male Hoggs, forward in condition; 50 B.F. Ewes, in lamb to Leicester Tup.
　Additional Entries expected and taken up to Day of Sale. Sale to commence at 12 o'Clock, Trucks at Station.

WEEKLY SALE, Monday, March 21st. Present Entries comprise a number of Choice DAIRY COWS and HEIFERS, 19 Fat CATTLE, 80 Fat SHEEP; CATTLE SPICE SHOVELS, GRIPES, &c.
　Sale at 12 o'Clock with Fat Stock; Cows at 2.30. Entries to day of Sale. Trucks at Station.

On December 19th 1887, Joseph Vickers hosted his Third Christmas Prize Show and sale of fat stock at Tow Law Mart. Seventy head of cattle and 350 sheep were put into the ring with a large crowd in attendance. At a luncheon at the Cattle Mart Hotel, the chairman and owner of the auction mart site, George Taylor-Smith JP, proposed a toast to Joseph Vickers and the success of Tow Law Mart, noting that he knew of no other northern mart which had achieved such success. In reply, Joseph said that when he started in 1882, he never anticipated the enterprise would be so successful.[154]

As Francis mentions, his son Frank Vickers and his wife Elizabeth (Sanderson) were at Ox Close House, located about 25 miles east of Stanhope at Shadforth, where they had moved in the early 1880s. At the time of the 1887 letter, they had three children: five year-old Thomas Herbert, and infants Mary Edith and Francis.

Daughter Isabella Vickers, named after her maternal grandmother Isabella (Dawson), is mentioned by Francis for the first time in the 1887 letter. She is married to bank-clerk

---

[152] Mingay (1998) Op cit, p 165.
[153] *Northern Echo,* March 19, 1887
[154] *Northern Echo,* December 20, 1887

John Crawhall. It was John's second marriage. In 1874, he married Annie Currah, the daughter of Joseph (deceased) and farm manager Frances Priscilla Currah, and the following year they had a son, Thomas Currah Crawhall.

A few months later in August 1875, Annie (pictured) died aged twenty-five years. Three years later, John Crawhall and Isabella Vickers were married at Stanhope St Thomas and by 1887 they had three children: Charles Edward, Judith Maud, and Mary.

## *Thomas Crawhall: "a Worthy Citizen"*

John Crawhall's father Thomas, an accountant, was living next door to them in Quaker's Square, Stanhope, in 1881. His first wife Esther (Raine) died the following year, and he then married Margaret Ridley in 1885. Francis reports that Thomas had had a stroke and was very poorly. After four years of ill-health, Thomas died on 24 March 1891 aged 75 years. An appreciation appeared in *The Northern Echo*:-

We regret to record the death, on Tuesday night, of Mr Thomas Crawhall, The Square, Stanhope, an old and respected resident, and a representative of an old local family. Mr Crawhall had been infirm for a few years, prior to which he was connected with the principal local movements in Stanhope for over a quarter of a century. He was representative and local agent of the Weardale Iron and Coal Company for many years and on his retirement was succeeded by his son, Mr John Crawhall, the present agent. The deceased gentleman had reached the age of 75 years. He was of a genial, generous, and kind disposition, having a fund of local and general knowledge, and full of anecdote, and as a worthy citizen had a large number of friends. Deceased had been attended by Dr Livingstone.[155]

Francis's strong faith is again evident when he talks without regret about the 'debt we all have to pay'. He uses the expression "tottering down the hill", a well-used phrase employed by Samuel Cowan in a poem, *The Passing of Yule,* published at Christmas 1886:-[156]

>And are you tottering down the hill?
>Old friend! I cannot stay you:
>O, were my power but half my will,
>I would, for aye, delay you!

---

[155] *Northern Echo*, March 26 1891
[156] *The Belfast Newsletter*, December 25, 1886

Knowing that his brother Joseph and his Canadian cousins had done well in new lands, Francis is keen for them to visit Stanhope to meet family and friends, and to see the great changes that have taken place in Weardale over the last four decades. After telling Thomas of the death of Joseph's wife Bridget (nee Brennan) in Australia, he mentions Joseph's intention to travel from Australia to England for an extended visit, and he lets Thomas know that George had promised he would return for a visit. Joseph did make the trip from Australia (See page 103), but why did George and Thomas never return? An obvious attraction for Joseph was that his mother was still alive, as well as a sister and two brothers, including Francis. In contrast, George and Thomas's parents were long dead, and they only had one brother alive, Frank of Dean Head, and they had no direct correspondence with him, only finding out about his remarkable exploits from Francis's letters.

## *"A Lover of Cattle all his Days"*

Francis reports the death of his father *"just a week turned of 95 years"*. Joseph Vickers of Howl John, 3x great uncle of the author, died on October 24 1885 at Howl John, Stanhope. According to his grandson, Joseph Vickers of Tow Law, "he retained every faculty to the last, and simply fell asleep, worn out" (See page 154). The obituary appeared in *The Northern Echo*:-

5-4 Joseph Vickers (1790-1885)

DEATH OF MR JOSEPH VICKERS, OF HOWL JOHN, WEARDALE.

We regret to record that on Saturday last Mr Joseph Vickers, of Howl John Farm, near Stanhope, the oldest inhabitant, we believe, in Weardale, died at the advanced age of ninety-five years. Deceased belonged to an old Weardale family, and during a very long residence at Howl John was an industrious, active, and much respected farmer, who during that period was eminently successful as a stock breeder, having bred, amongst other famous animals, the celebrated *Duke of Howl John*, the champion bull of England in 1880, when it took first honours at the Royal Agricultural Show at Carlisle, the *"Duke"* being then the property of Mr John Vickers of Mown Meadows, now of Catchburn, Morpeth, also an eminent stockman in the North of England. Of late years Mr Joseph Vickers has not taken part in farm management owing to his advanced age, but in the management of his youngest son, Mr Wm Vickers, Howl John has kept up its well-earned reputation for stock, as is shown in the most successful career of the Prince of Howl John at the agricultural shows during this season, having been proved a prize bull at local and county shows, and has also beat a Royal winner. Mr Joseph Vickers, who leaves a widow, was the oldest tenant on the extensive Weardale estates belonging to Mr JRW Hildyard.[157]

Two months later, under the headline "A Tribute to Weardale", *The Northern Echo* republished an obituary of Joseph Vickers which had appeared in an Edinburgh newspaper, noting that not only was the name of Weardale honoured in the Southern Metropolis (London) but also in the northern "Modern Athens", Edinburgh:-

> One by one the oldest of our breeders pass away. When improved breeding was in its infancy – when the now household word shorthorn was unknown – Mr Joseph Vickers was born. Though always humble he was one of the patrician farmers, not a man of yesterday. During his long life he saw many changes in the social, political and agricultural world. He was, comparatively speaking, an elderly and experienced man before Messrs Booth and Mr Bates founded the noted herds, tribes, and types with which their names will be for ever inseparably associated[158]. He was twenty-two years of age at the time of the famous "Ketton Sale"[159], and if not personally, he knew in a sense all the noted breeders who for three generations have made the "shorthorn" what it is. Always of a retiring disposition, he could view with equanimity (like the sage in 'Rasselas') 'the scenes of life changing beneath him,' and when he spoke attention watched his lips, and when he reasoned conviction closed his periods. Such a man was the venerable patriarch, who on Saturday left this earthly soil at the long age of ninety-five years. Before him his family had tilled the soil in Weardale for ages, and like a typical Englishman he was rooted in the soil. Yet, while connected by early associations with a bygone age, he had an ardent sympathy with more modern and everyday life. A lover of good cattle all his days, the 'sere and yellow leaf' of which was crowned by the advent of *Duke of Howl John* (33674) to the show yards of the country. This noted bull was symbolic of the old man's tastes – his lineage dating back anterior to the first Killerby Sale – a strain yet retained by the sons of Mr Vickers. The deceased was the oldest resident in Weardale, and leaves a widow aged eighty-five years.[160]

Thomas learns in the letter of the death of Francis's sister Margaret. Margaret Vickers was born in 1837 and married George Reed in 1868. They farmed at Emms Hill near Hamsterley where Margaret died on February 10 1887, leaving her husband with three young children. At the 1891 Census, George Reed was visiting his brother-in-law Francis Vickers at Belle Vue. He died the following year at Staindrop Field House, West Auckland.

---

[157] *Northern Echo*, October 29, 1885. (See page 99 re JRW Hildyard)
[158] 'Messrs Booth' were Thomas Booth of Killerby, North Yorkshire, and his sons, Richard and John, who were celebrated breeders of shorthorns during the nineteenth century. Thomas Bates, born 1775, was a noted Northumberland breeder of shorthorns.
[159] The Ketton Sale: shorthorn breeder Charles Colling (1751-1836) farmed at Ketton, Darlington, and in 1810, sold his bull *Comet* for the unprecedented sum of 1000 guineas
[160] *Northern Echo*, January 1, 1886

## "One Farmer Undermining Another"

Having brought Thomas up-to-date with news of family matters, Francis unburdens himself about the bad prospects of farming in England, giving a few local examples of the impact of the agricultural depression: farmers being forced by circumstance to give up tenancies, some having been in the same family for generations, and other farmers willing to pay high rents, thereby undermining any campaign to achieve the sorely-needed rent reductions from landlords – in effect, a Victorian version of gazumping, with one farmer being played off against another.

Farmers were faced not only with a succession of seasons with disastrous weather but also by increased imports of cheap produce. The consequence was a general agitation for reduction of rents and many good farmers surrendering long-held tenancies and moving to more affordable farms, giving up farming altogether, or migrating to the Colonies. In the mid-1880s, the *Northern Echo* published several stories highlighting 'agricultural distress' but encountered criticism from many landlords who maintained that the examples quoted applied to only 'a very narrow district (North Yorkshire and South Durham where there had been an exceptionally bad season) and not to farming generally'. The *Northern Echo* responded by interviewing Samuel Rowlandson of Newton Morrell, described as "an eminent agricultural authority... with wide experience in agricultural affairs and well-known accuracy in statistics". Rowlandson quoted detailed trend data which demonstrated that farmers were growing wheat at a loss if they had not had a reduction in rent. In response to the charge that losses were caused by the "dilatoriness of farmers in the spring", Mr Rowlandson asked, "How is it that many of our very best and most active farmers are in the same plight?" He continued, "Are they slothful in business? No Sir; use what endeavours they could, it has been impossible for any man to cope with the season."

Mr Rowlandson painted a gloomy picture across all aspects of farming: heavy losses of sheep and lambs in the Spring storms, a fall in beef prices as a result of cheap American imports, and poor barley, oats, turnip and potato crops. As to where to look for relief, he suggested that there is nothing else than a 'serious and permanent reduction in rents'. He noted, "I am aware that many landowners have already nobly borne their portion of the loss, yet the tenant has had the heavier load, and unless the load is reversed I am sadly afraid next year will strike off the list many thousands of worthy hard-working farmers."[161]

Addressing Francis's complaint about "one farmer undermining another", a *Northern Echo* editorial in July 1887 pointed out that "in an age when every trade and profession – workmen and shopkeepers, lawyers and publicans, and even parsons – are banded together for their common benefit, farmers alone are disunited", and that "a federation of farmers, standing by and trusting each other and working for the interest of all, could soon bring grasping landlords into line with the generous."[162] One such generous landlord was former Liberal MP and friend of the tenant farmers Sir Frederick Milbank, Bart, who stated in a speech at the Middleton-in-Teesdale Agricultural Show Luncheon on September 2, 1887 that he had told his tenantry recently that "sooner than see any of

---

[161] *Northern Echo*, November 25, 1886
[162] *Northern Echo*, July 6, 1887

them come to grief, I would rather become a pauper". To loud cheers from the assembled farmers, he suggested the way forward: "There must be a reduction of rent, and the landlord must pay all the tithes and taxes of the farmers", concluding, "If landlords would make reductions, and fix their farms at a fair rent (rather than hanging on to too much of the profits), I firmly believe they would hear little more of agricultural depression."

It is interesting that Finlay Dun, writing in the *Newcastle Courant* in 1879, had argued for rent reductions (see page 58), but believed that a federation of farmers would do more harm than good, arguing that "they will develop coolness and suspicion instead of kindliness and confidence between landowners and tenants....By their joint cooperation landlords and tenants will be mutually benefited"[163]. A problem with this idea was that many landlords were not remotely like Sir Frederick Milbank in their approach to their beleaguered tenants.

At the Wolsingham and Wear Valley Agricultural Show on September 7, 1887, the agricultural depression was a major subject of discussion at the luncheon – attended by multiple prize-winner William Vickers of Howl John amongst others. A Fellside farmer, John Oliver declared that land in America was very cheap and that the 'cardinal remedy' for agricultural depression was for the rents to be reduced more to the value of the land the farmers were competing with. If there was a level playing field, he believed British farmers could compete with farmers the world over.[164]

In a speech at Stanhope Agricultural Society Show on September 9, 1887, and in the presence of Weardale landowner and President of the Society, JRW Hildyard, JP, DL, Arthur Pease JP compared the plight of the landlord with that of the tenant farmer. He noted the landlord classes had recently seen the value of their land diminish by about 30 percent, but he added to cheers that "whatever had been the decline in the value of landed property, there had been even greater depreciation in the value and capital of the tenant". His advice to the farmer was to look not only to the generosity of his landlord, but to "exercise intelligence, and apply to his own use all that science and knowledge had put in his way".[165]

In the 1887 letter, several tenant farmers are mentioned by name. Francis reports that Allendale-born Thomas Patrick, aged 45 when this letter was written, had given up Steward Shield Meadows, a farm which would be well-known to the Canadian cousins because their uncle, Thomas Vickers of Stotsfield Burn, was farming there from the 1830s. Ralph Patrick and his younger brother Thomas came to Steward Shield Meadows in 1867 when John Roddam, also born in Allendale, relinquished the farm and sold off the stock and farm implements.[166] Thomas was there in 1871 assisting his older brother Ralph with farming 129 acres. After Ralph's death in 1875, Thomas took over the farm and married Margaret Philipson from Rookhope in 1876. Thomas and Margaret were at Steward Shield Meadows in 1881. *The Newcastle Courant* in an article entitled *Rambles around Stanhope* notes:-

> Steward Shield Meadows, the farm on the east side of the (Stanhope) burn on the moor, is the place evidently named in 1380, and called Stewardshell,

---

[163] *Newcastle Courant*, March 14, 1879
[164] *Northern Echo*, September 8, 1887
[165] *Northern Echo*, September 10, 1887
[166] *Newcastle Courant*, April 26, 1867

where there were eighty acres of wasteland then held by Bertram Moonboucher, Knight. Nearly three hundred years ago, there was a cottage in this neighbourhood called Catcleugh Shield.[167]

Francis reveals that John Collingwood has taken Steward Shield Meadows. John, in his sixties in 1887, was Francis's cousin – his father Francis Collingwood and Francis Vickers' mother Elizabeth Collingwood were brother and sister who had been brought up on a farm quite close to Pease Myers and Belle Vue.

Next Francis mentions William Watson. Born in 1847, William took the tenancy of White House, a farm situated just west of Howl John, in the 1870s. He was still at the 126-acre farm in 1884 when he spoke at the Wear Valley Farmers Club Meeting in Stanhope (See page 81), but as Francis indicates, he gave it up because of the high rent. There may have been more to it than the rent. Before he left White House, William Watson put in a claim of £51 against the landlord JRW Hildyard, who then made a counter-claim of £37. The Arbitrator Samuel Rowlandson determined that the landlord's net liability was for £6.18s.8d. With costs of £14 shared equally, William Watson was out of pocket by 1s.4d. for his trouble. But William Rippon, a Stanhope farmer, flour merchant and distant cousin of Francis through William's mother Isabella Vickers, was not deterred from taking over the tenancy.

Perhaps an important factor for those taking over tenancies at a difficult time for farmers was that they had more than one string to their bow, not just as lead miners or quarrymen but in occupations connected with farming. For example, William Rippon was also a flour merchant and Thomas Sanderson of Thimbleby Hill, mentioned in the 1881 letter, was also a butcher.

Francis informs Thomas that Featherston Collingwood, the brother of John Collingwood and another cousin of Francis Vickers, is leaving Eastgate for a farm only 20 acres larger in East Durham.. This appears not to have been a successful move, as by 1891 he has relocated with two of his sons to Job's Hill, Crook.

## *The Variable Weather of 1887*

Displaying the farmer's natural interest in the weather, Francis describes a severe January, a warm February, and a frosty and fine March, a pattern of variation which continues throughout the year. *The Northern Echo* reported the disastrous effect of heavy snowfalls in Weardale in early January, with mountain passes blocked and hay in short supply.[168] A few days later, there were further heavy snowstorms, blocking main roads and bye-roads and preventing carriers moving goods. It was reported that "calamity is within measurable distance to the sheep farmers whose stock, after the ordeal through which they passed last winter, are not able to withstand the present strain. The hay is rapidly diminishing, and their means are, it is to be feared, too limited for purchasing more in consequence of bad crops and the low prices of stock".[169] Severe snow storms were again reported in mid-January with farms in Upper Weardale cut off by deep drifts of ice-bound snow[170]. After a respite in February, Weardale farmers became increasingly

---

[167] *Newcastle Courant*, November 23, 1883
[168] *Northern Echo,* January 6, 1887
[169] *Northern Echo,* January 10, 1887
[170] *Northern Echo,* January 18, 1887

concerned in March about the effects of the 'terribly severe' weather on the lambs.[171] And when the farmers might have expected the warmth of Spring, the Arctic weather returned with a vengeance in May, with "snow falling at frequent intervals, accompanied by bitter north-east winds, which culminated in a terrific storm of wind, snow and sleet. Sheep farmers experienced the greatest difficulty in collecting their hill flocks. Many lambs are missing, having doubtless perished."[172]

> I am anxious of hearing from you all what sort of a Winter have you had in America. We have had both rough and fine Jan'y was a very severe Month, big storm with hard frost. Feb'y quite the extream fine weather and a hot sun. now a fostnight with the ground cover with Snow, frosty nights and sunny days, now I must conclude with best wishes from all to all.
> (Friends
> your affectionate Cousin
> Francis Vickers

5-5 Francis invariably mentions the weather in his letters

But then June brought a heatwave to Weardale, "four weeks of glorious and health giving weather". The excellent crops of hay are gathered, having dried "almost as fast as it falls beneath the sweeping scythes". And once the hay was in, there was widespread grumbling about the oppressive heat – 114 F was recorded at Hartlepool on July 3rd - and the farmer, praying vainly for rain to swell his barley and oats, was faced with a premature harvest of exceptionally thin crops – recalled by Francis in his letter of 1889 (See page 102) The news reporter, probably not a farmer, urges everyone to take the weather as it comes "serene in the certainty that all kinds of weather are satisfactory to somebody".[173]

By early September, the continuing drought was disrupting work in the mines. At Rookhope, there was no water to wash the ore and hydraulic machinery stopped working, resulting in 300 men being laid off.[174] A month later, winter came early with very severe

---

[171] *Northern Echo,* March 15, 1887
[172] *Northern Echo,* May 14, 1887
[173] *Northern Echo,* July 2 and 4, 1887
[174] *Northern Echo,* September 6, 1887

snow, sleet and bitter winds. In early December, a day-long snowstorm blocked many outlying roads and the rail line of the Weardale Iron Company.

5-6 Winter in Stanhope (courtesy of June Crosby)

## 6.  EIGHTEEN EIGHTY-NINE

> *are you any way near where those hurricanes is that one reads of in the papers, they must be something dreadful where they take place to drive every thing before them causing great destruction to both life and property.*

6-1 Francis would see reports of hurricanes not only in papers sent by Thomas but also in *The Northern Echo* and other local papers.

February 9, 1889, the day the letter was written, was the day that US President Grover Cleveland signed a bill elevating the United States Department of Agriculture to a Cabinet-level agency. The United States giving such high priority to agriculture was not good news for tenant farmers like Francis Vickers, already long concerned about the damaging effects of imports of cheap foreign stock and produce on British farming.

Closer to home, Bishop Auckland Football Club celebrated their triumph over Darlington FC in the County Challenge Cup at Darlington's ground, all the more satisfying because of Darlington's sneers at Bishop Auckland being 'the dirty little colliery town'. At a reception at the Waterloo Hotel in Newgate Street, Bishop Auckland, it was proudly pointed out to great cheers that the team were "Wear-water lads, born, all of them, in the town, or within two miles of it, and without any imported Scotchmen."[175]

### *Support for Irish Home Rule*

Despite the defeat of Gladstone's Irish Home Rule Bill in 1886 (See page 70), this issue continued to attract widespread support in England, and not only amongst the large numbers of Irish immigrants. In July 1889, Sydney Morris, a Unitarian Minister from York with his Home Rule Literature Van was received enthusiastically as he toured Weardale, making speeches and distributing instructive literature at Stanhope, Wolsingham, St John's Chapel and Frosterley. At the Frosterley meeting on the village green, with School Board member Joseph Maddison presiding, Mr Morris provoked laughter and applause when he wondered aloud what use was the Home Rule Van where all the people (of Weardale) were Home Rulers. Answering his own question, he said that it was necessary to sustain public interest and to continue to educate people about the issue. Addressing "a difficulty which was labouring in the minds of some of the

---
[175] *Northern Echo,* February 1, 1889

electors", i.e., the position of the "so-called" Loyalists under Home Rule, he argued that Gladstone's 1886 Home Rule Bill had given too much consideration to "a minority which had not been very loyal and had used its Protestantism for persecuting the Catholics." He maintained, to applause, that there was no such thing as "Protestant Ulster": not only were the numbers of Nationalist electors in the county similar, but also the Nationalist Party in Ulster had a clear majority of seats. His concluding remarks illustrate the depth of nationalist feeling in Ireland and the antipathy towards the "so-called Loyalists", not only in Ulster but in Dublin itself:-

> When you remember that there are as many Protestants in the aggregate in the other parts of Ireland as there are in Ulster, you cannot but come to the conclusion that the proposal to make special provision for the Ulster Protestants would not be fair to the Protestants scattered in little colonies, as it were, all over Ireland (applause). The fact was that many Nationalist members, including Mr Parnell himself, are Protestants, and in the case of Mr Abraham, who has a seat for a Limerick constituency, his Catholic constituents have shown marked and exemplary consideration in their desire not to embarrass the relations between themselves and their member as regards differences of religious opinion (Applause). A tradesman I worked with in Dublin last year confessed to me with shame that when the Protestants on the City Council were in a majority they did not treat their Catholic brethren fairly; whereas when the Catholics were in the majority, they showed every consideration for all (applause).

In conclusion, a motion of "full sympathy with the Irish cause", proposed by Joseph Maddison and seconded by Richard Emerson, was "carried very heartily".[176] An insight into why Weardale was in such sympathy with the Irish cause can be seen in the following observation from Jacob Ralph Featherston of Blackdean in 1840:-

> Weardale may justly be denominated the Ireland of England as it regards the residence of the proprietors, and is yearly becoming worse. Scarcely anyone who owns land to any extent lives upon his estates. In consequence of which land-stewards have to be appointed, and they invariably lean to the side of their employers. One of them, not long since, was attacked (Irish like) with loaded guns in an open pasture. By timely flight, and under the kind of protection of some feeling persons, he escaped.[177]

## *The Mayor of South Melbourne*

Like George and Thomas Vickers, many from Weardale migrated to seek a 'hame far o'er the deep'. One such was John Philipson who migrated to Victoria in 1857, a year before Francis's brother Joseph made the same journey, and rose to be Mayor of South Melbourne. In 1889, 32 years after he departed Weardale, he returned to visit his kith and kin. John, the second son of Ralph Philipson of East Blackdean, came from a family which had been in the building trade for many generations. When he reached Victoria, he began business in North Melbourne, and soon became involved in the building trade in Emerald Hill. When the Port Curtis gold rush took place in 1858, John headed for

---

[176] *Northern Echo*, July 17, 1889
[177] Featherston, Jacob Ralph (1840) *Weardale Men and Manners*, Durham, Francis Humble.

Queensland, but only reached Sydney as he met disheartened miners returning empty-handed. He panned for gold at Mudgee and other places in New South Wales before returning to Victoria in 1859. With a natural aptitude for designing and drawing, he worked hard until he was regarded as an expert on these matters and was often consulted on the design of local public buildings. After becoming a Councillor for Emerald Hill in 1871, he became Mayor for the first time in 1877.

Whilst in Weardale, he was treated like a celebrity, making a number of speeches at various gatherings to great applause.[178] At the 1889 Weardale Agricultural Show at St John's Chapel, a Cup for leaping was donated by the ex-Mayor, and won by Mr Parker of Haydon Bridge's "splendid animal", *Timber Topper*. Amongst the other prize-winners was William Vickers of Pease Myers who won 1st Prize for a "horse or mare of any size", and 1st Prize as the best rider.[179]

## *Death of a Champion Wrestler*

In Stanhope in October 1889, the celebrated Weardale wrestler Joseph Allison died at the age of 47. His obituary noted that: "Mr Allison was a man well respected not only in his native dale but at various other places, and especially at Barrow-in-Furness", where he had many friends. It continued, "Joseph Allison was a man of splendid build, and these tributes of respect, and the trophies won, speak highly for the acknowledged skill displayed in the wrestling ring, and for the straightforwardness and honesty of character of one of Weardale's greatest wrestlers."[180]

Wrestling ability proved to be useful to Thomas Whitfield, a former employee of the Weardale Iron Company who had recently left the dale to work in Blaydon. One dark night in March, 1889, he was walking home to Blaydon from Newcastle when he was accosted by a 'big burly fellow' who demanded his money. As the would-be robber grappled with him, Thomas simultaneously stooped and turned in with his buttock, throwing him onto the hard surface of the turnpike road. When he got up, the assailant was again thrown to the ground. Seeing the advantage his skill gave him, Thomas was all the more confident, and applied the *coup de grace* throw which left the ruffian "stunned and still". When Whitfield reached his destination, he reported the encounter, but an examination of the route revealed nothing but a few drops of blood and marks on the road.[181]

## *Skeeing (sic): The National Sport of the Dale*

Wrestling had been popular for many years in the northern dales, but half a century earlier according to William Morley Egglestone, skiing was a popular sport in Weardale:

> One of the most striking instances of the Norwegian element in Weardale is what was forty or fifty years ago the 'national' winter sport of the dale. This was *skee*ing, the national sport of Norway. Within the memory of a few of the oldest

---

[178] *Northern Echo*, June 5, 1889
[179] *Northern Echo*, September 2, 1889
[180] *Northern Echo*, October 22, 1889
[181] *Northern Echo* March 12, 1889

inhabitants no snowy winter passed in Weardale without this sport being practised to its full extent.

*Skees*, Norwegian *skees*, are a sort of snow shoes made of ashwood, beech or plaintree, the best, however, were made of black oak. They were, as a rule, about six feet long, four inches broad, half an inch thick, except that where the foot rested was an eighth of an inch thicker, and the toes were turned up, the wood sometimes being boiled to facilitate the process. The foot of the *skee*-runner rested a little nearer the heel of the *skee* than the toe, and it was kept in place by a leather heel-guard fixed to the *skee*, and two ears on the sides to tie over the forefoot.

The Weardale and Norwegian *skees* were identical in shape: those of Norway, however, were frequently ornamented and more a finished article than the home-made ones of the Weardale lead-miners, but the miners could produce these snow shoes so pliable as to touch heel and toe.

When the snow was in good order and the field walls were covered, groups of villagers gathered at various places in the dale for exercise in this most invigorating sport. An indispensable accompaniment was a guide-pole about six or seven feet long and locally called a *pleat*. Putting their *skees* over the pole which was placed on the shoulder, the villagers, old and young, would start for the top of some hill side and, after fixing on their feet their wooden shoes, they would start down the mountain side with alarming rapidity. On came the racers, avoiding hills and holes with tact and skill, and on nearing the foot of the hill side, the speed would be checked by throwing the weight of the body upon the pole, the end of which grazed the ground. Weardale skee-runners have *skeed* as far as three miles in a stretch, and a mile a minute was no uncommon speed. The quickest time I have on record is a mile in 45 seconds.

About a hundred years ago, a barrel of ale was one winter given as a prize for *skeeing* at Cowshill, a village midst the western hills of Weardale. The lead miners frequently having to cross the fells to other dales to their work, the *skees* in suitable seasons were always brought into requisition, and carried the miners down the snow-covered sides of the mountains.

On one occasion some forty or fifty of the dwellers of Allendale and Rookhope searched the fells for a missing dalesman by aid of skees. In those days a pair of these snow shoes were indispensable to the Weardale miner, and they provided an invigorating exercise, which in Norway has contributed to strengthen the bone and muscle of a people famed for their vigour and endurance.[182]

This is "Penny-a-Line" William Morley Egglestone at his best. The idea of lead-miners hurtling down the un-pisted Weardale hills at speeds of up to 80 miles-an-hour on home-made skis is a scary thought, and if true, these fearless dalesmen would have left the modern-day Olympic down-hillers trembling in their wake.

---

[182] Egglestone, William Morley, Excerpt from Chapter 4 of *Weardale Names of Field and Fell*, Reprinted in *Newcastle Courant* July 31 1885.

6-2 William Morley Egglestone (courtesy of June Crosby)

## *Opening of Eastgate Memorial Church*

Less than two months before the 1889 letter was written, a new church was opened at Eastgate in memory of Mr John Richard Westgarth Hildyard JP of Horsley Hall. The much honoured gentleman, a major landowner in Weardale, died following a 'paralytic stroke' on October 24, 1888, aged 75 years – two months before the formal opening of the church. Two days before his death, Mr Hildyard had visited Eastgate to see the progress with the church which was being erected at his expense. It was near completion and he and his family and the residents of Eastgate were greatly looking forward to the opening. It was reported that all his local tenants awaited the opening with eager anticipation, but many of them would have been dissenters and perhaps would have preferred less exacting rents than to have had the profits generated by them spent on a new church.[183]

---

[183] In a letter to the *Northern Echo* on December 27, 1890, a Weardale correspondent complains of money being wasted "on the erection of churches and palatial vicarages (Eastgate to wit)"

There follows an extract from the newspaper report about Eastgate Memorial Church:-

> Today (Thursday December 20, 1888) will be a 'red letter' day – we might add, with a mourning margin – in the eastern part of Weardale, on the occasion of the opening of the new church at Eastgate, associated as it is with the immortal exit of its founder, the late Squire of Horsley Hall, and the jubilee of our Sovereign. .... A feature of the structure is the belfry, which rises from the roof without the massive, lumbering masonry being visible for its support, which is covertly supplied by the arched interior, dividing the nave and the chancel....Entering the porch, our attention is arrested with the font of mottled Frosterley marble, with its cover of chaste design. On the left of the chancel arch stands the beautiful carved pulpit, and on the right a lectern of oak....A costly stained memorial window threw its fascinating shadows of the winter's sun o'er the altar. ...The cost of the church will exceed £5,000, only some £200 of which is contributed by the Ecclesiastical Commissioners, the remainder being borne by the heirs of the deceased Mr JRW Hildyard".

Named "All Saints", the church held a ceremony on December 19th, 1889 for the dedication of a new organ presented by Mary Hildyard, the widow of Mr JRW Hildyard. The organ was described as "a beautiful and fine-toned instrument, built by Messrs Foster & Andrews, Hull, and is a great acquisition for the very handsome church." [184]

Several members of the Vickers family would attend a wedding at All Saints Church eighteen months later, a joyful occasion tinged with sadness (See page 117).

## *Admiration for Primitive Methodists*

The local Primitive Methodists did not have such generous support from wealthy benefactors like JRW Hildyard, and had to rely on relatively small donations and income from the many events organised by energetic society members. One such event was a fund-raising bazaar and exhibition on Christmas Day, 1889, opened by Councillor (Dr) Livingstone. The exhibition consisted of "curiosities, old china, stuffed birds, collections of fossils, and various specimens of handiwork", and for the bazaar, there were five neatly-draped stalls on which were a choice selection of fancy and ornamental articles". Mary Vickers of Belle Vue presided over one of the stalls.

In his speech, Councillor Livingstone spoke of the "solidity" of Primitive Methodism in the dale, and contrasted this with the uphill struggle of the few adherents from the 1820s: meetings were held in the market shed, then in the Long Barn at Stanhope Hall until a chapel was built in 1846. And now they had property valued at almost £3,000, although the real value was in the adaptability of the premises for the society's work. Councillor Livingstone continued:-

> The chapel is a handsome building, comfortable and attractive, and it is filled Sunday after Sunday with the strains of a well-trained choir under the leadership of (local schoolteacher) Miss Harriet Temperley. Then the adjoining school, with its lecture hall and six classrooms, is the college where

---

[184] *Northern Echo,* December 20, 1889

the 300 children are taught and trained, and from whose ranks bright men and women will eventually come forth to guide onward and upward Primitive Methodism in Stanhope and elsewhere. It is gratifying indeed to view the higher standard established and maintained by this society, and our admiration is none the less when we consider that the resident minister, the Rev Emmerson Philipson, who commands with such tact and skill the onward movements of the society, is a Weardale man.[185]

## *The Letter to Thomas Vickers*

*Belle Vue     February 9th 1889*

*Dear Cousin,*

*I was very glad to hear from you once again or rather from your Daughter which is the same thing. You say you are not so strong as you used to be. Well, you see, old age is creeping on, you cannot always expect to keep clear of afflictions of various kinds. I may just say I have had 9 or 10 weeks of affliction and was never out of the House till last week. You know we are fast working up to our promised years. I am in my 68th year and you are a little older. We ought to be thankful to our Heavenly Father for sparing us till now while he has been taking as many of our friends and acquaintances away. The only thing for us is to try and be ready when he calls.*

*You want to know how brother Joseph's wife is, well I really cannot give you any information as I have not seen any of them for a long time. The last time I heard from them, Jane Ann the oldest daughter and her mother was living at Shildon. The other two daughters is married. Frank is still at Dean Head. I don't think I have seen him since John was buried. You say George has gone to Meaford to live. I suppose he has retired from farming. Would you be kind enough to give me his exact address as I perhaps might write to him. You say you intended coming over to see us last summer, perhaps you will be able to get this next summer to see Old England and a few of your friends that is left. You want to know how mother is. Well, considering her age, she is very fresh, although she has got very little now, she is in her 88th year.*

*We had brother Joseph over from Australia. He landed a year last May and stayed till the middle of August and then returned home again. I had two letters from him after he got back.*

*I am sorry to have to inform you of the death of our daughter, Isabella Crawhall. She had a fine strong boy 8 years old who got inflammation of the brain and died on the 6th of January and his mother Isabella on the 28th of July last. Just at that time, I received a letter from Australia, very unexpectedly, informing me of the death of my brother Joseph who had died of two days illness, inflammation of the bowels. (He) died on the 14th of June, so you see his time on earth was over, after being over to see us all that were left. He said he saw a great deal of alterations about Stanhope this last 29 years. Are you any way near where those*

---

[185] *Northern Echo*, December 30, 1889

hurricanes is that one reads of in the papers? They must be something dreadful where they take place, to drive everything before them, great destruction to life and property.

With respect (to our weather), we have had a very stormy winter. Summer before last was a very dry summer, and crops light. Last summer was a very cold summer and very wet, crops good but badly won, no sun to dry hay, corn crops was good but never got filled for want of sun and fine weather. Continued wet till the end of November. December and January remarkable fine weather, better weather than we had in summer, but this month has come in very rough, with strong winds, three very rough days last weekend, rather changeable this week but part snow lying yet. Of course the road is blocked through Kockels Cut if you know where that is. Stock with us has been very low for 2 or 3 years, but since there has been a good crop of hay, they have advanced in price very much.

I hope you will oftens write and not be as careless as I have been. I would have answered your letter sooner but I have not been able – you will see I don't write very well yet.

I must conclude with all our best wishes to you all.

Your Affectionate Cousin

Francis Vickers

PS I will sometimes send you a paper and you will see how the Markets are.

## "Working up to our Promised Years"

The ageing process is beginning to tell with Francis and his cousin. Thomas has disclosed that he is not as strong as he used to be and 67 year-old Francis is just emerging from an extended period of 'affliction'. But Francis, a Primitive Methodist for 30 years, a man of deep faith who has witnessed the deaths of many friends and close family members, including four of his own children, is approaching old-age with an attitude of grateful acceptance of his lot. He recognises the inevitability of declining powers and death, and just feels fortunate that he is within reach of the 'promised years' of Psalm 90,10:-

> The days of our age are threescore years and ten; and though men be so strong that they come to fourscore years: yet is their strength then but labour and sorrow; so soon passeth it away, and we are gone.

Francis's serenity also requires that he must "try and be ready when He calls". An insight into what 'being ready' meant to him is provided by an extract from the *Newcastle Courant* a few months before this letter was written:-

> Man has three friends in this world. How do they bear themselves in that hour when God calls him to judgement? Money, his best friend, leaves him first, and will not go with him. His relations and friends, who are second in his regard, go with him to the door of the grave, and then turn back to their homes; the third, whom in life he well-nigh overlooked, are his good deeds. They alone accompany him to the throne of the Judge – they go before him and speak for him, and are heard with favour and love.[186]

# EIGHTEEN EIGHTY-NINE

## *News of Family and Friends*

Thomas enquires about his sister-in-law, Jane, the widow of Joseph Vickers the Miller of East Thickley. Francis reports that the last time he heard from them Jane and her daughter Jane Ann Pearson were living at Shildon. This is the case two years later at the time of the 1891 Census, with Jane living on her own means and her daughter Jane Ann, a dressmaker, resident at Magdala Terrace, Shildon. Jane Ann's son Joseph Vickers Pearson had left home by 1891: like his father he worked for the railways, becoming a locomotive fitter. His work took him to Hull where he married Gertrude Fish in 1898. His grandmother Jane Vickers died in 1893 at Magdala Terrace.

Francis also tells Thomas that Joseph's other two daughters are married: Mary married locomotive stoker Edward Dunn in 1870, and in 1871, they were living in Magdala Terrace, two doors away from the house that her mother would move to in the 1880s after Joseph's mill was sold. And daughter Margaret married farmer George Heslop in 1878.

Francis informs Thomas that he hasn't seen his brother Frank of Dean Head Farm "since John was buried" – that is, about eleven years since the funeral of Thomas's brother in 1878. Given Frank's controversial marriage to a niece forty-seven years his junior in 1880, it is quite possible that very few of his kin had seen much of him in the last decade.

In reply to Thomas's enquiry about the health of his mother Elizabeth (pictured), Francis explains that she is 'very fresh', that is, in good health, but that 'she has got very little now", a reference to her size being diminished with age.

In April 1891, 89 year-old Elizabeth was living 'on her own means' with her daughter Elizabeth and son-in-law Joseph Walton at Thornley Hall, near Tow Law.

6-3 "Very Fresh". Elizabeth Vickers nee Collingwood

Joseph Walton was an experienced auctioneer and it is likely that he moved to Thornley Hall in about 1882 to assist his brother-in-law Joseph Vickers in establishing Tow Law Auction Mart. And following the death of Joseph Vickers of Howl John in 1885, his widow Elizabeth moved to Thornley Hall, Tow Law, to be looked after by her daughter, Elizabeth Walton.

Francis repeats his plea to Thomas that he and George should come "to see Old England and a few of your friends that is left." He tells of the visit of his brother Joseph from Australia in 1887, and only reveals that Joseph died at Locksley, Victoria in June 1888 in a later paragraph, concluding, "so you see his time on earth was over, after being over to see us all that were left". To his Canadian cousins, this may have suggested that

---

[186] *Newcastle Courant*, September 21, 1888

death quickly follows a visit to the Old Country, a thought unlikely to have encouraged them to make the journey that Francis is so keen on them making.

6-4 Joseph Vickers of Victoria – visited Stanhope the year before he died

Again, it is curious that he leaves it late to mention the death of his daughter Isabella and grandson Charles Edward Crawhall, "a fine strong boy" who had died of inflammation of the brain – encephalitis, which can be triggered by more than a dozen viral diseases such as chicken pox and measles.

To lose his son and then his second wife within months would have been devastating for John Crawhall, who was also now faced with raising four motherless children. John met the challenge, becoming a pillar of the community in Stanhope: a JP, Chairman of Stanhope Urban Council and a member of Stanhope Local Board of Guardians in the 1890s.

Francis was naturally preoccupied with telling the tragic news of the passing of his brother, his daughter and his grandson and does not mention his other children in the letter. The only change to note since the last letter is the birth of another grandchild, Joseph, to Frank and Elizabeth Vickers of Ox Close Farm, Shadforth.

# EIGHTEEN EIGHTY-NINE

## *Death and Destruction in America*

Francis, having read graphic accounts of the devastating hurricanes in North America, asks Thomas if he's had any experience of them. There were regular reports of the disastrous effects of hurricanes and floods in North America throughout the 1880s. A few days before this letter was written, one newspaper reported:-

> A terrible hurricane has swept over large parts of Nebraska, scattering rain before it. In various towns, public buildings, schools, and houses have been wrecked, and there have been many fatalities. One report records the death of a number of children by the fall of a school building, and from Omaha it is telegraphed that five people have been killed and several injured by the fall of a house"[187]

And in June 1889, the local newspaper headline was "UNPARALLELED DISASTER IN AMERICA. FLOODS SWEEP TOWNS AWAY." Very heavy rainstorms swept through Pennsyvania, deluging whole districts and leaving towns and villages submerged. As many as 25,000 were feared dead. A large reservoir above Johnstown burst its banks, the resulting floods wiping out the town and killing two thousand of its citizens. Francis would have read the report with a mixture of fascination and horror:-

> The reservoir, the bursting of which swept the town away, is five miles long and two broad, and in some places as much as seventy feet deep....Hundreds of houses, their foundations sapped by the water, were seen floating down the flood with people clinging to them for life, and holding out despairing hands, appealing for the succour which it was impossible to afford them.[188]

For those who stayed at home, there must often have been a feeling that the grass was greener for those who had migrated – and cousins George and Thomas undoubtedly waxed lyrical about their success in the New World. So perhaps news of the effects of hurricanes and other natural disasters in North America made them feel that staying at home had its merits.

## *The Markets*

Francis promises to send a newspaper occasionally so that Thomas can see how the Markets are. Local newspapers regularly listed prices for a wide range of agricultural produce. For example, in August 1890, *The Northern Echo* listed Home Market prices for, inter alia, Thirsk Wool, London Corn, Darlington Corn, Berwick Cattle, Thirsk Pig, Cork Butter, and Hartlepool Fish. Also listed were Tow Law Auction Mart Prices, where calved cows made up to £25, cows to calve up to £23, fat cattle up to £17, calves to 66s, and fat half-bred shearlings to 49s.[189]

---

[187] *Leeds Mercury*, February 6, 1889
[188] *Northern Echo*, June 3, 1889
[189] *Northern Echo*, August 26, 1890

## The Weather in Weardale

Farmers' lives are governed by the rhythms and vagaries of the seasons, so it is natural that the weather usually features in the letters. In the 1889 letter, Francis summarises the weather and its consequences for the farmer over the past two seasons. He recalls the summer before last (1887) being very dry with light crops (See page 102), but does not detail the severe weather of the winter of 1887-88. In the third week in February, an incessant snowstorm caused massive snowdrifts in Weardale with all the bye-roads to the numerous settlements and the Weardale Ironstone Company railway track blocked:-

> Traffic is wholly suspended, and it was only by dint of fresh relays of horses that the mails were carried on horseback up the valley. The ordinary post carrier, "Little Jimmy" was snowed up with the mail coach at Cowshill. At Ireshopeburn, houses by the roadside were completely enveloped, and a road had to be cut to allow of the exit of the occupants....The flocks from the hills have been brought home where they could be reached, but many of the latter it is feared will be overblown and perish. Snow is still falling heavily.[190]

The winter culminated in another severe storm in mid-March, with the mountain roads blocked and sheep farmers experiencing great difficulty with their hill stock.[191] The summer of 1888 was 'very cold and very wet', with no sun to dry the hay – one of the most important crops of Weardale - and good corn crops, although "never filled for want of sun and fine weather". He reports a wet Autumn but doesn't refer to the severely cold weather throughout the north-east district in early October, with snow falling in many areas. It was reported that octogenarian farmers couldn't remembered snow falling so early. Those who attended Brough Hill Fair were caught in the storm, and farmers were fearful because of a well-known saying which predicted that if snow fell on Brough Hill Fair, a severe winter would surely follow.[192] And he doesn't mention that in mid-November, there were the most severe westerly gales ever remembered over Northern England. Much damage was caused in Weardale, including the destruction of Dr Charles Arnison's hayshed at Stanhope.[193] The remarkably fine weather in December and January, according to Francis even better than the weather of the previous summer, demonstrated the shortcomings of proverbial predictions, although Francis in his summary does maintain that it has been a very stormy winter. February 'came in very rough' with snow and strong winds, blocking "Kockels Cut" or "Cockles Cut". Frosterley marble was known by local quarrymen as "Cockle" because it is speckled with the remains of prehistoric fossilised seashells. Cockles Cut is likely to refer to a quarryman's cut through the cockleshell limestone, and the best guess to location, according to David Heatherington from the Weardale Museum, is close to the junction of Reahope Burn with Stanhope Burn where there is a deep cut through the cockleshell limestone. This location is less than a mile from Belle Vue Farm.

---

[190] *Northern Echo,* February 21, 1888. See page 140 for more on "Little Jimmy"
[191] *Northern Echo*, March 16, 1888
[192] *Northern Echo*, October 3, 1888
[193] *Northern Echo*, November 17, 1888

# EIGHTEEN EIGHTY-NINE

## *"Tom Tiddler's Ground for Tramps"*

In December 1874, the Weardale Guardians of the Poor were praised for their warm hearts (See page 26), but fifteen years later their approach to the poor, particularly the itinerant tramps (the 'casuals'), appeared somewhat less generous. The December 1889 meeting of the Guardians was reported in the *Echo* under the headline "Tom Tiddler's Ground for Tramps".[194]

The Guardians clearly felt that the tramps were taking advantage of the generosity of the Weardale Union, heading straight to Stanhope and avoiding places such as Alston and Lanchester. William Vickers of Howl John believed the reason they were drawn to Stanhope was that they were well fed, with a soup diet when elsewhere they had bread and cheese which was fivepence per head cheaper. They also enjoyed free beer at Christmas. George Curry (Wolsingham) caused laughter when he described the tramps as professionals and "men of money" who were always smoking when he saw them. In other words, he was categorising tramps as the "undeserving poor", in modern terms, "welfare scroungers".

William Watson's proposal that bread and cheese be substituted for soup was referred to the Local Government Board. In the meantime, Stanhope Workhouse remained Tom Tiddler's Ground for Tramps.[195]

George Curry's dry wit had been evident at a meeting of the Guardians in August, 1884. At the end of the meeting, he questioned the authority of the overseers of Tow Law in sending Mrs Ann Robinson from Elm Park to the workhouse. He pointed out that her son Robert, the Land Agent for the Wilkinsons of Harperley Hall, was well-to-do and that the workhouse was not a place for his mother, drawing laughter when he reminded the guardians that the workhouse was "for the destitute and not for independent people":-

> Stanhope is getting, as you all know, quite a fashionable place. Lodging houses are full, public houses over-crowded, and the only place left for visitors is the Workhouse (renewed laughter). This old lady has been there during the summer, and as the weather is now turning cold, I have great pleasure in proposing that she be now sent at her son's expense down to her winter's quarters on the very first fine day (laughter).

It was agreed that Mr Robinson would be requested to make alternative arrangements for his mother.[196]

It seems unlikely that the clerical Wilkinsons would have approved of Mr Robinson allowing his elderly mother to languish in Stanhope Workhouse: George Pearson Wilkinson was Vicar of Thornley for many years, and his brother was a Roman Catholic Bishop.

Ann Robinson died in 1887, aged 91 years.

---

[194] Tom Tiddler's Ground is an old children's game in which one player, "Tom Tiddler," stands on a heap and other players rush onto the heap, crying "Here I am on Tom Tiddler's ground," while Tom tries to keep them off. By extension, the phrase has come to mean the ground of one who is easily taken advantage of – in this case, Stanhope Workhouse (Wikipedia).
[195] *Northern Echo*, December 14, 1889
[196] *Northern Echo*, August 30, 1884

## Plight of the Elderly Poor

At this time, progressive politicians increasingly spoke out about the plight of the elderly poor who often ended their days in the workhouse. William Gladstone in December 1891 succinctly articulated the concern:-

> It is a lamentable fact if, in the midst of our civilisation, and at the close of the nineteenth century, the workhouse is all that can be offered to the industrious labourer at the end of a long and honourable life. I do not say that it will be solved in a moment; but I do say this, that until society is able to offer to the industrious labourer at the end of a long and blameless life something better than the workhouse, society will not have discharged its duties to its poorer members[197]

In 1908, the Old Age Pensions Act came into law during the Liberal government of David Lloyd-George and means-tested pensions of 5 shillings per week were introduced from the age of 70 on January 1 1909 - "Pensions Day".

Post Office clerk Flora Thompson described the reactions of the aged cottagers when they first received a pension payment:-

> When Old Age Pensions began, life was transformed …They were relieved of anxiety. They were suddenly rich. Independent for life! At first when they went to the Post Office to draw it, tears of gratitude would run down the cheeks of some, and they would say as they picked up their money, "God bless that Lord George!" (for they could not believe that one so powerful and munificent could be a plain "Mr") and "God bless you, miss!" and there were flowers from their gardens and apples from their trees for the girl who merely handed them the money….If such a small sum of 5s per week could be greeted in this fashion, the extent of the hardships endured by old people in pre-pension days becomes painfully clear.[198]

---

[197] *The Times*, 12 December, 1891
[198] Flora Thompson, *Lark Rise to Candleford: A Trilogy*. Penguin Books, 1973

# 7. EIGHTEEN NINETY

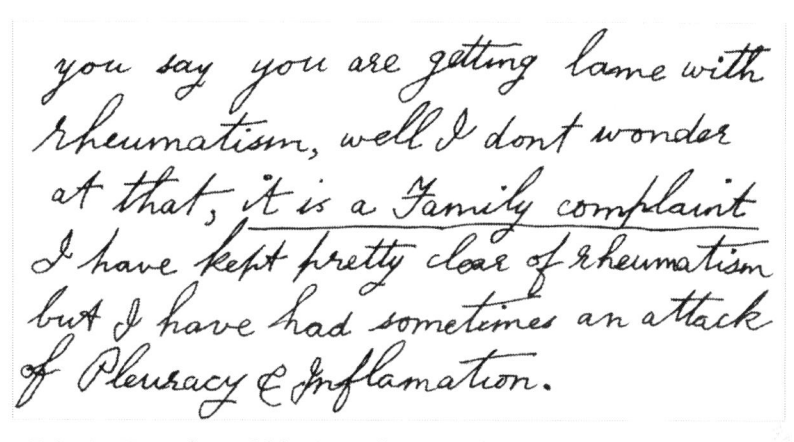

> *you say you are getting lame with rheumatism, well I dont wonder at that, it is a Family complaint I have kept pretty clear of rheumatism but I have had sometimes an attack of Pleuracy & Inflamation.*

7-1 As Francis and his Canadian cousins get older, they become more preoccupied with matters of health

In Weardale, the mild weather of 1889 continued into the New Year, with reports of primroses in bloom and whin in flower at Stanhope. There was the customary first-footing in spring-like weather on New Year's Day, which was observed as a holiday with all the quarries and mines closed for the day. In Upper Weardale, the ironstone mines had been closed not just for the day but for more than six months, and were not opened again until the summer. The frequent stoppages in the mines ultimately had some positive consequences for Weardale (See page 134, Weardale Extension Railway).

## *A Fracas and a Horse-whipping in Weardale*

Two interesting and related cases were heard at Stanhope Sessions, one in December 1889 and the other in January 1890, and both involving members of the Watson family from Short Thorns Farm, Ireshopeburn (See case of the stolen heifer, page 74). In the first case on December 20th, farmer William Watson was charged with assaulting Isaac Thompson, a joiner and cabinet maker, on the 23rd November, and Watson entered a cross-summons against Thompson. Charles Dix from Newcastle prosecuted and Mr John Thomas Proud from Bishop Auckland defended. It was claimed that Watson called at Thompson's house in his absence, and again when he was in, complaining that Thompson had said that Mrs Watson, in marrying the defendant, had married into a bad family. When Thompson denied having said this, Watson allegedly used bad language to Annie Thompson, and was ordered out of the house. The next evening, Watson returned and allegedly seized Thompson by the throat, hurling him against a bookcase. Constable Sedgwick, who lived nearby, was summoned and noted that William Watson's shirt collar and cravat were torn before hearing him issue more threats. In questioning, John Proud said that the two had always shown each other respect before and suggested that his client was annoyed because Isaac Thompson had taken Mrs Watson's furniture to Allenheads. He felt that the case was trivial, a 'storm in a teapot' which should never have come to court. At this stage, Watson offered another reason for calling on Thompson - he called to accuse him about a man named Bell, and after being given "a nap on the head" by Thompson, he reacted by pushing him back against his chair. After hearing the evidence, the Bench found Watson guilty of assault, but that it was very trivial, and fined him 2s 6d and costs. The cross-summons was dismissed.[199]

The suggestion that William Watson was annoyed about his wife's furniture being taken to Allenheads is plausible. William had married at the age of 45 a year previously and was probably not very happy that his wife was departing to Allenheads. Thereafter, they appear to have been estranged.

As to the significance of "the man named Bell", a little light was shed on this by the case involving William's brother John Walton Watson. On Friday January 17th 1890 at Stanhope Town Hall, there was much excitement in court when Joseph Dawson, a carrier from Ireshopeburn, and John Walton Watson a cattle-dealer of Redgatehead, came before the Justices of the Peace, Mr Charles J Backhouse and Dr Charles Arnison. Dawson and Watson had accused each other of assault, and many spectators were present to witness the proceedings.

7-2 "I learned him not to do so". John Walton Watson

At the outset, John Walton Watson admitted assaulting and pulling Joseph Dawson out of his cart, but Mr Charles Dix for Dawson stated that it was not just ordinary assault as it had been preceded by Watson making a threat to one of Dawson's brothers that he would "let the blood out of Dawson before night", and then afterwards boasting about it. It was

---
[199] *Northern Echo*, December 21, 1889

also pointed out that Watson's counter-claim of assault against him had only emerged some days after Dawson's summons.

Dawson's evidence was that as he travelled down the dale in a heavy cart, Watson followed him in a spring trap. Near Westgate, Watson jumped out of the trap, took off his coat and challenged him to a fight. When Dawson refused, Watson pulled him out of the cart, struck him, knelt on his body and threatened to murder him on the spot. Dawson managed to get hold of a stone and said he would use it if Watson came near him again. He claimed that he then drove off but that Watson came alongside him again and flogged him with a horsewhip for quarter of a mile before driving ahead. Under questioning by Mr John Proud for Watson, Dawson denied agreeing to fight, denied using his horsewhip, and said that he had not spoken to Watson for four years and didn't know why the altercation started.

There were several witnesses, one of whom was William Vickers of Pease Myers, the Stanhope Waywarden. It was obvious that William was a reluctant witness, perhaps not least because John Walton Watson's wife Ruth and his brother Joseph's wife Jane were sisters. He said that on the day of the alleged assault, he and his brother Joseph, the owner of Tow Law Mart, had spoken with John Watson at the mart. Watson explained to them that a man had been "ill-using old Willy Bell", a 60 year-old pony breeder from Upper Weardale, and that he had "learned him not to do so". Watson had not mentioned a stone, but claimed that he had been 'brayed' with a whip by Dawson.

On oath, Watson said that when he asked Dawson about ill-using Willy Bell, Dawson asked what he had to do with it. Watson then left his trap at Dawson's invitation and was struck on the hand with the butt end of Dawson's whip. He claimed he took a stone from Dawson who then reached for a knife. Questioned by Mr Dix about the relative strength of himself and Dawson, Watson replied that he was prepared to lift weights against him. Mr Dix replied "London's the place for strong men!", and Mr Proud interjected, "My client could lick Sandow out and out if he had the chance!" The Bench noted that Watson had admitted the assault and, concluding that it was not as bad as made out, they fined him 20 shillings with costs. The case brought against Dawson was dismissed.[200]

Seven and a half years later, Joseph Dawson was near Ireshopeburn in his cart when he was overtaken, knocked down and run over by a trap, and was struck in the back by the shaft of the trap, sustaining a compound fracture of the ribs.[201] There is no suggestion that John Walton Watson was driving the trap.

The reason for the particular local interest in this case was that John Walton Watson was a big powerful man, six feet four inches tall and twenty two stones, and well known in the dale for his prodigious strength – by all accounts not acquired through hard work. His grandson John Ross tells of him picking up and carrying two 16-stone bags of cement under his arms as if they were feather cushions. And once at a local fair, after he'd bought some beasts from two Irishmen, they made the mistake of demanding more money. Somewhat annoyed, John picked one up in each hand, banged them together and dropped them in a heap on the ground.

---

[200] *Northern Echo*, January 18, 1890
[201] *Northern Echo*, October 30, 1897

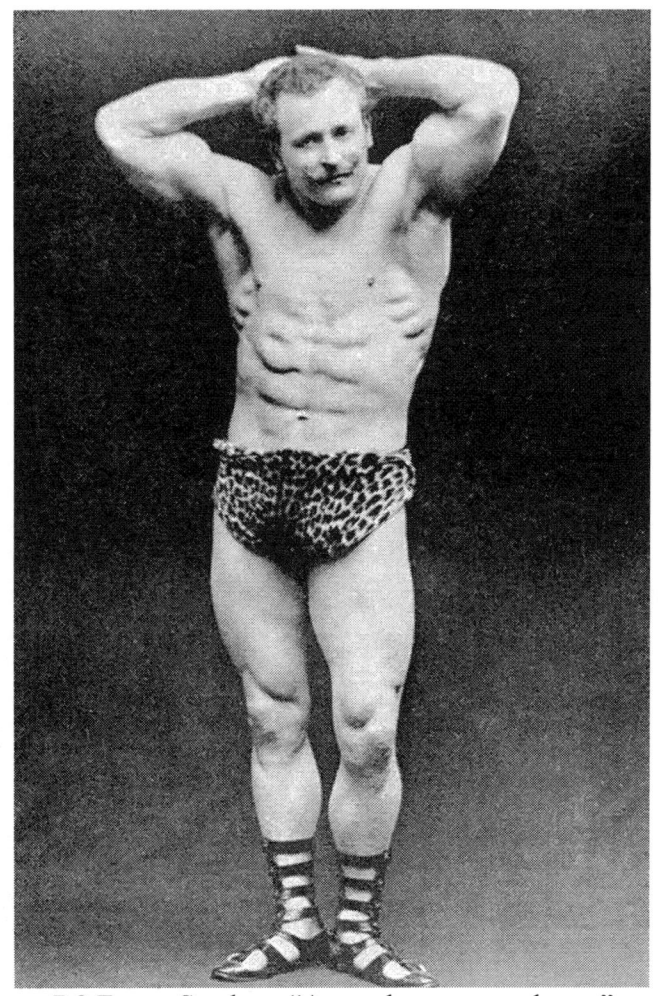

7-3 Eugen Sandow: "As cool as a cucumber…"

As for Sandow, he was a Prussian strongman who had caused a sensation two months earlier in London when he had beaten "Samson", celebrated as "the strongest man on earth".

David Chapman observes:-

> Eugen Sandow changed the way we see and think about our bodies…He made physical fitness palatable to the multitudes…He burst upon the athletic scene with all the force and brilliance of a shooting star, blazing as if from nowhere into the Victorian sporting and theatrical world.[202]

*The Graphic* reported:-

> After Eugen Sandow had defeated Cyclops, Samson's pupil, last week, he was challenged by Samson himself. On Saturday night, The Imperial Theatre was crammed to suffocation. The Marquis of Queensbury and Lord de Clifford acted

---

[202] Chapman, David, *Sandow the Magnificent: Eugen Sandow and the Beginnings of Bodybuilding.* 1994, University of Illinois Press.

as judges, and Captain Molesworth held the stakes. In turn the strong men bent iron bars, broke chains, and snapped wire ropes. As each of his feats was capped by Sandow, Samson grew more and more excited, the manifest bias of the audience in favour of his rival, who was as cool as a cucumber, adding fuel to the flame; and when Sandow himself took up the running and lifted full-grown men as if they were babies, and played with 150lb dumb-bells as if they were cricket balls, Samson retired in a huff..."[203]

His extraordinary feats were reported in the local press and he actually performed at Bishop Auckland Town Hall in October 1892.

## *Another Crisis in the Mines*

As the latest crisis in the ironstone mines ended in the summer of 1890, another crisis began. In response to a notice from the County Council prohibiting the pollution of the Wear with lead hush (waste) from the mines, the mine owners laid off hundreds of men in mid-1890. According to County Councillor Dr Thomas Livingstone who addressed a miner's gathering at St John's Chapel in September, this was an unnecessary response to what was only a notice and not a summons. He explained that the Council had not been "precipitate" in using its powers under the River Pollution Act, and he questioned why the Lead Company had laid men off rather than challenge the order of the Council.[204] A month later the matter was still unresolved, and there was little optimism on the part of the workless miners as winter approached. At Christmas, one correspondent dismayed by the abject poverty in Weardale, suggested that an "Emigration Club" should be established: a small sum deducted from each man's weekly wages, together with larger donations from richer men, would provide a 'respectable sum' each year to allow "twenty or thirty, or even fifty" young men to be sent to one of the colonies where "they could easily make more than 30 shillings per month." Emigration continued apace but there was no enthusiasm for this particular idea.

## *Death in the Workhouse*

A few weeks before the 1890 letter was written, a man named William Hammond Ambler died in Stanhope Workhouse aged 79 years. He was an unusual inmate in that he had been a very able and successful man, an owner of several large drapery establishments in London and elsewhere, the owner of several properties including a large estate in Carlisle, and married to the daughter of the famous Shildon steam locomotive engineer Timothy Hackworth. But largely as a consequence of the failure of the North of England Joint Stock Bank at Newcastle, he fell on hard times. His wife and only child having been dead many years, he was forced to enter Stanhope Workhouse at the age of 73:-

> To the last he was polite and gentlemanly; and though he remembered well his former state of affluence, he maintained an air of philosophic contentment....The Master and Matron knew well the old man's story, and ever showed him the consideration to which his misfortune entitled him. His transactions at one time

---

[203] *The Graphic,* November 9, 1889
[204] *Northern Echo,* September 18, 1890

represented thousands of pounds. *Sic transit Gloria mundi.* After life's fitful fever, he sleeps well.[205]

## *Broken Leg at Shaftwell Head*

A month before Francis's letter was written, his brother William Vickers senior of Howl John suffered a nasty accident. He and some friends had attended a sale at Middle End Farm in Teesdale and they were returning home over Bollihope Common. When they reached the mountain pass of Shaftwell Head, the horse stumbled, the shafts of the conveyance broke, and the passengers were propelled onto the road. As William attempted to get hold of the horse's head to calm it, he received "injuries of a serious character, one of his legs being broken below the knee". As luck would have it, Thomas Sanderson of Thimbleby Hill was coming up behind in a trap and was able to take William home to Howl John where he was attended to by Dr Livingstone. The newspaper report concluded "Much sympathy is felt for Mr Vickers, who is a Weardale guardian and a member of other boards, and is widely known in the dales".[206]

Road accidents like this, not infrequently resulting in fatalities, were quite common in Victorian Britain. It was twelve miles from Middle End Farm over the fell to Stanhope on a rough track which followed the line of a Roman road. It would not have been well maintained at the best of times, and is likely to have been in a poor state after a dales' winter.

7-4 The road to Stanhope over Bollihope Common, near Shaftwell Head.

---

[205] *Newcastle Courant*, April 19. 1890
[206] *Newcastle Courant*, April 5, 1890

# EIGHTEEN NINETY

## *The Letter to Thomas Vickers*

*Belle Vue     June 3rd 1890*

*Dear Cousin,*

    *Yours duly to hand last March. I have not had much time to write as I have been very busy kept during lambing time[207]. We have had betwixt 2 and 3 hundred ewes to lamb, which kept son William and me very busy during that time. I may just say that my wife has had a very bad finger for about eight weeks and not quite better yet. There has three pieces of bone come out, looks like some more to come yet.*

    *You say you are getting lame with rheumatism, well I don't wonder at that, <u>it is a Family complaint</u>. I have kept pretty clear of rheumatism, but I have had sometimes an attack of pleurisy and inflammation.*

    *It appears your family is trying to make a home for themselves, which you cannot blame them. I suppose you will have some left at home to support you in your old age. I am not sure about your age but I think you will be 69 or more. I think you will not see your daughter Alice every day if she has gone fifteen hundred miles away. Are you still farming or have you retired? Is your sons in the farming line? <u>What is Charlie going to do in Manitoba?</u>*

    *I think I told you about my brother Joseph's death and our daughter's death. Our oldest son Joseph is Auctioneer at Tow Law. You will see his name in the newspapers I send you. I think I asked you for your Br George's address, but you have not told me in your letter. You ask where Joseph's widow is living – she is at Shildon, but I have not seen her nor any of them for a long time. Frank is still at Dean Head with his wife and 3 young children, his sons have all left him and are on for themselves. It appears you have had the influenza bad in America. Well, we have had it just as bad all over England.*

    *We have had a very fine winter, never saw so little snow since I can remember, only once a few inches but lay none[208]. And a very fine spring up to last week when it has set in very cold. Farmers are well forward with their work, and crops of all kinds are looking very well.*

    *Do you ever see George or any of the family? If you do, give my best respects to them. Since he has removed, I have not got his address, therefore I cannot write to him.*

    *Now I must conclude with kind regards to you and Mrs, and wishing your family much success in their new undertakings. I will send you a newspaper with this letter and then you will see a little how things are going. So no more at present from your loving Cousin*
    *F. Vickers*

Francis proclaims "an exceptionally good lambing season", confirmed by a report in the *Newcastle Courant* that "the crop of lambs in Weardale this season has been

---

[207] "I have been very busy kept" – An archaic way of saying, "I have been kept very busy".
[208] *"..only a few inches* (of snow) *but lay none."* Another archaic expression

exceptionally good, the lambs being both numerous and strong."[209] The weather was clearly an important factor. He also mentions with obvious pride that he has been "very busy kept" with the lambing, indicating that he has recovered from the afflictions of the previous year and that despite his age, he can still make a significant contribution to the work on the farm.

A year later, the variable weather demonstrated how difficult farming could be in the dale. After the good lambing season in 1890, a similar season was in prospect with exceptionally fine weather in February 1891. It was reported that thrushes were singing day after day and that farmers were well advanced with their Spring work.[210] But a report at the beginning of May told a different story:-

> The oldest residents in Weardale scarcely remember a colder or more cheerless spring time. Day after day the weather is bleak, and intensely cold for the time of the year. Cold easterly and northerly winds prevail, with occasional showers of snow. The trees are naked, the fields are little more attractive, and there is a prospect of a poor turn-out for stock. There is nothing growing in the gardens, and the seeds sown in the fine weather in February are barely making their appearance.[211]

Francis reveals that his wife Mary has had "a very bad finger", the only time in the letters that her name is directly mentioned. The photograph (below), taken a few years after the 1890 Letter, would suggest that Mary's fingers are affected by arthritis, with several fingers being noticeably misshapen. As for "pieces of bone" discharging from the finger, this seems unlikely, with the condition perhaps being caused by gout.[212]

7-5 The misshapen fingers of Mary Vickers

The previous Christmas Day, Mary Vickers presided over a bazaar stall at the Primitive Methodist Chapel (See page 100) where she was a member of the congregation along with husband Francis. Money raised was for the new school which had just been completed – "a handsome building consisting of one large lecture-room with six

---

[209] *Newcastle Courant*, March 29, 1890
[210] *Newcastle Courant*, February 21, 1891
[211] *Newcastle Courant*, May 2, 1891
[212] Dr Paul Mullen suggests gout as a possible cause for the discharge.

classrooms above, all heated with hot water, lighted with gas, and otherwise well furnished and finished".[213]

Francis, increasingly concerned about health and coping with old age sympathises with Thomas about his rheumatism, a "family complaint" he himself has not experienced, although he tells Thomas about his pleurisy and inflammation. Being cared for by family in old age was important to Victorians, (See page 126), and Francis hints at concern for his cousin, with his daughter Alice being 1500 miles away ("I think you will not see her every day"). In his letter of March 1890, Thomas told Francis about the marriage the previous month in St Vincent Township, Ontario, of his daughter Alice (Maria) Vickers to Canadian-born Lemuel (Lem) Booth McLean, a farmer from North Dakota. After the wedding, Alice and Lem settled in North Dakota, about 1500 miles from St Vincent. Francis also asks what son Charlie will be doing in Manitoba – a year later, the 1891 Canadian Census reveals that Charles is living in St Vincent Township which suggests that whatever plans he had in Manitoba had been either completed swiftly or abandoned.

## *A Wedding and a Funeral*

Francis records that his son William of Pease Myers was kept busy with lambing in the Spring. Three months after this letter was written, by an unhappy coincidence William lost his wife on the same day that his brother-in-law John Crawhall gained a wife. Suffering from tuberculosis, Sarah Vickers died on September 14, 1890, aged 36 years. John Crawhall, whose first wife, William's sister Isabella, had died two years earlier, married Annie Dixon Moore at Eastgate Church. The local paper reported the wedding under the headline "Fashionable Marriage at Eastgate":-

> Yesterday morning (Sunday, 14th September), at the pretty village of Eastgate, in Weardale, the church was filled with friends and well-wishers, who had assembled to witness the marriage of Mr John Crawhall, local agent of the Weardale Iron and Coal Co, Stanhope, and Miss Annie Dixon Moore, daughter of Mrs Ann Moore of Eastgate. The handsome new church was beautifully decorated with ferns and flowers for the occasion. The service was full choral, and Mr John Bell, organist of Stanhope Church, presided at the organ. The Vicar of the parish the Rev J Eddowes officiated and was assisted by the Rev J Schofield, Vicar of Westgate. The bride, who wore a tastefully-arranged dress and veil and carried a bouquet, was given away by her brother, Mr John Moore, a younger brother, Mr Tom Moore, acting as best man, while five little girls – the two Miss Crawhalls, daughters of the bridegroom; the two Miss Vickers, daughters of Mr W Vickers, Howl John; and Miss Morley, daughter of Mr (William) Morley – dressed in white, with red sashes, acted as bridesmaids. As the wedding party left the church, the organist played the "Wedding March", and the bells sent forth a merry peal. After breakfast at the bride's mother's[214], the happy pair left, amidst a shower of rice, for Keswick, where they will spend their honeymoon.[215]

---

[213] *Northern Echo*, December 27, 1889
[214] *The Cross Keys Inn*, Eastgate
[215] *Northern Echo*, September 15, 1890

The bridesmaids were Misses Judith and Mary Crawhall, Misses Emily and Ethel Vickers, and Miss Annie Morley. Annie's father William Morley junior, the erstwhile Poor Rate Collector in Stanhope and by then Inspector of Nuisances in Houghton-le-Spring, was married to Hannah Moore, the sister of bride Annie Dixon Moore.

It would have been evident that Sarah Vickers was close to death that weekend, so unless she had died in the early hours, some members of the family would have maintained a vigil at her bedside at the time of the wedding. Her uncle, William Vickers of Howl John, was at her bedside when she died and may have missed the wedding, although two of his daughters were bridesmaids at Eastgate Church.

William Vickers of Pease Myers was left to bring up seven young children. So it was no real surprise to see that by 1891, his brother Joseph Vickers and his wife Jane had two of his children, 11 year-old Elizabeth Eleanor and 7 year-old Mary Annie, living with them at Grove Villa in Tow Law. It was a happy arrangement as Joseph and Jane had no children of their own, but the happiness was not to last (See page134 134).

## *The Influenza Epidemic of 1889-90*

Francis is determined not to be outdone, even when it comes to influenza! The 1889-90 Influenza Pandemic originated in central Asia and followed a path through Russia and Europe, reaching North America in December 1889. A total of one million people died world-wide. All over the continent large numbers of people suffered from it and many died. There were major outbreaks in Belgrade, Copenhagen, Vienna, Berlin, and Paris where "scarcely a household has not furnished a victim"[216]. On December 28, the *Newcastle Courant* reported that the epidemic "which seems to be another name for a bad cold" had reached London. But in Paris, the "bad cold" was being likened to cholera, with nearly 600 deaths reported in 24 hours.

By early January, influenza had reached Tyneside and by mid-January, *The Northern Echo* reported that a number of Stanhope quarrymen were suffering from the illness, amongst whom were several members of Stanhope Band[217]. Within a week Stanhope, Wolsingham and Frosterley had over 100 cases each, and the epidemic remained prevalent in Weardale throughout February. The *Newcastle Courant* reported that: "No one can ever remember as many workmen (in Weardale) being on the sick list. The Sick Benefit Societies … have suffered much in consequence of the extra drain of the funds."[218] Local collieries were losing 1000 tons per day of production and schools in Upper Weardale and Witton-le-Wear were closed. In March, the *Newcastle Courant* reported that the epidemic was abating in Stanhope, Frosterley and Wolsingham, "but is still very prevalent at Tow Law, Witton le Wear and Upper Weardale - at Tow Law, it has even prostrated the doctors"[219].

No doubt the epidemic had a very disruptive effect on the people and economy of Weardale, but the influenza was generally of a mild type in England, resulting in relatively few deaths. This contrasts with the continent where large numbers of deaths occurred, and with North America where there were a large numbers of victims of "very severe" influenza – 25,000 in Boston alone.

---

[216] *Northern Echo,* December 26 1889
[217] *Northern Echo*, January 13, 1890
[218] *Newcastle Courant*, February 15, 1890
[219] *Newcastle Courant,* 8 March 1890

# EIGHTEEN NINETY

It would seem that Francis Vickers' claim that the influenza epidemic was "just as bad all over England" as it was in North America was not accurate. Francis's judgement would appear to have been influenced by the fact that Weardale was more badly affected by the epidemic than many other parts of England.

The epidemic also provided an insight into Victorian humour, as evidenced by reports in *The Northern Echo*. Following advice in a leading medical journal that a tot of rum in the morning and several tots in the afternoon would keep the flu at bay, a lady correspondent claimed that she and several friends had avoided "the well-nigh universal affliction" by acting on the advice. The *Northern Echo* report concluded: "So firm is her own faith in it that she has decided to replace her five o'clock tea by a 'five o'clock grog' while the epidemic lasts."[220]

And on a slightly more serious note in April, 1890:-

> It would be comforting to accept the ingenious theory that the increased consumption of rum…was due to the prevalence of influenza but the theory will hold no water. In the first place, the doctors have as a rule prescribed not rum but whisky for the disease; in the second place, the increased consumption is mainly in the seaport towns, which have not suffered exceptionally from the epidemic; and in the third place, its increase is altogether too large to be explained away in this manner."[221]

And finally:-

> Some good anecdotes are already being told about the influenza epidemic, but the following caps any that I have hitherto seen. It happened in Germany. One of the railway employees of a much-frequented line, whose duty it was to stand at a level crossing, flag in hand, when the train passed, thought he had influenza, and applied to the authorities for a visit of the company's medical adviser. The latter, however, was extremely busy and could not see his way to travel to the out-of-the-way village where the flagman lived. He was, however, a man of resources, and ordered the patient to stand at his post when a certain train came by in which the doctor was travelling, and to put his tongue out as far as he possible could, in order that the medico might see what was the matter. The flagman, nothing daunted, obeyed the order, with the result that the company received no end of letters in which complaints were made about the extreme rudeness of one of the company's employees. Those who witnessed the occurrence from the flagman's point of view described the scene as most dramatic."[222]

## *"Few Prettier Places"*

Just a few months after the 1890 Letter, an article appeared in *The Newcastle Courant* promoting Stanhope as a health and pleasure resort. An extract follows, which perhaps helps to explain why so many of the Vickers family, including Francis's father, Joseph, were long-lived:-

---

[220] *Northern Echo*, 2 Jan 1890
[221] *Northern Echo*, 22 Apr 1890
[222] *Northern Echo*, 16 Jan 1890

There are few prettier places than Stanhope. It is situated in a picturesque valley on the banks of the Wear, in the southern division of the county of Durham, and is surrounded by high hills and wooded dells, through which numerous streams leap and dash over moss and lichen-covered stones as they wind their circuitous way down from the heather-clad hills around it....Its air is pure and bracing and fresh from the mountains. ...Its water supply is good, being brought in earthenware pipes from the adjoining moors, and is cool, clear, and sparkling, very soft in its nature, nice to taste, and excellent for either drinking or washing purposes. The sanitary arrangements for Stanhope are excellent. The drains are well looked after by an energetic Local Board. Its footpaths are all asphalted. It streets are lighted with gas. Its death-rate is low, varying from 10 to 14 per 1,000. Sometimes it is as low as 8 per 1,000. Only last autumn, there was not a single death in the Stanhope Local Board district from August until November...it goes to prove the healthiness of the place. The people invariably live to a good age. Its oldest inhabitant to-day is 97 years of age.[223]

7-6 Few Prettier Places: Stanhope from the South-West

---

[223] *Newcastle Courant*, March 21, 1891. Unattributed, but likely to have been written by William Morley Egglestone.

# 8. EIGHTEEN NINETY-SIX

> *Second son William took East Gate Farm went to it 2 years last May since, the place where George Little had, so you see, we are left with a lot of care in our old ages.*

8-1 Many old people in Victorian England faced ending their days in the dreaded Workhouse.

Since the last letter to Canada, William Gladstone had returned to power in 1892 and the following year introduced the second Home Rule Bill which was passed at the second reading. However, the Conservative dominated House of Lords had the ability at that time to veto any legislation, and they duly blocked the bill. In 1894, Gladstone resigned the premiership at the age of 84, gave up his seat the following year, and died of old age at Hawarden Castle in 1898. His passing was mourned in staunchly Liberal Weardale.

## *Assaults and Threats at Sandedge*

John Walton Watson was again making headlines in the local papers. A farmer and cattle-dealer, he had established an auction mart at St John's Chapel in partnership with John M Dalkin, with the first sale taking place on April 22, 1896. This development no doubt created unwelcome competition for his brother-in-law, Councillor Joseph Vickers, owner of Tow Law Mart. So perhaps it was no coincidence that in July 1896 John Walton Watson was in court as a result of a dispute with Joseph Vickers. At Wolsingham Petty Sessions in the presence of a large crowd of farmers, John Walton Watson of Redgate Farm near Wolsingham, was charged with assaulting William Robson on Sunday May 24th on the moor near Sandedge, Wolsingham Park. John Teale prosecuted and Thomas Jaynes defended. Watson had fell rights for grazing and because his sheep kept jumping a wall into Joseph Vickers' adjoining allotment, the latter engaged Robson to look after his sheep and keep Watson's sheep out. On the day in question, when Robson was chasing seven of these sheep away from the wall, it was alleged that Watson came up and struck him and threatened to "knock out his brains and bury him among the ling". Watson claimed that ninety of his sheep were injured by being chased about so much. Two policemen, William Briens and John Wood said they witnessed the assault and the verbal threat from Watson. Having heard the evidence, the Bench concluded that an assault had been committed and fined Watson £1 and costs.

121

The Bench then heard a curiously similar case, this time an employee of Joseph Vickers being the alleged assailant rather than the victim of an assault. Robert Mewburn, a hind for Councillor Vickers was charged with assault on Thomas Dawson at Sandedge on Sunday May 10th, 1896. Dawson who had an allotment on Wolsingham Moor said that his sheep were driven off a part of the moor where he had put them, and that when he took them back, he had an argument with Mewburn who he alleged barged him with his horse, knocking him down and threatening to kill him and bury him on the fell – a threat which was suspiciously like that allegedly made by John Walton Watson in the previous case. Dr Thomas Devey confirmed that Dawson had bruises on the day of the incident. Robert Mewburn was fined 2s 6d and costs, and a cross-summons against Thomas Dawson was dismissed[224]

## *Sir Joseph Whitwell Pease in Weardale*

In July of the previous year, Sir Joseph Whitwell Pease visited Weardale during the Liberal campaign for the 1895 General Election. He had represented the Barnard Castle Division, which included Weardale, for 30 years, fighting elections in 1868, 1874, 1880, 1885, 1886, and 1892. William Gladstone having resigned in 1894, the Party was now led by Lord Rosebury.

At a constituent's meeting in Stanhope, Dr Thomas Livingstone in the chair heartily endorsed Sir Joseph as "one of the very best candidates in the party of liberty and progress". Sir Joseph in a speech which would have struck some chords with the Weardale tenant farmers present, said that "men are never made one in their views and their nationality by force of arms, by armed police, or by unjust laws which allowed the landlords to confiscate all the improvements of their tenants. That class of law brought about feelings of disloyalty, rebellion, and conspiracy in Ireland." Sir Joseph was in favour of government by conciliation, and not by coercion. His views on the evils of drink would also have gone down well with the many teetotallers in the district such as Francis Vickers – he said that evidence suggested that up to 80 percent of the inmates of the workhouses, lunatic asylums and gaols were there through the effects of drink.[225]

The 1895 General Election was won by the Conservatives led by Lord Salisbury, with a large majority over the Liberals. For the Liberals, Sir Joseph Whitwell Pease retained Barnard Castle and his brother Arthur held Darlington.

## *The Star of Tow Law*

On Saturday afternoon, December 5, 1896, there was a meeting of the Weardale Naturalists' Field Club at Tow Law Vicarage at the invitation of the vicar, the Reverend Thomas Henry Espinell Compton Espin. As well as being a highly respected cleric and an accomplished pianist who for many years was his own organist at Tow Law, the Rev Espin was also a noted amateur scientist with expertise in Botany, Geology, Photography, Microscopy and Astronomy. Born in 1858, his interest in astronomy began at school and remained a passion for the rest of his life. He studied Theology at Oxford and then took Holy Orders. During his time as a curate at West Kirby and Wallasey, he founded and became President of the Liverpool Astronomical Society. When he moved to the Parish

---

[224] *Northern Echo*, July 8, 1896
[225] *Northern Echo*, July 15, 1895

of Wolsingham in 1885, he purchased a 17¼-inch Calver reflector which led him to make many important discoveries of red stars and double stars. He became President of the Newcastle Astronomical Society and was recognised as the best amateur astronomer in the country. In 1888, he became Vicar of nearby Tow Law where he stayed until his death in 1934. His obituary noted:-

> In addition to his exceptionally keen sight, he was possessed also of great powers of endurance. He was known on occasions to continue to work for as long as thirteen hours without a break, and his usual hours of observation were from sunset to 3.00 or 3.30 the following morning. [226]

He was also a pioneer in the construction of X-Ray apparatus, and used his X-Ray machine mainly to examine bones of people referred to him by a doctor, but he was also able to locate a number of coins swallowed by children.[227] X-Rays and astronomy were the subjects of his talk to the Weardale Naturalists' Field Club in 1896. The following is an extract of the afternoon's proceedings:-

8-2 Rev T.H.E.C. Espin

The company visited the apparatus and experimental department room. A quantity of electric appliances and scientific instruments stood about. Small wires were attached to the electric jars, and the host attached two wires to a small glass tube about six inches long, inside being a small plate of platinum and some other metal. He then made the room dark, after which he turned on the electricity. A beautiful greenish light filled the glass tube. A number of other glass tubes were hung up against the wall, and by simply turning a little handle an inch or two, each tube became filled with electric sparks. Then Mr Espin held his hand before the X rays. And the company could see every bone and even every finger point distinctly. He put his arm before the rays with his coat on, and the visitors could see the bone all the way up his arm. The joints at the wrist and elbow were very distinct….A foot was placed before the rays with the boot and stockings on as well. Every bone and joint in the foot was plainly visible, and what was more surprising still, the bones were transparent. A big book was then brought, about two inches thick, bound in calf. The entertainer put into the middle of the book a small drawer key and then

---

[226] Report of the Council to the 115th Annual General Meeting of the Royal Astronomical Society, February, 1935, page 319 ff
[227] *Northern Echo,* A Star of Tow Law, by Keith Proud, 20 May 2011.

held the book to the rays. The key was then seen quite clearly just as if nothing was in front of it at all. But the biggest wonder of all was with a boy about 10 or 11 years of age, son of J Littlefair of Stanhope[228], who was placed before the rays, and his friends could see every bone in his breast, also his backbone, every joint of which was visible…

After a hearty tea, The Rev Espin took the group to his observatory to show them the two-ton Calver telescope:-

The telescope is like a huge cannon in shape and size, and had the night only been starry the company would have enjoyed a peep at the vast worlds above us. Mr Espin explained the manner of working, how it could be turned easily to any part of the heavens.[229]

The Rev Espin's father, The Rev Chancellor Thomas Espin of Wolsingham, found himself in disagreement with William Vickers of Howl John at a meeting of the Weardale Guardians in January 1892, when the "chaplaincy issue" was discussed. The Chairman, Dr Livingstone, had received a letter from the Bishop of Richmond indicating his willingness to be appointed as chaplain for the Board. Mr George Curry moved that a chaplain be appointed and this was seconded by William Snowball, Wolsingham. But William Vickers of Howl John, displaying typical lack of deference to the representatives of the established church, thought the matter should be left open because of the sensitivities of the Dissenters who were not only numerous throughout the Union but were also large rate-payers. He argued that to appoint a chaplain would be an insult to them. Dr Livingstone reminded them that the Local Government Board's inspector had said that it was the duty of the Guardians to allow the inmates to have "spiritual consolation from their own Church." The Rev Espin, said that he did not wish to be disrespectful to Nonconformists, but chaplains were appointed because "75 per cent of the inmates of every workhouse were members of the Church of England." With Rev Espin's support, George Curry's motion was duly carried, and the Bishop of Richmond was elected to the office of Chaplain.[230]

William Vickers of Howl John had long been in conflict with the Church Party in seeking to have the interests of rate payers fairly represented. During his successful Stanhope School Board Election campaign of 1883, he assured a public meeting that, as a large rate payer, he would be economical with expenditure "consistent with thorough efficiency", and questioned whether those in holy orders "who have their living safe and had not to struggle with depression and hard times," could be trusted to use the rate payers' money wisely.

The underlying tension between dalesmen and the local establishment was alluded to by William Vickers of Howl John at the 1893 meeting of Stanhope Agricultural Show, albeit in a good-natured and humorous way. [231] At the luncheon where there was the usual succession of toasts, William proposed a toast to the vice-chairmen, the Rev John Eddowes, Vicar of Eastgate, and John W Roddam, Land Agent for John Arundel

---

[228] The boy was Joseph WS Littlefair, born in 1884, the son of Joseph Littlefair, an Engineman.
[229] *Northern Echo*, December 8, 1896
[230] *Newcastle Courant,* January 16, 1892
[231] *Northern Echo*, September 9, 1893.

# EIGHTEEN NINETY-SIX

Hildyard. William declared himself to be in a difficulty, "One vice is my landlord's agent, and the other is my parson. I dare not say anything bad about either; and if I said anything good they would say it smelt of shop (Laughter and cheers)."[232]

## *The Letter to Thomas Vickers*

*Belle Vue   January 8th 1896*

*Dear Cousin,*

*I have just been thinking it is a long time since I have heard from you. In looking over your letters, I see the last I have received has been wrote at Christmas 1888. I think I would answer that, if I did not you must excuse me. At any rate I have wrote to George since then, so you would hear from him.*

*Well we have had a great many deaths about Stanhope this last year. Joseph Heads of Greenfoot died a year last September. You would know Thomas Baty: I think you once lived with them over about Lead Gate. He came to Stanhope some years ago, died last Spring. Frank Brown died last October, his widow sold all off except cows and a few young stock. She will be selling them in the Spring. John Henry Stephenson (Henry Stephenson's son) has taken Green Head, so you see it has to go out of Brown's family after being there for generations. F. Tinkler's wife was at Funeral (and) only a few days after, she died very suddenly, found dead in bed. So you see in the midst of life we are in death. I think I told either you or George about our son Frank: he died four years since. His widow is keeping shop at Stanhope. She has two sons and two daughters. Our second son William took East Gate Farm, went to it two years last May since. The place where George Little had, so you see we are left with a lot of care in our old ages. We have both a boy and girl hired, and a Hind at Pease Myers. Brother William left Howl John a year last May since. He gave up for a reduction of rent. He could not take it at what they wanted for it, so he went to West Country and took a Large House, formerly a Gentleman's Residence, close to Ullswater Lake, and has taken in visitors that comes to the Lake. Mary and I were there to see them a year past September, it is a large house with pleasure grounds and a carriage drive. A Steamboat runs from there to a place called Patterdale, about 10 miles long. He is 5 miles from Penrith. We have got a Railway from Stanhope to Wear Head, opened out 2 months since. You would not know Stanhope now if you saw it. There is twice as many houses now.*

*You must get your daughter Alice to write and let me know how you are all getting on, as I would like to hear from you all. I expect that you will be getting rather feeble by this time. I think you will be in your 75th year. You are a little older than I am. I was 74 last December. I don't know what age your brother Frank is but he must be going up to 90 years of age. Last account I heard of him he was managing his place himself, but I think he will have got his second family up now.*

*We have very fine weather just now. This year has come in very mild, last year came in very rough. There was never known to be as much snow in Weardale as there was last winter. We were blocked in at our place for 11 weeks. We had to go*

---

[232] If something 'smelt of shop', it was conveying an impression of obsequiousness.

*over top gates and walls with the horses to get to any place. We had a heavy stock (of) sheep. We took about 300 to East Gate beside 300 we had at home. There was nothing to get but what was given to them. Had it not been that William had plenty of hay we would have had £50 worth to buy. There is a great difference betwixt last winter and this so far. While I am writing the sun is shining like a summer's day and quite mild.*

*Now I have not much more to say at present. If there is anything you would like to hear about, just let me know. You will see by my writing my hand is rather shaky.*

*Now give my kind regards to George and Family and accept the same yourselves. Wishing you all a happy and a prosperous new year.*
*I remain your loving Cousin,*
*Francis Vickers*
*Write soon*

## Age Taking its Toll

The 1896 letter reveals that age is taking its toll on the 74 year-old Francis Vickers. Reflecting on the waning of his own physical powers, and mindful of the deaths of increasing numbers of his contemporaries, he tells the marginally-older Thomas, "I expect that you will be getting rather feeble by this time" which is another example of the disarming directness of country people in Victorian times (See page 78). Francis didn't quite realise how feeble Thomas was: a month after Francis wrote him the letter, Thomas died on February 7, 1896, and is buried in Lakeview Cemetery, Meaford, Ontario. His wife Alice died in April, 1898 and is buried beside him.

Francis relates that Frank of Dean Head is still managing the farm himself, despite approaching 90 years of age, adding "but I think he will have got his second family up by now". In fact, Frank was a mere 86 years of age, his eldest daughter was just turned 16 and Jane the youngest was six years old.

How they would cope in their old age was a particular concern for people in Victorian Britain. If they did not have family to support them and had not accumulated savings, they were likely to become outdoor paupers, or if incapable of fending for themselves, inmates of the Workhouse. So with son William close by at Eastgate and his widowed daughter-in-law Elizabeth and her children living in Stanhope, Francis expressed his pleasure to Thomas that he and Mary are "left with a lot of care in our old ages."

## "A Great Many Deaths about Stanhope"

Francis recounts the deaths in the dale of people that Thomas would have known in his youth. One such was Joseph Heads, a farmer at Greenfoot. He was twice married, firstly to Hannah Brown, sister of Frank Brown, in 1849. Following Hannah's death in 1857, Joseph married Mary Burdus, a 35 year old farmer's daughter from Slaley, in 1864. Joseph died at Greenfoot in 1894 and was buried at Stanhope St Thomas. Frank Brown, husband of Mary Reed who he had married in 1861, was 67 years old when he died in October 1895, to be succeeded at Greenhead by his nephew Michael Heads. His obituary appeared in the *Newcastle Courant*:-

# EIGHTEEN NINETY-SIX

There died at Greenhead Farm near Stanhope on Saturday a well-known and highly respected farmer named Francis Brown, at one time a Newcastle and Weardale carrier. He had farmed the Greenhead Farm a great number of years. The interment took place at Stanhope Church on Tuesday (8 Oct 1895) amidst many signs of sympathy and respect.[233]

Amongst the many mourners at Frank Brown's funeral was "F Tinkler's wife". Francis relates that only a few days later, Mary Jane Tinkler was found dead in bed, having died very suddenly. Francis Tinkler, a Cabinet Maker born in 1824 and a cousin of Francis Vickers, had married Mary Jane Wearmouth from Cumberland in 1849. A year after Mary Jane's death, Francis Tinkler died and was buried on 10th October 1896.

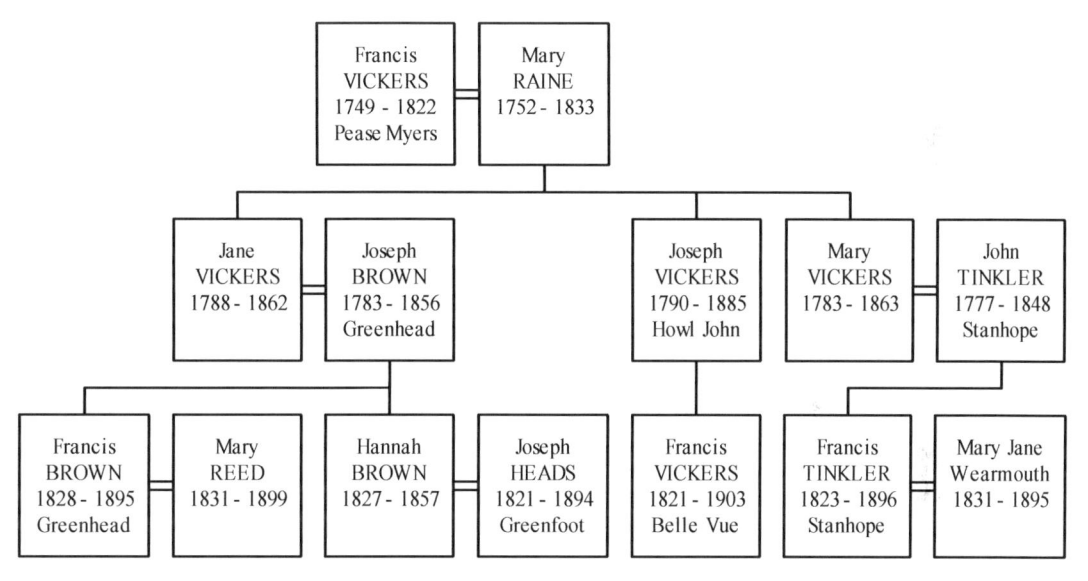

8-3 Links of Vickers Family with Brown, Heads and Tinkler Families.
Francis reports the death of Joseph Heads, Francis Brown, and Mary Jane Tinkler.

As a young farmer, Thomas Vickers had lived with Thomas Baty at Leadgate, about 20 miles north of Stanhope, and Francis inform him of his death "last Spring". He died at The Square, Stanhope, not in the Spring but on July 4 1895, aged 79 years. His daughter Margaret married the letter-writer's brother William Vickers of Howl John in Lanchester in 1879, and his son William Thomas Baty married Sarah Ann Sanderson, granddaughter of John Sanderson and Margaret Vickers.

---

[233] *Newcastle Courant,* October 12, 1895

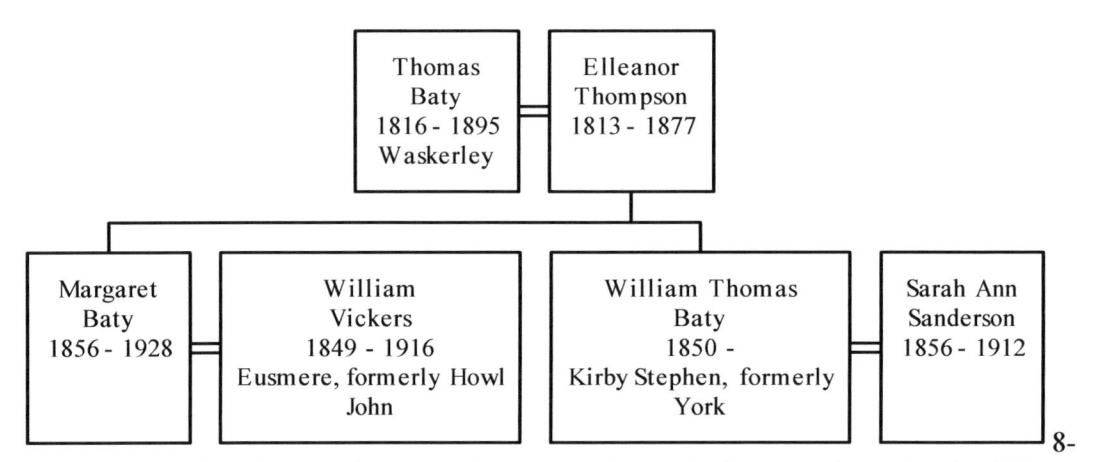

```
                    ┌─────────────┬─────────────┐
                    │  Thomas     │  Elleanor   │
                    │  Baty       │  Thompson   │
                    │  1816-1895  │  1813-1877  │
                    │  Waskerley  │             │
                    └─────────────┴─────────────┘
```

8-4 Vickers/Baty/Sanderson Links. Sarah Ann Sanderson is the second cousin of William Vickers of Howl John.

| Margaret Baty 1856-1928 | William Vickers 1849-1916 Eusmere, formerly Howl John | William Thomas Baty 1850- Kirby Stephen, formerly York | Sarah Ann Sanderson 1856-1912 |

John Henry Stephenson took over the tenancy of Greenhead after the farm had been in the Brown family for generations. John Henry was the son of Henry Stephenson, a farmer at Billingshield who had the distinction of having been an exhibitor at the first Stanhope Agricultural Show in 1834 and was still exhibiting 50 years later. John Henry lived at the family farm at Billingshield until he married schoolteacher Mary Jane Philipson, daughter of Eastgate butcher and flour dealer Thomas Philipson, in the summer of 1886. Shortly after they married, he and Mary Jane emigrated to Canada where children Eleanor and Annie were born. By 1891 they were back in Stanhope living with Mary Jane's widowed mother Sarah at Eastgate, before moving to Greenhead in 1896.

Francis reminds Thomas about the death of his son Frank "four years since". Frank Vickers, son of the letter writer, followed in his brother Joseph's footsteps, making rapid progress as a farmer and auctioneer. In March, 1891, he was the auctioneer conducting a large sale of stock and implements at Thornley Hall, following Joseph Longstaffe's departure. Part of the farming operation had been sub-let to him by Joseph Walton[234] who lived at Thornley Hall with his wife Elizabeth nee Vickers. As previously mentioned, Elizabeth's mother, 89 year-old Elizabeth Vickers was living with them, her husband Joseph having died at Howl John in 1885. Also present was 9 year-old schoolboy Lawrence William (Lawrie) Vickers whose mother Sarah had died at Pease Myers about 6 months earlier (See page 117). At Thornley Hall, Lawrie had the highly unusual experience at that time of actually getting to know his great grandmother, who was 80 years old when he was born.

Later in 1891, Frank Vickers' promising career came to a tragic end. He contracted pneumonia and less than a week later, his 3 year-old son Joseph died on November 29 1891. Doubly stricken with illness and grief, Frank died four days later of acute pneumonia and pulmonary congestion at Ox Close House, Shadforth, aged 33 years. His family were with him when he died and they took him home to Stanhope for the funeral and burial on 8th December.

---

[234] *Northern Echo*, March 18, 1891

His wife was Elizabeth Sanderson of Thimbleby Hill – they were married in 1880 and had 5 children, 4 of them surviving in 1896. To support herself and the children, Elizabeth opened a drapers and grocers shop in Stanhope. By 1901, three of her children were still at home, and the eldest, Thomas Herbert (Tom) Vickers, was an apprentice at Messrs Bainbridge & Company Department Store in Newcastle[235] (See page 168).

## *Pease Myers to Eastgate*

In his 1896 letter, Francis mentions that his second son William Vickers junior had left Pease Myers and taken a farm at Eastgate previously tenanted by George Little, presumably a name known to Thomas. George Little born in 1808, unmarried and a distant cousin of Francis, farmed 326 acres at Eastgate House until he died in 1877. According to William Morley Egglestone, he was the owner of the last set of Carrier Galloways in Weardale - "a hardy shaggy pony of some 13 hands" originally imported from Scotland and which had been employed for centuries to carry the mineral wealth of the dale to Newcastle.[236]

After George Little's death, Eastgate House was farmed by William Morley's sons William junior and Henry. By 1891, Henry had moved to nearby Broad Law Farm, whilst his brother William was dividing his time between Eastgate Farm and his role as Inspector of Nuisances in Houghton-le-Spring (See page 76). In 1893, William Morley and family moved to Houghton-le-Spring and William Vickers took over the tenancy of Eastgate House on May Day, 1893. Shortly afterwards, William was helped out by his friends with the traditional Ploughing Day support:-

> This very desirable Farm on the Horsley Estate has just been let to Mr William Vickers of Pease Myers, Stanhope. On Saturday a large number of Mr Vickers' friends turned out with their teams, and a capital day's work was done, notwithstanding the very dry condition the land is in. The farm has been for fifteen years in the hands of Messrs Morley, previous to which it was for a long time occupied by the late Mr George Little. It is well known in the county as the homestead of many first-class shorthorns and border Leicesters. We wish Mr Vickers every success.[237]

By 1901, William Morley junior and family had moved to Houghton-le-Spring, Henry Morley was at Middlehope Farm, Westgate, William Vickers at Eastgate House, and Matthew Reed Jnr at Broad Law with his wife Mary Hannah, two children, and his 73 year-old mother-in-law, Mary Heads nee Burdus.

William Vickers of Pease Myers followed in his brother Joseph's footsteps in becoming an auctioneer in the 1890s. He also continued to be active politically in the interests of tenant farmers, making an impassioned speech at the 63rd Stanhope Agricultural Show which took place at the Castle Grounds in September 1896. After the moor sheep of his brother Joseph and his cousin John Edward Nicholson of Lanchester had notably swept the board, William urged farmers to give thought as well as exertion to their business, and for those who were ever ready to criticise to step forward and help

---

[235] Now John Lewis Store.
[236] *Newcastle Courant*, The Carrier Galloway by WM Egglestone, October 7, 1887
[237] *Northern Echo*, May 8, 1893

find solutions to the problems they faced. In an echo of the "pity without relief" comment of his father in the 1874 letter, William said that he appreciated the sympathy for farmers but that he found that whatever was profitable, "something always came in the way of advantage". Rent and rates were far too high but landlords and agents were not to blame. The main problem was lack of solidarity amongst farmers "who were only too ready to cut each other's throats". To laughter and cheers, the Bishop of Richmond, John James Pulleine, concluded the speeches with his tongue firmly in his cheek; he felt that the farmer had to be "a very exceptional man" – he had to endure the hardship of rates, taxes and the costs of freight with the consolation that if he didn't get any benefit out of his business, the country did.[238]

On Boxing Day, 1893, the eligible William married the equally eligible Annie Clayton in her home town of Farnley, near Leeds. After attending Ripon Diocesan Training College, Annie became a schoolmistress and by 1891 was teaching at Eastgate School. The Wedding took place only six months after William moved to Eastgate, suggesting either a whirlwind romance or, more likely, a closeness which developed over a longer period through their shared political interests - Annie was as a prominent member of the Women's Liberal Association of Stanhope.[239] In 1898, she stood for election to the Stanhope School Board but failed to achieve sufficient votes.

## *Howl John to Ullswater*

As previously mentioned, the agricultural depression caused many tenant farmers in Weardale and elsewhere to agitate for rent reductions, but as long as the landlords had farmers willing to take over tenancies, i.e., "willing to cut each other's throats", many of them did not see the need for rent reductions. William Vickers senior, a highly experienced and able farmer, must have reached the point where he felt worn down by the accumulation of adverse circumstances. Perhaps the rent demanded for Howl John was the final straw that caused him to surrender the 42-year tenancy in May 1894 to run a guest house in the Lake District, but other factors may have may have played a part. In 1890, he broke his leg quite badly which may have affected his ability to meet the physical demands of farming. The death of his mother Elizabeth in December 1892 may also have had a bearing on his decision to leave Weardale. Another factor was his relationship with the new landlord of Howl John, Mr JA Hildyard, JP, the son of the recently deceased JRW Hildyard. William was a man of strong convictions and did not see eye to eye with John Arundel Hildyard on the future of the Stanhope Agricultural Show. At the 1892 show, Mr Hildyard, the President of the Stanhope Agricultural Society, repeated a long-held view that there were too many shows in a small area and that by amalgamation, "larger prizes could be offered and competition greatly improved in a way not practicable to a smaller or local society." Responding, William argued that that the Stanhope Agricultural Show would stand comparison with the County Show in all respects except horses, and that they had better Shorthorns. He felt that it would never be practicable to combine the three local societies[240] because "the members might not then work so energetically as they did for their own societies."[241]

---

[238] *Northern Echo*, September 12, 1896
[239] *Northern Echo*, October 19, 1896
[240] Stanhope, Weardale (St John's Chapel), and Wolsingham Agricultural Societies.
[241] *Northern Echo*, September 10, 1892

On April 30th, 1894, notice of an auction appeared in *The Northern Echo* (right). William Vickers of Howl John was fortunate that his nephew Joseph Vickers of Tow Law happened to be the best auctioneer in South Durham.

The auction at Howl John was a success, attracting leading farmers from far and wide. *The Northern Echo* reported that "the away-going sale of the well-known cattle and sheep breeder, Mr Wm Vickers, was conducted by Mr Joseph Vickers, Tow Law, at the above Weardale farm. There was a very large attendance, embracing all the leading shorthorn and cattle farmers of the kingdom. The bidding was spirited for the pedigree animals, and good prices were realised."[242] The farm at Howl John was taken over by William's cousin, John Collingwood junior.

> MR JOSEPH VICKERS, acting under instructions from Mr William Vickers of Howl John, who is relinquishing this Farm after completing a 42 years' tenancy, will DISPERSE BY PUBLIC AUCTION the whole of this NOTED STOCK, on Thursday, May 3, 1894, comprising 37 Head of Superior Shorthorn Cattle, some of which are pedigreed; 40 Splendid Young Border Leicester Ewes and Followers; 16 Border Leicester Ewe Hoggs and Followers; 1 Border Leicester Shearling Tup; 1 Border Leicester Tup Hogg; 5 Horses, including 2 Handsome Clydesdale Mares. A Large Field of MODERN AGRICULTURAL IMPLEMENTS, by the most eminent makers; Dairy Utensils, and Part HOUSEHOLD FURNITURE.
> 
> Sale to commence with Implements at 11 a.m. prompt.
> 
> Full particulars in Circulars to be had of the Auctioneer. - Mart Office, Tow Law.

8-5 Sale at Howl John, 1894

Before he left Stanhope for Ullswater, William's immense contribution as a stock breeder, a campaigner for the interests of farmers, and as a public servant on various parish authorities was recognized by his many friends and admirers. A Parish Committee was established to organize an appropriate send-off, and on Thursday 10th May at Howl John Farm, "a large and influential gathering assembled to present the departing tenant with a public acknowledgement of his services". Sir Joseph Pease was unable to attend but sent a cheque along with his apologies.

The Vicar of Eastgate the Rev JGB Knight presided and expressed his gratitude to William, who was the warden-in-charge of Eastgate Church when he arrived, and introduced the Rev James Schofield of Westgate to make the presentation:-

> The Rev Schofield expressed his regret that Weardale was to lose so faithful and worthy a son as Mr Vickers of Howl John (applause) – a name in which every sphere of parish offices commanded their respect (applause). Mr Vickers's services to the Church bespoke an ideal official (applause) – whose place would be hard to fill (applause) while his departure from Weardale would, he was afraid, tend to lessen the notoriety of the acumen and ability of its stock breeding and culturing of celebrity in the show rings of the North (loud applause). Mr Vickers and his good wife embodied socially all that was requisite to make life happy if possible to their fellows (loud applause) and in their home he hoped the blessing of God would rest upon them, and the prosperity which it incorporated by theirs (loud and prolonged applause). He had pleasure in handing Mr Vickers a purse of

---

[242] *Northern Echo*, May 5, 1894

gold (£35) and the following address as a memento of their regard for him and his (loud applause).

The illuminated citation, over which there was a painting of Howl John, with the *Duke of Howl John* and the Leicester ram with which Mr Vickers is identified, "chastely and massively mounted by Mr WB Bird, West Hartlepool" was as follows:-

> *Presented with the purse of gold to Wm Vickers on relinquishing the 42 years' tenancy of the paternal farm of Howl John, Weardale, in recognition of his political and public services on the parish Boards, and as churchwarden. Also for successfully enhancing the stock-breeding reputation of the district; together with a timepiece and standard bearers for Mrs Vickers and family, in token of their social worth. Wishing them "Long life and happiness" – signed on behalf of subscribers to the Committee.*
>
> RALPH WATSON, *Irestone, Treasurer,*
>
> THOMAS PENTLAND, *Ireshopeburn, Secretary.*

William, deeply touched and struggling to keep his emotions in check, returned the thanks. Close friend Annie Dixon Crawhall handed Margaret Vickers and family the beautiful timepiece and standard bearers, and spoke touchingly of the esteem in which they were held. This was wholeheartedly endorsed by her husband John Crawhall (soon to become a Weardale Guardian and a JP) and by local farmer William Watson of Winter Gap, on behalf of the neighbours. The heartfelt thanks of the Vickers' family to the committee were gracefully acknowledged by Ralph Watson of Irestone, William's Guardian colleague, and after warm thanks to the Rev Knight and the Rev Schofield, the event was closed.[243] Days later, William and his family left Howl John[244] for Eusemere House in the Lake District, described by Francis as "The West Country", nowadays associated with the South-West of England, but Cumberland had long been known in the dales as "the west countrie". Eusemere House is recently described as: "A large, comfortable residence, near the shores of Ullswater, and boasts superb views out over the lake and towards the fells beyond. It has big bedrooms, many of which also look out over the lake, and also has a huge garden and patio area. Once owned by Thomas Clarkson, who campaigned to end slavery and was a friend of the Wordsworth family..." It is also where Wordsworth began his famous poem *Daffodils*. It is not hard to see why William would forsake the perpetual struggle to make a good living from tenant farming in Weardale to pursue a quite different and less physically onerous challenge in the idyllic setting on the shores of Ullswater.

Francis notes that he and Mary had visited Eusemere House in September 1894 a few months after William and family had taken up residence. They will have travelled by train to Darlington and from there, a 2½ hour journey to Penrith. A horse-drawn cab would then have taken them on the scenic 6-mile trip to Pooley Bridge, either the direct route through Redhills and Dailmain Park, or an alternative route via Lowther Park and Askham.

---

[243] *Northern Echo*, May 12, 1894
[244] John Collingwood Junior took over the tenancy of Howl John. He was first cousin once removed of William Vickers of Howl John

The Ullswater steamboat service, inaugurated at Eusemere in 1859, was a great attraction for visitors and the Vickers brothers would have enjoyed the journey to Patterdale and back on the steamboat *Raven*. The Shildon Show Committee certainly enjoyed their day-trip to Ullswater in August 1895, not least their cruise on the *Raven* where "the scenery *en route* was much admired by the delighted trippers, many of whom had never had a previous opportunity of visiting the Lake District."[245] Of course, William would have known that trips from County Durham to Ullswater were becoming popular at that time, and this may well have been a factor in his decision to take over the guest house at Eusemere.

## *From Strength to Strength*

Francis's son Joseph, not mentioned in the 1896 letter, was going from strength to strength. He had become a leading exhibitor of black-faced sheep, carrying off most of the prizes at the 131st Wolsingham Show in 1894. He also delivered a speech in which he revealed that the first show was held in Wolsingham Market Place and originated because of a bet between two farmers as to who had the best beast.[246] The following year at the South Tyne Agricultural Society Show at Haltwhistle, the *Newcastle Courant* reported that Joseph's blackfaces "carried all before them, as they have done at many shows this year, among their trophies being first at the Royal and the Yorkshire".[247]

On December 14, 1896, Joseph wielded the hammer at his Twelfth Christmas Prize Show and Sale at Tow Law Auction Mart. With a large crowd all day and the stock in prime condition, the sale was a great success and judged to be even better than in previous years. The luncheon was held at Robert Wheatley's Cattle Mart Hotel where chairman Mr John D Taylor-Smith of Colepike Hall presided. Joseph's brother William (vice-chairman) proposed a toast to "The Judges", and Thomas Starforth, a butcher from Spennymoor, responded, praising the "straightforward" way in which Joseph and his staff operated – high praise in a business where shady practices were commonplace.

The chairman, in proposing the "Success of the Mart", said that Durham-bred cattle were world renowned. He recalled a recent visit he and his wife had made to Dublin where the hotel menu boasted *"beef a la Durham"*, an anecdote which drew loud cheers. Councillor Vickers, "replying amid a volume of cheers", declined to take credit, attributing the great success of the mart to "the necessity for an outlet for stock in this district". Perhaps so, but Joseph Vickers was the one who saw the opportunity and followed it through, in the process making his fortune and providing a long-term boost to the economy of Tow Law and district. The high quality of the black-faced sheep on the day made him proud, no doubt particularly so because of his special interest in the breed. The luncheon concluded with enthusiastically received songs and duets.[248]

At the thirteenth Christmas Show the following year, the mart was "tastefully and seasonably decorated, while the show of fat cattle, sheep, pigs, etc., was one of the best seen in the district, giving ample scope to the feeding and fostering stock *cognoscenti* who occupied to suffocation the tiers of seating round the rostrum of the above popular auctioneer, which included buyers and vendors from all parts of the country, and the task

---

[245] *Northern Echo*, August 30, 1895
[246] *Northern Echo*, September 13, 1894
[247] *Newcastle Courant*, September 21, 1895
[248] *Northern Echo*, December 15, 1896

– a herculean one for the judges – was keenly watched and endorsed, and the bidding and prices were lively and large."[249]

Not long after sister-in-law Sarah Vickers of Pease Myers had died in 1890, Joseph and Jane adopted William and Sarah's daughter, Mary Annie. It was a happy arrangement, at once relieving the pressure on his grieving and hard-pressed brother and also providing he and Jane with the child they had prayed for. In the early 1890s, Joseph, Jane and their adopted daughter moved to the "big house" at Elm Park, but the happiness was shattered on April 8th 1897 when Mary Annie died at Westholm Nursing Home, Bishop Auckland, of pneumonia aged 13 years. She was buried on April 10th at Stanhope St Thomas where her memorial reads:-

> Loving Memory of/ MARY ANNIE,/ BELOVED DAUGHTER OF/ WILLIAM & SARAH VICKERS/ OF PEASE MYRES/ DEARLY BELOVED NIECE/ AND ADOPTED DAUGHTER OF/ JOSEPH & JANE VICKERS/ ELM PARK/ BORN JAN 24TH 1884/ DIED APRIL 8TH 1897

The death of Mary Annie will have been a devastating blow to not only her father William but also to her adoptive parents, Joseph and Jane. And as if that was not enough to endure for one year, Jane's father John Sanderson died three months later at Broomley Farm in Tynedale.

## *The Weardale Extension Railway*

There had been talk of a railway extension up the dale from Stanhope to replace the packhorses and carts as far back as 1845, which was two years before the railway reached Frosterley and seventeen years before it was extended to Stanhope. At the 1864 Dinner of the Weardale Agricultural Society at St John's Chapel, Mr Wentworth Blacket Beaumont, MP, raised the issue of the railway extension to St John's Chapel which he felt would add to the prosperity of the district by giving better access to the vast mineral resources. For this to happen, he believed that the people of Chapel must "bestir themselves" and demonstrate that they took a real interest in promoting this objective, rather than just standing by until the railway company saw fit to construct a line. Responding, Henry Pease MP, of Stanhope Castle, indicated that the subject had previously been considered by the directors of the North-Eastern Railway, but "they could not, after due inquiry, see such a prospect of a remunerative return for the capital required to be expended in the construction of the line, as to justify them in recommending to the shareholders the carrying out of such a project". He suggested that if the men of St John's Chapel worked together to construct a line, then maybe the NER or some other company might purchase it from them. In effect, both Mr Beaumont, the lessee of the lead mines, and Mr Pease, director of the NER, were placing the onus of responsibility for acquiring a railway extension on the shoulders of the local population.[250]

The subject was not raised again until plans were exhibited to the public by a London firm of engineers at St John's Chapel Town Hall on April 9th,1870. This proposal for a

---

[249] *Northern Echo*, December 14, 1897
[250] *Newcastle Courant*, September 2, 1864

line from Stanhope to Westgate and onwards over Killhope Moor, costing about £100,000, also failed to get off the ground. In November 1886, *The Northern Echo* reported the results of a survey commissioned by Sir Joseph Pease on the proposed railway from Stanhope to Wearhead. The new railway would be used for the conveyance of minerals out of the dale – transport costs would be cheaper than carting - and for the benefit of the estimated 10,000 population beyond Stanhope, living mainly between Westgate and Copt Hill – and very many in small holdings, spending half their time raising cattle and sheep, and the other half in the lead mines, and in the ironstone and limestone quarries. It was argued that this community would benefit because their "wants…are almost wholly supplied from outside", and the coaches which passed between Stanhope and Cowshill were "frequently insufficient".[251]

Then in 1887 William Morley Egglestone made a presentation to the directors of the North-Eastern Railway Company on behalf of the Weardale Railway Committee. The proposed line had been surveyed by civil engineer Edward Lyall and the cost estimated at less than £50,000. Mr Egglestone pointed out that "a dale famed for its short-horned cattle, its black-faced sheep, its limestone, and with such a large proportion of pasturage and moors, was a dale capable of vastly increasing its rateable value and consequently its agricultural produce, and this desired improvement would be greatly facilitated by a railway which would bring the products of the dale within touch of better markets".[252]

Not everyone was convinced: in 1890, one correspondent stated, "It is idle to expect that a Weardale railway will ever resuscitate the trade of the dale when ten or twelve Galloway carts can easily carry away daily all the lead and iron found there. Railway directors are business men too".[253]

In 1891, yet another sudden stoppage of the Weardale Iron Company's ironstone mines as a result of adverse trading conditions gave renewed impetus to the idea. A meeting of workmen and property owners of the district resolved that a railway was the only sustainable solution to the difficulties caused by the frequent industrial suspensions. In 1892, a bill authorising the construction of the line was carried through Parliament. And on October 21st 1893, a procession headed by the Weardale Brass Band and the Stanhope Saxhorn Band left St John's Chapel at 1.30 p.m. for the field where Sir Joseph Whitwell Pease cut the first sod with a ceremonial silver spade.

Tea and entertainments were provided for the large crowd in the afternoon, there was a fireworks display in the evening, and commemorative medals were presented to the school children in the dale.

The construction phase was not without incident, with at one stage the men going on strike for better pay and conditions. They had a point as many of the men were receiving only 2s10d per day, and working a 58½ hour week, excluding meal breaks. A deputation was then appointed to meet the management and not only raise the wage and hour questions but also raise the conduct of the gangers towards the men. They were rebuffed, being told that they would now only employ their own navvies and not dalesmen. Feelings then ran high and the windows of the navvies' lodge at Westgate were smashed and some of the navvy gangers were jostled by the crowd.[254]

---

[251] *Northern Echo*, November 3, 1886
[252] *Northern Echo*, October 21, 1896
[253] *Northern Echo*, December 27, 1890
[254] *Northern Echo,* June 18, 1894

Despite the setbacks the line was completed on time, and in September 1895, a month before the official opening of the extension railway, *Northern Echo* correspondent William Morley Egglestone accepted an invitation to travel on "the prettiest bit of railway extension in the country" in the company of several NER staff, including the civil engineer, Darlington-based Edward Lyall :-

> In a few minutes we were forging ahead at what one may call a nice little trot....The luxury of the Pullman car was not to be compared from the sensation derived from the full free flow of the mountain air as, resting leisurely on the fore end of the truck, we made our way along the new line, full as it is at every turn of scenic beauty of the most enchanting kind. River, burn, moor, wood, copse, stream, cliff, ravine came under the eye in charming succession, and one's rapture at the loveliness of a particular point was only enjoyed the while some even more surpassing scenic beauty striking the eye and excited fresh admiration....Here and there one could see where the spirit of engineering genius had achieved a triumph, and even thereby added to the attractive pictures which this bonnie bit of railway presents on every side. Just out of Stanhope, one is struck by the number of crossings, necessary of course for the perpetuation of old rights of way. Now and again we ran along close to the river; and anon through a plantation; while on either side rose the hills beyond which the becking grouse fatten themselves for the guns which await them in due course....Beautiful little structures are the four new stations, each of which is fitted with the most modern fixtures for safety, comfort, and convenience. At length we reached St John's Chapel, the capital of the upper dale – once in the far off days when lead was gold, a place of some consequence, judging from the number of shop premises to be seen in the long main. The ride thence to Wearhead was the final stage of a most delightful journey. The bright-looking dwellings, many of them of the old 'villa' type, nestling in all sorts of pleasant nooks, gave a most charming character to the whole scene. The drip-white blinds of the houses, the quaint-looking farmsteads, and here and there an ancient cottage or two invest the entire valley with a deliciously rural character; and one could see that at some day not far off the volatile tripper will make the welkin ring with his jocund cries and merry refrains....At one place the course of the Wear has been diverted, and the line runs along a solid embankment of masonry, from which can be seen the river as it gurgles along over the fantastic boulders without which no country stream would be worth looking at. It only remains for the dalesfolk to put their house in order, so to speak, for the rush there will be into a land which up to now is as little known, twenty miles away, as Devonshire or Suffolk. Weardale then will be a new land to thousands of trippers who have never been beyond Stanhope, or even so far. The whole country is an artist's paradise, and in a short time the dalesfolk will find their immemorial seclusion and quietude gone for ever! They will become, what they are not at present, citizens of the world at large, and will derive thereby advantages which will more than compensate them for the old-world solitude in which the dale has so long and so complacently existed.[255]

---

[255] *Northern Echo*, October 3, 1895

# EIGHTEEN NINETY-SIX

On Monday, October 21st, 1895, the second anniversary of the sod-cutting, the line was opened to the public for traffic, the *Northern Echo* observing, "without being too sanguine, there is good reason for believing that the new line will not only prove a boon to dwellers in the dale, but will be sufficiently remunerative to reward the North Eastern Railway Company for the step they have taken. It cannot fail to materially improve the industries of the dale, besides opening up to tourists an historic and romantic dale, to the visiting of which the great obstacle has hitherto been the lack of a railway service".[256]

The opening ceremony was conducted by Sir Joseph Pease, the local MP and chairman of the North-Eastern Railway Company Company. Rain fell heavily all day but it did not dampen the enthusiasm of the crowds who turned out to cheer the progress of the train up and down the dale. The new track covered a distance of about 9½ miles, and was constructed at a cost of around £50,000[257]. The line followed the course of the River Wear, but because of the many windings of the river, 21 small bridges had to be built to allow the track to maintain a straight course. There were new stations at Stanhope, Eastgate, Westgate, St John's Chapel, and Wearhead.

8-6  Sir Joseph Whitwell Pease, MP

The report of the opening appeared in *The Northern Echo* the following day:-

Despite the terribly depressing downpour of rain which continued from the earliest hour on Monday until evening, the residents in Weardale did not allow their enthusiasm in regard to the new Wear Valley Extension Railway to be one whit lessened. Nearly 400 persons assembled at Stanhope new station to make the trip to Wearhead by the first public train on the new line, and every succeeding train – both ordinary and special – carried a numerous freight of passengers. There was little or no attempt at any set public rejoicing over the event, but at intervals along the new railway, and especially at Westgate and St John's Chapel, there was a somewhat pretentious display of bunting.

Alike in his capacity as member of Parliament for the division and as chairman of the North-Eastern Railway Company, Sir Joseph Pease was peculiarly fitted to perform the opening ceremony. Sir Joseph Pease travelled by special train which, leaving York at 10.45, stopped at Darlington at 11.45 for the convenience of other guests invited to participate in the ceremony….On arriving at Stanhope, the special was brought to a stand, and Sir Joseph Pease alighted to greet the Local Committee who were awaiting the arrival of the train. Leaving Stanhope exactly at one o'clock the party proceeded up the

---

[256] *Northern Echo*, October 21, 1895
[257] *Newcastle Courant*, 26 Oct 1895

line, stopping at each station en route to allow Sir Joseph and the other directors to inspect the station buildings. At Westgate, a considerable crowd had assembled on the platform and greeted the arrival of the visitors with loud cheers; and at St John's Chapel several hundred persons had congregated, notwithstanding the heavy rain. On the arrival of the train a hearty cheer of welcome went up, and the strains of the Weardale Brass Band intensified the greeting. Only a brief stop was made her and the train proceeded to the terminus at Wearhead, where another large gathering awaited it and indulged in similar demonstrations of welcome. Stopping just sufficiently long to enable the engine to be detached and coupled on the other end of the train, the party proceeded to St John's Chapel, "and on alighting, were preceded by the Weardale Band to the King's Head Hotel, in front of which there was a great gathering."[258]

Sir Joseph was welcomed by a group of dignitaries, amongst whom was William Vickers senior, late of Howl John and now of Eusemere, Ullswater who attended the lunch at the *King's Head Hotel*.

The following snippet from the *Newcastle Courant* provides an insight into regional politics.

There are many funny stories being told at the expense of Weardale folks in connection with the opening of the new railway. Among them is the following: An old lady (from Weardale) who had never been in a railway carriage before, took a ticket to Darlington to see some friends. Her fellow-passengers noticed she looked uneasy on getting into the train. But they were shocked on the train entering Shildon tunnel to hear her exclaim, "Lord hae marcy o' ma; aw've nivver been in a train afore, but aw've gone stone blind.[259]

The country folk of Upper Weardale would no doubt be the butt of jokes for the "sophisticated" town dwellers not only from Darlington and Bishop Auckland, but also from Stanhope. There would also be local jealousies: many villages throughout the region would have lobbied for a railway connection without success.

### *Postscript 1: Death of a Stationmaster*

On Wednesday February 5th 1896, William Charlton, the long-serving stationmaster at Stanhope died. The *Northern Echo* reported that he contracted a chill on the opening day of the new Weardale Extension Railway from which he never recovered. He was described as "of a frank and cheerful disposition...., courteous to all in the discharge of the onerous duties devolving on him as stationmaster."[260]

### *Postscript 2: Richard Mews unamused*

Understandably, the owner of the Stanhope Coach was not pleased with the arrival of the railway in the upper dale, as illustrated by the following story. Just after the opening of the Weardale extension Railway, on what was probably their first journey by rail, a gentleman and three ladies from St John's Chapel travelled down to Stanhope with the

---

[258] *Northern Echo*, October 22, 1895
[259] *Newcastle Courant*, 26 Oct 1895
[260] *Northern Echo*, February 6, 1896

# EIGHTEEN NINETY-SIX

intention of making the return journey on the last train up the dale. Unfamiliar with this new form of transport, they missed the connection which left from the opposite platform, and were breezily told by a porter that the next train would be on the following morning. Undaunted, they sought out the coach proprietor Richard Mews to arrange transport back to St John's Chapel. Mr Mews asked them how they had travelled to Stanhope, and they replied, "By train, but we missed the last train back." "Well then," said Mr Mews, turning on his heel, "you travelled here by train, so you had better go back by train". Despite the inclement weather, they walked the eight miles home, "wetter, sadder but wiser".[261]

### Postscript 3: Sale of Horses, Cobs, and Vehicles

Just over a month after the opening of the railway, Auctioneer John Myers Dalkin placed the following notice in the *Northern Echo*:-

The Wear Valley Extension Railway now being complete, necessitates the Proprietor of the well-known Weardale Coach to have the above brought under the hammer. The Auctioneer can recommend the Horses as very useful, and in the best of hard fed condition and ready for immediate work, being at their respective jobs up till day of sale. The young horses (being bred by the owner, whose long experience, together with the sound judgment possessed by him as a breeder, cannot be denied) are a fine lot, several of which have taken prizes during the show seasons.

8-7 John Myers Dalkin
(Courtesy of Brian Dalkin)

### <u>Pack Horse Inn</u>, Stanhope

**MR JOHN M DALKIN, favoured** with instructions from Mr Richard Mews, will SELL BY AUCTION within the above yard on Saturday, Nov. 30th, 1895, the following HORSES, COBS, VEHICLES, HARNESS, &c., viz:-

HORSES – *Tommy*, black horse, 8 yrs old, 16 h.h.; *Billy*, chestnut horse, 7 yrs old, 15.3 h.h.; *Bella*, grey mare, 8 yrs old, 16 h.h.; *Charlie*, brown horse, 8 yrs old, 16 h.h.; *Dick*, grey horse, 7 yrs old, 16.1 h.h.; *Jess*, chestnut horse, 7 yrs old, 16.3 h.h.; *Hack*, bay horse, 5 yrs old, 16.1 h.h.; *Daisy*, grey mare pony, 6 yrs old, 12½ h.h.; *Snow Flake*, piebald cob, 3 yrs old, 12 h.h. Bred by Owner:- *Buck*, dun gelding, by *Sir William*, 4 yrs old, 15½ h.h.; Chestnut Brood Mare Cob, 14 h.h., stinted, by

---

[261] From *Weardale memories and traditions*. John Lee, 1950.

*Reedham Shales*; Chestnut Cob Colt, 2 yrs old; Chestnut Cob Filly, 1 yr old – both by *Reedham Shales*; Draught Filly Foal, by *Howard*.

VEHICLES– 1 Stage Coach (Rob Roy), 1 Three-horse Bus, 3 Two-horse Buses, 1 Three-horse Brake, to carry 24 passengers; 3 Two-horse Brakes, with removeable tops, to carry 12, 16, 18 passengers respectively; 3 Four-wheel Phaetons, 2 Whitechapel Carts, 2 Gigs, 1 Double-horse bussette, in good condition; 1 Four-wheel Dog Cart, with reversible seat, pole and splinter bar (nearly new); 2 first-class Double-horse Waggonettes, 1 Spring Cart, 2 Snow Sledges.
Sale commencing at 10 o'clock a.m.
Luncheon at 12 Noon.
ORDER OF SALE, - Sundries, Harness, Vehicles, Horses. Terms cash.
Sale Office, Daley Villa, Westgate, Weardale[262]

## Postscript 4: The end of The Coach and Little Jimmy

Less than three months after the opening of the railway to Wearhead, the following item appeared in the local newspaper:-

The Weardale Mail Coach and the postman, Little Jimmy, finally disappeared from the road today (Sat) for the mails are to be transferred to the railway on Monday…the abolition of the time-honoured vehicle and driver will make a void in many ways. The quaint ride and the cheery chat of Jimmy will be much missed. It is to be hoped that some tangible mark of gratitude will be given by the public and the Post-Office authorities to one whose fidelity to duty, sobriety, and attentiveness, braving all weathers for so many years, merit well recognition.[263]

James Wilkinson, commonly known as "Little Jimmy", was regarded with great respect and affection in the dale. In 1887, William Morley Egglestone described a journey up the dale on the mail coach to Bents Show at Cowshill "with the portly son of temperance, 'Little Jimmy', as our guide, philosopher and friend."[264] He was born in Howden-le-Wear in 1854, becoming a coach driver for Richard Mews in the 1870s, driving the mail coach between Cowshill and Stanhope. Unmarried, Little Jimmy lodged at Cowshill and made two coach journeys each day to Stanhope. As a rural postman, he had only a modest wage, but his services were greatly appreciated in the dale, as evidenced by the gesture of Mr Walter Beaumont who in 1883 presented him with a cheque for £3 "as a personal recognition for his courtesy and attention to his duties".[265] In recognition of his long service, he was presented with a coachman's horn, inscribed "Presented to James Wilkinson, Mail Coach Driver, Weardale".[266] Like his boss Richard Mews, Little Jimmy would have found the passing of the mail coach sad and traumatic, and no doubt many would have had felt regret at the loss of so much colour from the dale in the name of progress. After Richard's death, Little Jimmy continued to work for the Mews family at the *Pack Horse Inn* in Stanhope. He died in Stanhope in 1920.

---

[262] *Northern Echo*, November 26th, 1895
[263] *Northern Echo*, January 18, 1896
[264] *Northern Echo*, September 24, 1887
[265] *Northern Echo*, December 29, 1883
[266] The inscribed horn may be at the York Railway Museum.

# EIGHTEEN NINETY-SIX

8-8 Richard Mews's horse-bus *Rob Roy*, pictured above outside *The Queen's Arms*, Richard Bright's Inn at St John's Chapel, travelled from Cowshill to Stanhope until the opening of the Weardale Extension Railway. It was then kept at the *Packhorse Inn*, Stanhope, and used until after the Great War for special occasions, which no doubt required the services of Little Jimmy (Photo courtesy of Weardale Museum).

## *Postscript 5: Death of Richard Mews*

After his dramatic change in fortune, Richard Mews' health deteriorated and he died in 1899 at the *Packhorse Inn* "at the advanced age of 71". He was well respected and there was an exceptional turn-out for his funeral with many prominent public figures present, including Councillor Joseph Vickers of Tow law, Alderman (Dr) Thomas Livingstone, John W Roddam, JP, William Vickers of Pease Myers, Councillor Thomas Pentland, and Richard Bright junior.[267]

Richard Mews was 68 years old at the time his coaching business was eclipsed by the arrival of the extension railway. After an early career as a lead ore carrier in Allendale, he moved to Weardale in the 1850s. In about 1860, he set up a coach business to challenge the NER monopoly, and eventually became the sole coach and cab operator for the dale until the opening of the Wear Valley extension line. He became a local Guardian and was a noted farmer, horse breeder, judge and exhibitor. At the 1870 Stanhope Show, he was in the newspaper headlines when two of his show horses bolted through the Castle Grounds, causing "a frightful accident". Blacksmith William Tweddle and another man were riding the horses and agreed to have a race, at which

---

[267] *Newcastle Courant*, April 29, 1899

point the horses "dashed off at a tremendous rate" and the spectators "looked on in breathless suspense at the race to the death":-

> On the horses sped through the inner gate at the end of the field, when, the horses turning to save themselves from collision with a stone hay-shed, the men both flew off, and Tweddle was dashed violently against the stone pillar of the hay-shed, whilst the other was thrown violently to the ground.

It is unclear what happened to the badly injured riders who were treated by Dr Arnison, but it was feared that the accident would "terminate fatally".[268]

## *The Snow Storms of 1895*

Francis recalls in the letter that "last year came in very rough. There was never known to be as much snow as there was last winter". The winter was notably severe throughout the country with the Thames freezing over and February being the second coldest ever recorded.

The *Northern Echo* reported on January 5th, 1895:-

> A heavy snowstorm has raged over Upper Weardale for the last twenty-four hours, blocking the bye-roads and tracks to the adjacent dales, and suspending the leading of ironstone on the main road, which is yet uncleared by the plough, although the mails were brought up with commendable promptitude by increased horse-power by Mr R Mews. A fierce wind is blowing, and the cold is intense, and the snow plough was busy. Tramps crossing the several moors are reported to have narrowly escaped perishing. Snow is yet falling at intervals, and the sheep and grouse are making for lower grounds.

On January 8th:-

> Another additional heavy fall of snow took place in Weardale on Monday, and the roadmen were kept busy cutting a track for vehicles to the neighbouring dales, the snow plough being taken on to the summit of Killhope and Allenheads fells. Birds are dying in large numbers, and all ore-washing operations are stopped....Domestic goods are being delivered on sledges by local tradesmen.

And on January 10, under the headline WEARDALE ROADS BLOCKED:-

> The snowfall continued throughout Monday night, rendering the roads impassable for the bus to catch the trains on Tuesday morning, and the snowplough had to be run down to Stanhope before the mails could be brought up on a snowsledge. The whole of the by-roads being blocked to great depths by drifts, all the leading of ironstone is stopped, as well as other vehicular traffic off the main track. A keen frost followed the downfall, and huge drifts are in constant evidence….. from twelve to twenty feet in depth in Teesdale.

Nearly three weeks later on January 28, the *Northern Echo* reported:-

---

[268] *Northern Echo*, September 10, 1870

# EIGHTEEN NINETY-SIX

Some three or four engines and a van, in trying to clear the road with a snowplough on Friday became firmly embedded in the snow between Waskerley and Park Head, where they remained all night, and were only dug out late on Saturday. ….Grouse were caught in Stanhope streets during the week, driven off the moors by the storm and lack of food.

A month later, *The Newcastle Courant* reported that Weardale farmers were still in the grip of the "Arctic winter", and warning that "their hay supplies are diminishing daily, and unless there is a decided change in the weather soon, the outlook will be serious indeed."[269]

Francis reveals that they were blocked in at Belle Vue for 11 weeks from early January 1895 until late March, and were fortunate that his son William had plenty of hay for the large stock of sheep at neighbouring Pease Myers, where a shepherd had been employed to look after the farm.

## *Stanhope Transformed*

Since George and Thomas left Stanhope, immense changes had taken place in the town. The coming of the railway in 1862 had opened up the Lower Dale to the world beyond, and now the extension railway promised to have the same effect on the Upper Dale. And Francis was keen to let his cousins know just how much Stanhope had changed, telling Thomas in the letter that the town now has twice as many houses. The change is evident from the maps of 1851 and 1896 respectively (see overleaf).

8-9 Stanhope transformed: This West End view would have looked very different in 1851 (Courtesy of June Crosby).

---

[269] *Newcastle Courant*, February 23, 1895

143

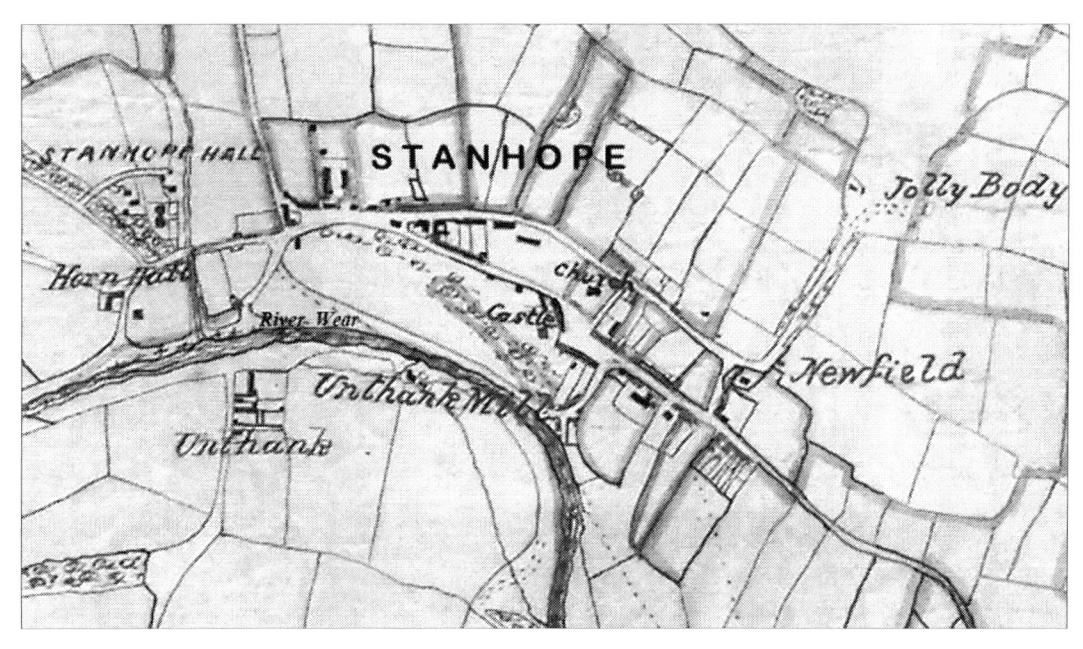

8-10 The 1851 Roddam Map was produced by Surveyor and Land Agent John Joseph Roddam, so well regarded by his fellow dalesmen that a Drinking Fountain was erected in Stanhope in his memory in 1877. (Detail reproduced courtesy of Weardale Museum)

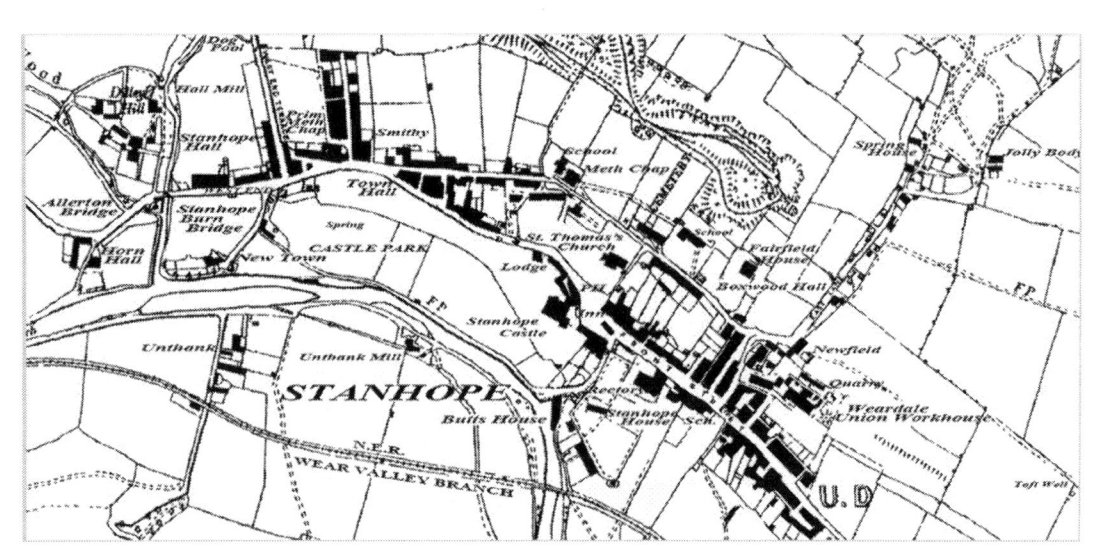

8-11 The adapted 1896 OS map provides an idea of the scale of the development of the town since the 1850s. Included on the map is the Weardale Extension Railway from Stanhope to Wearhead, opened in 1895 (Courtesy of Landmark Information Group).

## 9. NINETEEN HUNDRED

> he is remarkably well now, calm, contented, & peaceful, trusting in the merits of Our Saviour Jesus Christ in whom he has confided so long. & he believes he will gain by the Grace of God an abundant entrance into Heaven.

9-1 Joseph Vickers of Tow Law writing to George Vickers about his father, Francis Vickers of Belle Vue

Two days after Christmas, 1900, Joseph Vickers of Tow Law writes to George Vickers at the request of his father Francis whose rheumatism prevents him from writing himself. Just turned 79 years of age, Francis is anxious to maintain contact with his one surviving Canadian cousin.

Nineteen Hundred was notable for snowstorms early in the year and for the opening of two new Institutes in the dale.

### *"Terrible Night on Bollihope Fell"*

In February, 1900, the whole of the country experienced extreme wintry weather. In Weardale, there were heavy snowstorms on 9-10th February causing roads to be blocked and numerous sheep to be overblown. After a brief respite, there was a terrible snowstorm and blizzards in the dale on Thursday, February 15th, completely undoing all the work on opening the roads in the preceding days. With the storm raging, Emerson Currah, a 38 year-old shepherd from Woodcroft, set out late on Thursday morning for Scott Hill on Bollihope Fell with some hay for his sheep. The north-east gale increased until it became a blizzard, and the afternoon and night storms were among the worst ever remembered on the Weardale moors. Emerson had his two collies with him, and in the late evening, when one of them came home without its master, the alarm was raised. A search party of 22 men from Hill End and the neighbouring farm houses was organised and after scouring the moors for several hours, at 3 a.m. on Friday morning they came across his body buried in the snow in the Ridding House allotment, only half a mile from home. It was reported that "the attention of the searchers was directed to the place by the second dog, which had faithfully kept watch by his master's side during the lonely hours of a terrible night." The youngest of five brothers and unmarried, Emerson Currah was widely known and respected in the dale. The inquest concluded that he had wandered about until he had become exhausted, and had died from exposure.[270]

A quarter of a century earlier, Emerson Currah's sister Annie Crawhall died at the age of 25 years (see page 87).

## *Opening of Institutes in Ireshopeburn and Westgate*

Joseph Vickers of Tow Law wrote the letter in 1900 on behalf of his father to George Vickers towards the end of a month which began for him at Ireshopeburn.

On the first day of December, in his capacity as a County Councillor, Joseph chaired the proceedings at the formal opening of the new Ireshopeburn Institute. He was supported by the formidable Mrs John Marshall from Darlington who officially opened the Institute, George Race, a builder and county councillor from Westgate, Dr John Easton from St John's Chapel, John T Carr, postmaster at Cowshill, and Thomas Pentland, a tailor from Ireshopeburn who acted as secretary/treasurer to the Institute Fund. Conceived as a lasting way to commemorate the Jubilee Year, the Institute with its motto *"Knowledge is Power"* provided a meeting place for people to socialise and to gain knowledge from the library, a place where "the wisdom of old age, the experience and maturity of middle-age, and the energy and expectation of youth" would find expression. Addressing a large crowd of local residents and visiting dignitaries despite it being "a typical backend day", Joseph excused Sir Joseph Pease MP for his absence, pointing out that he had many claims upon his time and that they should "not expect impossibilities."[271] He praised the establishment of the Institute, believing that such places would help stem the migration of young people to the towns, and be "a counter-attraction against worse places". Not averse to name-dropping, he recalled a conversation with General William Booth of the Salvation Army which had touched on the land question, the migration to the towns and the consequent "wrecked humanity".[272] General Booth had addressed a large congregation at the Primitive Methodist Chapel in Tow Law on Tuesday, September 13, 1892, and it is likely that Joseph Vickers had the opportunity to speak to him on that occasion.

Mrs Marshall delivered a rousing speech. Mildred Dorothea Marshall, born in Belgium in 1859, was a more than capable substitute for Sir Joseph Pease. She was described in one tribute as having a "vigorous and well-trained intellect, and a rare impartiality of judgement". She was "an excellent and indefatigable" secretary to the Darlington Women's Liberal Association and had a reputation as a clear and "forcible" public speaker, "her success in this role being due to observance of one of the first rules of oratory – a thorough mastery of the subject in hand".[273]

---

[270] *Northern Echo,* February 24, 1900
[271] Mrs Marshall was third choice to open the Institute. Mr A. de Bock Porter, Secretary to the Ecclesiastical Commissioners, was excused the honour of opening the Institute as he was "sojourning in Lowestoft for a holiday".
[272] *Northern Echo,* December 3, 1900
[273] *Northern Echo,* April 20, 1900

# NINETEEN HUNDRED

Mrs Marshall had demonstrated this mastery the previous year when she gave a speech to the Darlington Women's Association in the Union Street Congregational Schoolroom at Darlington on "The Last Decade of the Nineteenth Century". Arguing that by looking back they were able to comprehend the present and construct the future, she described the 1890s as a new era in which daily life was characterised by "cleverness, energy, sharpness of wit, haste, turmoil, and hurry." She reminded her audience that Liberals believed in "liberty and progress for all, equal justice, opportunity to develop all that was best in men and women, and power to remove the many obstacles which prevented the realisation of such opportunity". Liberals also believed that "men and women should be invested with a fit sense of their responsibilities as citizens."

At the outset Mrs Marshall dealt with an issue close to the hearts of Liberals – the Irish Question (See page 95). She outlined the efforts of William Gladstone in the 1880 Liberal Government to address the issues arising from widespread hardship and injustice in rural Ireland and how he was frustrated by the actions of the House of Lords, adding, "It is recognised now that if Home Rule had been granted to Ireland at that time many a calamity and many a crime might have been prevented." How true: over 100 years later and after countless further political calamities and crimes, the on-going Peace Process offers a democratic way towards resolution of this enduring problem.

Mrs Marshall also touched on women's rights, describing a "gallant attempt" by the Earl of Meath to pass a bill allowing women to sit in the House of Lords, a bill which was defeated by "a vast majority, 108 ungracious peers voting against 23 gracious peers".[274]

The previous year had seen the opening of Westgate Institute by Sir Joseph Pease with Councillor George Race of Westgate presiding. In his speech, Councillor Race expressed his pride in the "splendid library" with its works on metaphysicis, science, and books of reference, including *Encyclopaedia Britannica.* Sir Joseph Pease termed the institute the "market-place of the minds of Westgate", and declared that the men who succeeded in life were those who cared for the mind. He illustrated the perils of ignorance with a story about a cattle dealer who had thought America and Belgium were geographically close to each other. When the facts were explained to him, he declared, "I thought all those foreign parts lied together"(Loud laughter).[275]

In October 1900, at the time of the General Election, Sir Joseph Pease toured Upper Weardale, repeatedly reminding his constituents that the policy of the Liberal Party was to distribute power over the largest number, to take power away from the few and put it in the hands of the many, "into the hands of the tradesman, farmer, and miner, who were as entitled to it as the landowner or the capitalist" (Cheers). They were for the masses, whereas the Tories were for the classes.[276]

## *An Enterprising Auctioneer*

Even by his 3rd Christmas Prize Show at Tow Law Mart in 1887 the contribution of Joseph Vickers to the regeneration of Tow Law was widely recognized (See page 86). By the 16th Christmas Prize Show in 1900, it had become one of the events of the year, with the *Northern Echo* acknowledging the amazing growth of the Tow Law Mart under Joseph Vickers's guidance.[277]

---

[274] *Northern Echo, January 10, 1899*
[275] *Northern Echo, February 6, 1899*
[276] *Northern Echo,* October 8, 1900

9-2  Joseph Vickers of Tow Law in 1893 after the move to Elm Park

At the well-attended luncheon, John R Hodgson, a butcher from Crook, proposed a toast to the success of the Tow Law Auction Mart, which he described as "second to none in the country", along with good wishes to Joseph Vickers who had put his life's work into the success of the mart. He added that in his 18 years of business with the Mart, he had yet to experience an unfair action. *The Northern Echo* reported that the popular auctioneer, who believed that he didn't have a single enemy as far as he knew, was "heartily received" when he made some very practical remarks in response to the toast:-

> Auction marts have come to stay. It is the duty of every man who attends an auction mart to be honest. There is one thing lacking in auction marts which I have found after twenty years' experience, and that is confidence. If there is confidence between an auctioneer and his customers, that is the best way of getting a fair price all round (Applause). [278]

---

[277] *Northern Echo,* December 17, 1900
[278] *Northern Echo,* December 18, 1900

# NINETEEN HUNDRED

Such was his success as a farmer, stock breeder, auctioneer and public servant, Joseph Vickers was widely respected and was a man whose professional opinion carried weight. The thriving Tow Law Mart was advertised prolifically by its founder in *The Northern Echo*, and it is not surprising that he and his business would be the subject of a feature in the newspaper at some stage. Under the heading, "An Enterprising Auctioneer", *The Northern Echo*, using the interview technique pioneered by WT Stead in the 1870s, published a profile in 1897 which provides a useful insight into the character and Victorian business acumen of Francis's son, Joseph Vickers:-

> Tow Law – what a name to conjure with, and how suggestive, as if it hadn't been for the 'tow' of a couple of North-Eastern locomotives, I, with hundreds more, would never have reached the 'law', or summit giving nomenclature to the place, so excellently adapted for the astronomical research of Canon Espin, our senior clerical scientist (See page 122). Where the now famous mart of Mr Joseph Vickers has risen phoenix-like from the ashes – for there are abundant slag heaps and ruins – of the whilom[279] busy scene of the Weardale Iron Company's blast furnaces, and inflated anew the commercial importance of Tow Law, which forms the apex to the Crook, Dearness, Lanchester, and Wear valleys (of which a capital view was obtainable at intervals yesterday when the smoke lifted), also forming a plateau terminus to the ridge Consettwards. Caught in the human vortex, on alighting, of bluff, blooming, bland and burly farmers and butchers one is whirled towards the well-known County Councillor's stock venue at the base of "Dans Castle" (whether the old prophet Daniel's keep once or no isn't known), in handy juxtaposition to the main line, where in active preparation for wielding the hammer and disposing of the mass of animals comfortably quartered in the surrounding sheds and cleanly-kept pens I espied Mr Vickers, who as yet seems on the sunny side of the meridian of life, and was soon in candid tete-a-tete with the scion of one of the best known Weardale farming families in the North.
>
> "How long has your mart been established in this, to the casual observer, out-of-the-way situation? was my first query.
>
> "Fifteen years," replied Mr Vickers with a smile begotten of success, "and relying on modest beginnings, attention to business, and integrity, I made the venture which many scouted at the outset. I foresaw the possible growth, now verified, of the coal and coke districts practically without an auction ring, easy of access by road and rail, and, as you'll see, have no cause to regret. But as you'll have noticed our business now extends over a large area both south and northwards. My acknowledgements are for the help I've received in the founding and ultimate development of the mart to Mr Taylor-Smith, Colepike Hall, from whom the ground is leased, and the many farmers and others, as well as the North-Eastern Railway authorities, who run a special on Mondays and to our special sales. The latter I have to subsidise. Only one gentleman came to meet me when I came to Tow Law, where we tried a sale monthly, then fortnightly, and ultimately, as you see today, weekly, with specials in season. I am glad to number among my patrons Lord Durham, Lord

---

[279] "whilom" is an Old English word for "formerly"

Londonderry, Viscount Boyne, Pease and Partners, the Weardale Iron Company, and the majority of known farmers in the North."

"I take it, from current observation, that your fount of food is fed from the large farming localities of Weardale, Teesdale, Allendale, Derwent, and Alston, who regard Tow Law Mart as a sort of price-fixing beacon and realising haven for their stock".

"Well in the main, yes, as the rich herbage and nature's verdure on the pastures in these dales, together with the excellent breeds, make the animals splendidly adapted for the cereal producing districts of a lower altitude, where they prove good thrivers, hence the demand, and I daresay the prices here are a fairly good market guide, as we have a good many migratory dealers as a rule who know the current rates all round."

"Would it be a breach of confidence were you to tell me approximately the number of head you sell at your specials I hear so oft spoken about elsewhere."
"At one of our recent Thursday sales we put 791 cattle through, and 5000 sheep at another, but of course that is a very unusually large consignment."

"Speaking of sheep I see you are a very successful exhibitor of black-faced ones."

"Yes, I take a deep interest in promoting that breed, they being so well adapted to the dales, and while I spend a good deal in giving large prices for good breeds in Scotland I give our customers the option of purchasing at the mart without reserve their descendants, and I'm glad to be able to do so. But my time is up for beginning the sale, and if you care to follow you can judge for yourself of the veracity of these remarks."

Subsequently I found everything arranged for man and beast, and had little difficulty in garnering full endorsement of the genuineness of the mart from buyers present, and left the busy scene a little surprised as well as pleased with the usefulness of Mr Vickers's concern and the candour of the councillor who invests Tow Law with an abnormal interest.[280]

A report in September 1900 of the Annual Pony Show and Sale at Tow Law Mart illustrates Joseph's reputation:-

> From frequent observations at the large gatherings, everything tends to establish the virtue of honesty which we all know is a small quantity in horse dealings at the usual trysts and fairs.[281]

These fulsome tributes gives an indication of the standing of Joseph Vickers in South-West Durham and beyond. Not surprisingly, he was a prominent freemason, connected with several lodges and Junior Warden of the Tow Law Lodge. As an elected Junior Warden, he was third in line in the lodge hierarchy and helped to ensure that the lodge ran smoothly. He was responsible for arranging refreshments for the Brethren at their meetings, and ensuring that there was no intemperance or excess.

Freemasonry suited the outgoing businessman perfectly, as explained by Roger Burt:-

---

[280] *Northern Echo*, October 26, 1897
[281] *Auckland Chronicle*, September 13, 1900

Fully initiated Master Masons attended frequently (usually monthly) meetings of their own lodge and had rights to visit and move between any other lodge at home and abroad. Their ritual embraced the egalitarian philosophy of the Enlightenment, and they were sworn to strict codes of moral conduct and were under an obligation to help other Masons, where there was no conflict with their own interests. In all aspects, Freemasonry was highly 'business friendly'. Membership was by invitation, but highly 'permeable', and offered both 'bonding' opportunities with others in the same profession, business, or locality, and 'bridging' to groups with which they may previously have had little contact. The formalised dining and socialising activities that followed every lodge meeting presented exceptional opportunities for networking between individuals and firms. Members could exchange information, seek credit, arrange capital movements, organise contracts, find employment, exercise influence, and ensure benevolent support against the unexpected... The opportunities for all forms of networking – consciously or unconsciously – clearly remained ever present.[282]

A picture emerges of an astute and highly respected businessman noted for his practicality, straight dealing, and integrity, an excellent networker, a man without a single enemy, and a man who takes great pride in his success.

## *Sensational Property Sale at Wearhead*

Joseph's brother-in-law John Walton Watson was the auctioneer at a crowded property sale at the *Queen's Head*, Wearhead in September 1900. Up for sale were a shop and two houses at Wearhead, eventually sold for £260. The "sensation" was caused by the unusual bidder, Patrick Burke, an Irish-born hawker and sometime wrestler from Wolsingham, whose reputation and appearance did not inspire confidence:-

The property sale at Wearhead was quite sensational in its way to the large company present, as none imagined that the dust-begrimed son of Erin, who preferred to "stand and not soil the chairs", was a genuine bidder and eventual purchaser, and it was only on the assurance of Mr JW Watson, the auctioneer, that the solicitor and the company truly "burked" in their speculations that the sturdy and thrifty "Pat", as Mr Burke is familiarly called, was booked as owner of the remarkably cheap bit of property.[283]

Five years previously, it had been reported in the local paper that Patrick Burke had sold a horse, warranted sound, to John Ferguson, a hawker from West Cornforth. Ferguson claimed at Auckland County Court that the horse kicked its stall to pieces and would have demolished the cart had it not been unyoked. The court found for Ferguson.[284]

The auctioneer appeared to be taking a risk, but if the sturdy Irish wrestler had not had the funds for the purchase, he would have had to answer to the even sturdier Mr Watson (See page 109).

---

[282] Roger Burt (2003) Freemasonry and business networking during the Victorian period. *Economic History Review,* LVI, 4, 657-688
[283] *Auckland Chronicle,* September 6, 1900
[284] *Northern Echo*, April 10, 1895

## The Letter to George Vickers

*JOSEPH VICKERS*        *Elm Park, Tow Law, Co Durham*
*AUCTIONEER & VALUER*
*Dec 27th 1900*

Mr George Vickers,

Dear Sir,

    My Father (your Cousin Frank Vickers of Belle Vue Stanhope) requests me to write you on his behalf, and he also sends you a photo of himself and mother taken recently. His hand is too shaky to write now. He is in his 80th year & mother is 8 years younger. They have given up farming and built a new house at the West End of Stanhope and came to live in it nearly a year ago. The photos are rather too small, having been taken outside in front of their house, a portion of which can be seen on the picture, but it is very like what they both are now, and father was very anxious for you to have a copy, and he has also sent a copy to your niece, Mrs McLean, Bournemouth. Father often talks about you and your Brother who also went to America and who is now dead we are informed. Three or four years ago Father got a heat behind his shoulder which gathered and from which there was a considerable discharge, and it has never fairly healed..., and has weakened his system considerably. But he has improved very much lately. I spent Christmas Day with him and he is remarkably well, now calm, contented and peaceful, trusting in the merits of Our Saviour Jesus Christ in whom he has confided so long, and he believes he will gain by the Grace of God an abundant entrance into Heaven when his journey here is finished. My sincere prayer is that you and all our friends may meet there.

    You are probably aware that your Brother Frank is still living on a farm called "Dean Head", Heighington, near Darlington. He is as fresh as a daisy and working every day on the farm. Father thinks he is 93 or 94 years of age. Nearly as old as the Century which is now closing. My grandfather Joseph Vickers, your uncle, was 95 when he died and retained every faculty till the last, and simply fell asleep, worn out.

    Father will be glad to have a line from you when convenient. Wishing you all a happy and prosperous New Year, and with united Kind regards and remembrances.

*I am Yours Sincerely,*
*Joseph Vickers*

Father's present address is: F Vickers, Belle Vue House, Stanhope, Co Durham

Just a week before Joseph wrote the letter, there had been a savage gale and heavy rain, followed by a fierce snowstorm which caused much damage to property in the dale:-

> Shortly after midnight the south-east roof of Midlothian House at Ireshopeburn was blown off, and much damage done to the interior from the torrents of rain, till daylight permitted temporary timbering till the gale subsided. In the rear of Mr

# NINETEEN HUNDRED

Pentland's premises also, the wet caused a subsidence, carrying away a portion of the coachhouse and stable.[285]

Yet by Christmas Day, the weather was unusually mild with temperatures as high as 50F, and "instead of frost and snow, buttercups and daisies dotted the pastures, while in the gardens roses, carnations, wallflowers and primroses were in bloom". The Weardale celebrations were reported by the *Newcastle Courant*:-

> Christmas was observed with customary zeal and goodwill throughout the dale. Upon the stroke of twelve the carollers commenced the rounds and the quiet valleys again echoed to song until daybreak. In the churches the occasion was marked by special services and the festivities everywhere were kept up with spirit until a late hour.[286]

Despite his busy lifestyle, Joseph was evidently a devoted son concerned for the welfare of his aging parents and spending time with them whenever he could. He reveals in the letter that he was with his parents on Christmas Day, and he writes in some detail about the health of his father. And knowing how much his father valued correspondence from Canada, he politely asks George to write a line "when convenient."

The 'Dear Sir' formality of Joseph's letter is understandable not only because of the prevailing formality in letter writing but also because George and Thomas Vickers, Joseph's first cousins once removed, had emigrated to Canada before Joseph was born.

Joseph enclosed a photograph of his parents, Francis and Mary Vickers, likely to be the one reproduced on page 157. It was taken outside the front door of Belle Vue Farm in Stanhope, and possibly commissioned for their Golden Wedding Anniversary on December 14, 1900, although by that time they had moved to Belle Vue House in Stanhope West End.

And Joseph lets George know that his niece, Mrs McLean, also received a copy of the photograph. In 1901 the McLeans were on an extended visit to England and staying at a boarding house in Bournemouth. Thomas A McLean, the son of a Scottish draper, was born in Bury, Lancashire in 1841 and migrated to Canada in the 1860s where he married George's niece Mary, the daughter of Thomas Vickers of Ontario.

It was not the first marriage between one of Thomas's daughters and a member of the McLean family –Thomas A Mclean was possibly a cousin of Canadian-born Lem Mclean of North Dakota who married Mary's sister, Alice Maria in 1890 (see page 117).

Joseph informs George that his brother Frank is still farming at Dean Head and is "as fresh as a daisy". He is not quite as old as Francis thinks he is, being only 91 years old, but he is still working on the farm every day, and he continued doing so right up to his unfortunate death in August 1901 (See page 161).

The Victorians, not least Primitive Methodists, were God-fearing, full of faith, and familiar with the Bible. Joseph tells George that his father believes he will gain by the Grace of God an abundant entrance into Heaven when his journey here is finished. This is from The Second Epistle of St Peter the Apostle, Chapter One, Verse 11: that by your good works, "…an entrance shall be administered to you abundantly into the everlasting kingdom of our Lord and Saviour Jesus Christ."

---

[285] *Northern Echo*, December 22, 1900
[286] *Newcastle Courant*, December 29, 1900

9-3 Stanhope West End with JJ Roddam Fountain in the foreground (June Crosby's Collection).

9-4 Blacksmith Robert Sisson had a forge at West End. The poster advertises an auction of property at Crawleyside on May 16, 1903. The auctioneer is Joseph Vickers of Tow Law (June Crosby's Collection).

9-5 Francis and Mary Vickers, at Belle Vue Farm on their Golden Wedding Anniversary.

## The Workhouse Diet

The meeting of the Weardale Guardians at Christmas 1900 demonstrated the customary seasonal goodwill towards the inmates alongside the constant drive to minimise costs  With John W Roddam presiding, the Master reported that inmates had received gifts from, amongst others, JW Roddam himself, the Bishop of Richmond and his wife, George Curry, and William Thomas Stead of London, formerly editor of the *Northern Echo* and by 1900 a world-famous journalist and peace campaigner.  Dr Thomas Livingstone and his wife had provided a knife and fork tea, and John W Roddam indicated that he would be providing the inmates with a dinner to commemorate the new century.

A decade earlier, the Guardians had sought to save costs by substituting bread and cheese for the more expensive soup diet.  Now Thomas Moses of Tow Law proposed that money could be saved by placing food on the tables for the inmates to help themselves rather than weighing out the food on a *per capita* basis.  Not only would this save money because of the poor appetites of some inmates but it would also make the Workhouse appear less like a gaol.[287]

## Dr Thomas Livingstone

Dr/Alderman and Mrs Livingstone's generosity to the inmates of the Workhouse may have been in thanksgiving for his recovery from a "complicated attack of influenza" in the Spring of 1900. In August, William Morley Egglestone reported that "the intellectual giant of parochial life" was rapidly recovering from his illness, and that the "intellectually contoured medical practitioner conveys the impression of the highest attributes in every sphere".[288]  Alas, Dr Livingstone died the following July, the funeral at Stanhope being conducted by the Bishop of Richmond, Dr JJ Pulleine.  Amongst the mourners was Councillor Joseph Vickers of Tow Law.

---

[287] *Northern Echo*, December 29, 1900
[288] *Auckland Chronicle*, August 23, 1900

## 10. NINETEEN HUNDRED AND ONE

> Your Brother Frank hapend a very bad accident on the tenth, of last month (august 10)th - he was on with his hay on the Hay Rake and was overtaken by a Thunder storm, it is supposed the Horse took fright and he got under the rake but no one saw it done. he only lived till the 12th.

10-1 Frank Vickers of Dean Head Farm was 91 when he died. He left a 45-year-old wife and three children, the youngest aged 11 years.

This momentous year marked the transition from the Victorian to the Edwardian era. On January 22nd, Queen Victoria, a close contemporary of Francis Vickers, died at Osborne House on the Isle of Wight aged 81years. She had served as monarch for almost 64 years, longer than anyone else in our history. Victoria was succeeded by her eldest son, Prince Albert Edward, Prince of Wales who became King Edward VII

The 1901 Census was taken on March 31st. Francis and Mary were now living in Stanhope at Belle Vue House in West End Terrace to which they had moved in early 1900. Looking after them in their retirement was grand-daughter Elizabeth Eleanor Vickers, the daughter of William Vickers junior. Further care was available next door from widowed daughter-in-law Elizabeth Vickers, a draper and grocer who still had her three children at home.

Francis's son William Vickers junior was still farming at Eastgate with his second wife Annie Clayton, and five children from his marriage to Sarah Petty. His father and mother having moved to the village, William assumed responsibility for Belle Vue Farm, which he sub-let to 28 year-old hind Joseph Stephenson, a farmer's son from Eastgate. At this time, William's eldest son Lawrence William was living at the family farm in Eastgate, greatly enjoying his work as an apprentice Engine Fitter, but he was coming under concerted pressure from his father and grandfather to take over at Belle Vue Farm. He reluctantly agreed to do so, and seems to have had misgivings about it for the rest of his life.

# LIFE AND TIMES IN VICTORIAN WEARDALE

The now prosperous Joseph Vickers of Tow Law Mart was living at 'palatial' Elm Park near Thornley Village, Wolsingham.

By 1901, Francis's 69 year-old brother John was farming at Churchfield, near Carnforth in Lancashire. His sister Mary was still his housekeeper, and his unmarried son Matthew was running the farm. Brother William senior was still running the Guesthouse at Eusemere Hill, Ullswater, with his wife Margaret and three of his children.

## *The Letter to Thomas Vickers*

*Belle Vue House     Sept 11th 1901*
*Stanhope*

*I am just going to try and write you a few lines but I have not very good news to tell you. Your brother Frank happened a very bad accident on the 10th of last month (August 10th). He was on with his hay, on the Hay Rake and was overtaken by a Thunder Storm. It is supposed the horse took fright and he got under the rake but no one saw it done. He only lived till the 12th. I think he could not tell how it happened. He has never had any servant man, done all the ploughing and carting himself except his three daughters to help him, the oldest about 20. It seems hard that he should have had to work till he was 93 or 94 and have to come to such an end at last.*

*We have had a very dry and droughty summer, very light crops all over, corn good but straw short and nearly all in and well won. We have had some very heavy Thunder Storms this summer and some damage done in places. There was one on the 10th of last month in Northumberland, Durham and Yorkshire. A great deal of damage done at Wolsingham and neighbour John Dowson at Newlands had nearly all of the panes broke out of the windows. Likewise Henry Pickern[289] of East Newlands the same. Both much damage done to both corn and turnips. One field, both soil and turnips washed away. At Wolsingham, scores of houses scarce had a whole pane left in. It was said the hail came down like great squares of ice. We had nothing like that at Stanhope, only a very heavy rain and some hailstones.*

*We are having a new Town Hall built at Stanhope where old John Benson's House stood. There is no public works about Stanhope except the limestone and whin quarries. Stanhope is three or four times larger than when you left. That place is all filled up between dark lane and the Bridge. Our house is the second from lane end.*

*Now I will have to close as I can scarce sit for rheumatism pains in my left hip and down the leg. Was it not for that, I am best now than I have been for three years. I have to walk with 2 sticks. For rheumatism I cannot steady my hand to write, but you can perhaps make it out. Now be sure to write soon as I am always pleased to hear from either you or Thomas's family. Give my kind regards to all friends and accept the same for yourself from your loving cousin.*

*    Francis Vickers*

---

[289] *Henry Pickering*

# NINETEEN HUNDRED AND ONE

## *The Deadly Thunderstorm*

Francis, who wrote this letter 100 years to the day before the world-changing destruction of the Twin Towers in New York, normally reported deaths of family members mid-way through his letters but on this occasion he tells Thomas about the death of his brother Frank at the outset. Early on Saturday August 10th, 1901, 91 year-old farmer Frank Vickers was hay-making at Dean Head Farm, Coatham Mundeville, near Darlington. It must have seemed like a good day for work on the farm, as there was a clear blue sky in the morning and the weather was very hot and sultry, the air soft. But by early afternoon, clouds had begun to gather on the horizon and not long after two o'clock, "the sky was covered by dark, yellowish, threatening clouds which betokened a storm". But Frank, perhaps anxious to gather the hay before the storm broke, made the fateful decision to continue haymaking. And then suddenly, "the rain came down in torrents and the lightning, both sheet and forked, was continuous, the peals of thunder being very loud".[290] In the Darlington district, the storm only lasted a quarter of an hour, but that was long enough for Frank to suffer critical injuries. Given the violence of the storm and the very loud peals of thunder, the horse would become unmanageable, and so Francis's assumption that the horse took fright with the result that his cousin was thrown under the hay rake, is reasonable. He died two days later from his injuries, his death certificate recording, "Accidentally killed whilst working a Horse Rake in Hayfield."

Frank Vickers (1809-1901) had a long and eventful life. Born at Greenhead, Stanhope, the eldest son of John Vickers and Jane Morgan, he moved with his father to farm at New Shildon in the 1830s. Frank married Mary Scott in Shildon in 1838 where his sons John and William were born. In 1842, Frank and family moved with his father to Dean Head Farm, where he had a further seven children. Frank took over the farm when his father died in 1855 and farmed Dean Head, with a brief interlude at nearby Humbleton, for the rest of his life.

Frank was a man of prodigious vitality. At the age of 71 and a widower for 12 years, when almost everyone who had been fortunate enough to have lived that long would be retired and in marked physical decline, Frank married 24 year-old Jane Davison at Darlington Register Office. Less than three months later, their first daughter, Frances, was born. Predictably, with all his children from his first marriage not only older than his new wife, but also in effect disinherited, there was "much quarreling" in the family. Under normal circumstances, Frank would have looked for care in his old age to his children and grandchildren from his first marriage, and he would have retired and left the farming to one of his sons. But now he had a young wife to fulfil the caring role, he had the motivation and physical stamina to continue farming until his unfortunate accident. He and Jane had two more daughters, the youngest being born in 1890 when Frank was 80 years old. At the time of the 1901 Census, Frank was still farming at Dean Head at the age of 91, and as Francis points out, "doing all the ploughing and carting himself except his three daughters to help him". He died just before his 92nd birthday.

---

[290] *Northern Echo*, 12 August 1901

## The Storm in Weardale

The storm on August 10th 1901 that led to Frank Vickers' death at Dean Head was experienced in varying degrees of intensity right across the North of England and South Scotland. In Weardale, the violent storm swept in from the south, and it seems that Frosterley and Wolsingham had the worst of the hailstones, variously described in the local press as "not much less than half an inch across", "more like pieces of loaf sugar than anything else", and "the size of large marbles". Three miles up-river at Stanhope, Francis tells us that the storm was less violent, "only a very heavy rain and some hailstones".

The *Northern Echo* reported that when the storm was at its height, "it seemed as though the whole atmosphere was on fire and the elements in the throes of dissolution. Chain, forked and sheet lightning flashed uninterruptedly and with startling vividness, and thunder pealed with deafening crashes in rapid succession. Tons of water were precipitated…" It was reported that:-

> The hailstones…smashed the windows of many houses in Wolsingham and around the locality. At East and West Newlands Farms, near Frosterley, almost every pane of glass was broken. Wolsingham Rectory and the West End of the town suffered hundreds of panes of glass being broken. The fruit crop in the track of the storm was also destroyed. The morning was close, sultry, and hot, the air soft. It began to thunder soon after 10 a.m., and between 1 and 2 p.m., the storm raged fiercely. The oldest inhabitants in Wolsingham have never seen its equal.[291]

Francis confirms the reports of the damage at Wolsingham and identifies the occupants of East and West Newlands Farms where nearly all the windows were broken: John Dowson at West Newlands who was 48 years old and farming with his wife Isabella, five young children, and five servants; and 73 year-old Henry Pickering who was farming at Newlands Hall (East Newlands) with his wife Emma and five adult children.

Some of Francis's information will have come from press reports but more than a month after the storm he would also have heard local word-of-mouth reports about the damage to property and crops down the dale.

## New Town Hall at Stanhope

Francis reports that a new town hall is being built on the site of Old John Benson's house. John Benson would have been known to both George and Thomas. He was born in Jarrow in 1798, and was Relieving Officer for the Weardale Union and Registrar for Births Deaths and Marriages for the Stanhope district when he married Jane Johnson of Mill Shields at Bywell St Peter's in 1846. Still working in 1871, he died six years later aged 79 years and was buried in Stanhope.

Thomas Crawhall[292], the Executor of John Benson's Will in 1877, gave instruction to Joseph Walton[293] to auction John Benson's property which was described as a "Valuable

---

[291] Northern Echo, August 12 1901
[292] Thomas Crawhall was soon to be the father-in-law of Isabella Vickers, the daughter of Francis of Belle Vue.
[293] Joseph Walton married Elizabeth Vickers, the sister of Francis of Belle Vue.

Freehold Dwelling-house" with Outbuildings and an extensive garden. It was stated in the newspaper announcement of the public auction at the Phoenix Inn, Stanhope, that the property was "suitable for building sites, in the front street, and in the centre of Stanhope".[294] Given these characteristics, it is not surprising that almost a quarter of a century later, the site was seen as an ideal location for a new Town Hall.

> **TENDER**
>
> CONTRACTORS wishing to TENDER for the various Works required in the ERECTION of NEW TOWN HALL, STANHOPE, can see the Plans and Specifications at the Board Room, Stanhope, from Monday, the 15th inst., to Wednesday, the 24th inst. Sealed Tenders, marked "Town Hall", to be sent to John Thompson, Esq., Solicitor, not later than Thursday, the 25th inst. The lowest or any Tender not necessarily accepted. CLARE AND MOSCROP,
>
> Architects, Darlington. – January 10th, 1900.[295]

10-2 Stanhope Town Hall, opened in 1901 (courtesy of Andrew Cunningham)

---

[294] *Northern Echo*, November 5, 1877
[295] Northern Echo, January 11, 1900

At the August, 1900 meeting of Stanhope Urban Council, with JW Roddam in the chair, it was announced that the Local Government Board had sanctioned the borrowing of £2,000 needed for the building of the Town Hall, but that the Public Works Commissioners had declined to make the loan. Despite the bureaucratic in-fighting, the funding was secured and the Town Hall formally opened in late 1901.

On the evening of Monday, 31st March 1902, not long after the opening, Stanhope Town Hall was the venue for the Coming of Age celebrations of Lawrie Vickers, son of William Vickers, farmer and auctioneer of Eastgate, and Tom Vickers, son of Elizabeth Vickers of Shotley House, Stanhope. About 150 guests attended the festivities and many of them enjoyed an all-night dance in the beautifully decorated Hall. A report of the event in a local paper noted that "the presents were numerous, handsome and costly".[296]

10-3 Lawrence William Vickers (1881-1867). After his grandfather Francis Vickers' death, Lawrie farmed at Belle Vue and was a respected member of the Stanhope Show Committee for 52 years and Secretary of the Wear Valley Beagles from 1918 – 1935. He wrote a monthly column for the *Northern Echo* under the by-line "Bogtrotter" about the various beagle meets.[297]

---

[296] *Auckland Times & Herald*, April 4, 1902
[297] Information about Lawrie Vickers was supplied by his granddaughter Sheila Potter.

## 11. END OF AN ERA

### *Francis Vickers: "A Man of Characteristic Generosity"*

In his 1890 letter, Francis sympathised with Thomas about his debilitating rheumatism which he described as a family complaint which he'd kept pretty clear of. But a decade later, the family complaint had caught up with him. In his last letter to Ontario in September 1901, Francis spoke of his painful rheumatism which caused him to walk with two sticks, but he nevertheless remained positive, reflecting that if not for the rheumatism, he had never felt so well for three years.

But his health soon began to fail, and he died on Saturday 24th October, 1903 at Belle Vue House at West End, Stanhope after "a lingering illness." *The Northern Echo* reported his death, noting that he was a Liberal in politics, and came "from a long-lived family, many of his ancestors having been octogenarians and nonagenarians". His obituary featured in *The Darlington & Stockton Times*:-

> A man of characteristic generosity and an expert in agriculture and business, in the person of Mr Francis Vickers, passed away at Belle Vue House, Stanhope, on Saturday night. He had reached the age of 81 years, and belonged to a family who had farmed in the Wear valley for upwards of 300 years. For over 40 years, he was a member of the Primitive Methodist Church. He leaves a widow and two sons, William of White House and Belle Vue Farms, and Joseph, the well-known auctioneer of Elm Park, Tow Law. The remains of the deceased were interred at St Thomas' Church on Wednesday. The Bishop of Richmond (Dr John J Pulleine) performed the last sad rites, extolling Mr Vickers' character, his kindly disposition and his charity. The funeral was an unusually large one, being attended by most of the leading farmers and citizens in the Wear Valley. Mr John Bell played the "Dead March" on the organ as the mourners left the church. Some beautiful wreaths were placed on the coffin, which was borne by a number of leading Primitive Methodists. The place of interment was behind the church, where members of the family for generations past have been buried.[298]

The beautiful words from another obituary, that of Featherston Philipson (1827-1881), a fellow Primitive Methodist born in Eastgate and well-known to Francis, are equally fitting for Francis Vickers:-

> In his death the church has lost a faithful Christian, his widow a loving husband, and his children a good father; but their loss is his gain. "They sorrow, but not as those that have no hope." Fallen he may be, but fallen in Christ.

> His mortal remains were laid in Stanhope Cemetery, on the green hillside, from whence may be seen the dark rounded moors, the murmuring Wear, and the dale he loved so well.[299]

---

[298] *Darlington & Stockton Times*, October 31, 1903

In the words of his son Joseph from the 1900 letter to George Vickers, Francis Vickers was no doubt "calm, contented and peaceful" to the end, trusting in his "Saviour, Jesus Christ, in whom he has confided so long." Joseph wrote that his father looked forward "by the Grace of God (to) an abundant entrance into Heaven when his journey here is finished", concluding, "My sincere prayer is that you and all our friends may meet there."

He made due provision for his wife Mary in his Will and, after a special legacy of £50 to his granddaughter Elizabeth Eleanor Vickers for her role in looking after him in his final years, the residue was divided equally amongst his twelve surviving grandchildren.

Just over 14 months after the death of Francis, his Canadian cousin George Vickers died of old age on January 2, 1905, aged 86, and was buried beside his first wife Mary Ann Bere in Fairmount, Ontario.

## *A Family Difficulty*

Joseph Vickers of Tow Law was a very powerful figure in County Durham by the time of his father's death. Tow Law Mart which he had established in 1882 had become a great success. With hundreds, sometimes thousands of stock sold at the weekly sales and special sales, and a commission of eight per cent on the selling price, Joseph had become a very wealthy man. He was widely admired for his integrity and fair-dealing, necessary qualities for a successful auctioneer. And he was a high profile public figure, a County Councillor for Tow Law and Wolsingham, frequently chairing meetings and making speeches throughout Weardale. His success was such that he increasingly lived the life of the county squire, residing with his wife Jane in a palatial mansion at Elm Park, becoming a Justice of the Peace, and serving on numerous public bodies. In short, he was a model Victorian farmer, businessman, and politician, proud of his success and widely admired for his outstanding achievements and his rectitude.

His unblemished reputation in Weardale and beyond came under significant threat when, not long after his father's death, he embarked on an affair with a housemaid at Elm Park. The threat became serious when the housemaid, Mary Elizabeth Hamilton, informed him in the Spring of 1905 that she was pregnant with his child.

Born and raised in Wolsingham where her father Joseph Hamilton was a tailor, Mary Elizabeth was well known to the Sanderson and Vickers families. As a 19 year-old in 1901, she worked as a maid in York for Sarah Ann, Jane Vickers' sister, and William Thomas Baty, a locomotive foreman originally from Waskerley, near Wolsingham. Also present was the Baty's 18 year-old nephew Arthur Vickers, the son of William Vickers of Howl John and Margaret, the sister of William Thomas Baty

Mary Elizabeth gave up her service to the Batys in York, probably returning to Weardale to work for Joseph and Jane Vickers at Elm Park when her father became seriously ill in 1903. Joseph Hamilton died of Pulmonary Phthisis, now known as tuberculosis, on January 31, 1904 at the age of 55. With Joseph likely to have been ill for several months before his death, Mary Elizabeth may have secured service at Elm Park so that she could be close to the family during a difficult time.

---

[299] *The Primitive Methodist Magazine*, 1883

# END OF AN ERA

11-1 Joseph Vickers of Tow Law (courtesy of Harry Vickers)

One scenario thereafter is that her employer Joseph Vickers, a man of similar age to her father, and a man of a "social, kindly disposition", may have provided a shoulder to cry on in her grief, and that the comfort he provided at a stressful time developed into a closer relationship.

Whatever the circumstances, as soon as Joseph learned of the pregnancy, he was naturally desperate to avoid a scandal in the family, preserve his reputation, and act as honourably as possible in the circumstances towards Mary Elizabeth Hamilton. He had a lot to lose and needed to call on all his considerable political experience to manage this extremely delicate situation.

Of course, he had the financial resources to pay off the Hamilton family, to handsomely reward them for their silence and to provide for the upbringing of the expected child. But this would have meant shame for Mary Elizabeth, the stigma of illegitimacy for the child, and the risk that the circumstances would become public knowledge and ruin his reputation. He quickly decided that the best solution was to keep the problem "in the family": he needed to find a way to incorporate Mary Elizabeth into the Vickers family, thereby protecting not only her reputation but also his own, and giving him the legitimate means of keeping in touch with, and perhaps supporting, the child's progress.

To keep it in the family he sought to persuade one of his young nephews to marry Mary Elizabeth, offering Thornley Hall Farm, Tow Law, as an inducement. First he asked his nephew, Minnie Farrage's father, Lawrie Vickers if he would marry Mary

Elizabeth, but Lawrie was already engaged to Annie Siddle[300] and declined the invitation. He then went to see Lawrence William's cousin and close friend Tom Vickers in Newcastle, where he was working at Bainbridges Department Store - which incidentally had been founded by Eastgate-born Emerson Muschamp Bainbridge in 1838, and whose brother Cuthbert Bainbridge had bred champion bulls at Howl John in the 1830s. It is not known how long Tom pondered this proposition, but the arrangement may well have been sealed not only with the promise of the farm but also with Joseph adopting his fatherless nephew (See Obituary of Joseph Vickers, page 171) and offering him an immediate partnership in Tow Law Auction Mart Company Ltd.

Tom Vickers, described as an Auctioneer on the marriage certificate, married Mary Elizabeth Hamilton, Domestic Servant, on September 19, 1905 at Thornley Parish Church. They were married by licence, thus avoiding the need for banns which would have caused delay and drawn unwanted attention to the wedding. It is noteworthy that the witnesses at the ceremony were Joseph Vickers himself and Frank Sanderson of Nafferton, the brother of Jane Vickers and whose prime motive would have been to protect and support his sister.

Joseph, a God-fearing man who for the most part had led an exemplary life, must have found the ceremony stressful. Any relief he felt when no just cause or impediment was declared will have been overtaken by an even greater feeling of relief once the minister concluded:-

> Forasmuch as Thomas Herbert and Mary Elizabeth have consented together in holy wedlock, and have witnessed the same before God and this company, and thereto have given and pledged their troth either to other, and have declared the same by giving and receiving of a Ring, and by joining of hands; I pronounce that they be Man and Wife together, in the Name of the Father, and of the Son, and of the Holy Ghost. Amen.

Whatever Joseph felt on that day, to the outside world appearances and family honour were officially preserved, although there would have been the inevitable gossip in such a close-knit community where everyone tended to know everyone else's business. The *Auckland Chronicle* appeared to acknowledge this, reporting that the marriage "had been the subject of much interest,"[301] when the family would clearly wish for a very low-profile event. Family members and close acquaintances will have certainly known the truth: Mary Elizabeth's puzzling pregnancy and the late and abrupt emergence of Newcastle-based Tom Vickers as the intended bridegroom would have raised questions. And no doubt to her great personal distress at the time, Jane Vickers will have known only too well of her husband's infidelity, particularly given that Mary Elizabeth was living at Elm Park before her marriage to Tom Vickers.

---

[300] Lawrence William Vickers married Annie Siddell (sic) in Houghton-le-Spring in 1906
[301] *Auckland Chronicle*, September 21, 1905

# END OF AN ERA

11-2 Sanderson Cousins: Frank Sanderson of Nafferton, a witness at the wedding; Ruth Kipling, married to John Walton Watson; Jane, wife of Joseph Vickers of Tow Law; and Tom Sanderson of Broomley Farm

And what of the feelings of Mary Elizabeth Hamilton when she found herself pregnant by Joseph? She will have known that such a prominent public figure who traded on his integrity and trustworthiness, would be desperate to avoid a scandal and that there would be no question of him giving up his marriage. Whatever she felt, she must have quickly agreed to Joseph's plan to find her a husband.

Less than four months after the wedding Mary Elizabeth gave birth to a girl, Jennie Hamilton Vickers, on January 13, 1906, at Elm Park. It is not known whether Thomas and Mary Elizabeth developed an affection for each other during their marriage, or whether it remained a strictly business arrangement. To the outside world, they will have presented themselves as man and wife, but the reality may have been different. If a genuine affection had developed between Mary Elizabeth and Joseph, then there is a remote possibility that the relationship continued after her marriage. We will never know the full story, but we do know that Tom's life was transformed: the career at Bainbridges abandoned, he was now a young farmer, an auctioneer at Tow Law Mart, and living at Thornley Hall with a wife and child he had acquired through an arrangement with his uncle.

Francis Vickers of Belle Vue who died in 1903 was spared the discomfort that may have accompanied these events, but what of his wife Mary? The family may have considered it wise to keep Mary in the dark, given her age and sensibilities. If so, she will have delighted in the birth of Jennie Hamilton Vickers as a great granddaughter rather than the granddaughter she was.

Tom Vickers' life was further transformed less than three years after the marriage when Mary Elizabeth Vickers succumbed, like her father before her, to Pulmonary Tuberculosis on 27th October 1908 at Thornley Hall, the death being reported by her brother-in-law, Francis Edwin Vickers who had been present at the death. Her unacknowledged mother-in-law, Mary Vickers of Belle Vue House, was spared some sadness: she died a few months before Mary Elizabeth and 18 months before the death of her eldest son.

Jennie Hamilton Vickers was adopted by Jane and Joseph at Elm Park, less than a mile from Thornley. To the world at large, Joseph and Jane had, admirably, adopted Jennie Hamilton Vickers following the tragic death of her mother. Jane may have felt at least some initial discomfort about this, but for Joseph, notwithstanding the sadness and regret he would have felt at the untimely death of Mary Elizabeth, it was a remarkably convenient outcome.

Given that there were no direct descendants to inherit his considerable wealth, is it possible that Joseph deliberately set out to produce a direct heir through his relationship with Mary Elizabeth? It is possible but unlikely, as the potential ruinous consequences would have been obvious to him, whereas the fortuitous solution he found could not have been foreseen. Nor could he have foreseen the tragedy of Mary Elizabeth's early death, which presented Joseph with the opportunity to adopt Jennie Hamilton Vickers and make her a major beneficiary under his Will. There is some irony in the fact that Jane the surrogate mother was actually related by blood to Jennie because of the earlier connection between the Sanderson and Vickers families: they were second cousins, once removed. And Joseph's untimely death four years later meant that Jane became the sole parent, responsible for raising Jennie Hamilton Vickers.

11-3 Jennie Hamilton Vickers on a postcard from Elm Park
sent to my grandfather, Frank Sanderson at Hamsterley in 1911.

# END OF AN ERA

## *Joseph Vickers: "An out-and-out public man"*

A year after Joseph and Jane formally adopted Jennie, Joseph Vickers died on Boxing Day 1909 at the age of 58. Under the headline "DEATH OF COUNCILLOR VICKERS: A Well-known Auctioneer and Agricultural Expert", his obituary appeared in a local newspaper:-

> Very general respect was expressed when it became known on Sunday afternoon that the death had taken place at Elm Park Hall of Councillor Joseph Vickers, JP. The deceased was a native of Weardale, being the eldest son of the late Mr Frank Vickers of Belle Vue, Stanhope. He was known throughout the North of England as an auctioneer and farmer, few men being more widely known. He came of a noted long-lived family who have lived for ages in Weardale. They farmed Howl John, Pease Myers, Guy's Close, Cold Knuckles, and other well-known Weardale farms.
>
> He was recognised as an expert and leading authority in all matters pertaining to agriculture and the breeding of horses, cattle, sheep, etc. He was famous as a breeder of cattle and sheep, and he bred the famous bull *Duke of Howl John*. His black-faced sheep were often successful at Royal Shows, country shows, and at practically all shows of merit on the country.
>
> He founded the Tow Law Auction Mart in 1882, which, under his supervision, has become one of the most popular marts in the North. He was a splendid judge of stock and an expert auctioneer, a born talker. He afterwards formed the mart into a limited company.
>
> Mr Vickers was county councillor for the Tow Law and Wolsingham division for several years, being succeeded by Mr A Wooler. At the time of his demise, he was a member of the Weardale District Council, sitting for the Thornley ward. He was also a member of the Weardale Assessment Committee up to last year. He was besides a member of the Joint Hospital Committee for Infectious Diseases, and was an out-and-out public man.
>
> Of a social, kindly disposition, he made hosts of friends all over the district, among whom his loss will be keenly felt. His residence at Elm Park was palatial, a veritable paradise on the sloping banks of the Wear. His widow who is left to mourn his loss, was, to her marriage with Mr Vickers, Miss Sanderson, of Bradley Hall. She also belonged to an old and respected farming family in Weardale. Mr Vickers had no family, but he adopted his nephew, Mr T.H Vickers, who has assisted him in his business. Mr Vickers was extremely well-known over a very wide area, and he was highly respected. He was a Freemason and connected with the Hudson Masonic Lodge, and also the Tow Law Lodge of which he was a Junior Warden, and also with the Crook Lodge.[302]

---

[302] *South Durham and Auckland Chronicle*, December 30, 1909

The obituary is accurate in all respects except perhaps one: although Joseph did become a very successful breeder and exhibitor in particular of black-faced sheep, it is not true that he bred the *Duke of Howl John*. Joseph was a 23 year-old farmer at the family farm at Pease Myers when the famous white shorthorn bull was bred in 1874 at Howl John by his grandfather Joseph Vickers and his uncles John and William Vickers.

Joseph's funeral at Thornley Church was attended by a large number of family members, Masonic brethren, farmers and cattle breeders, and also of friends and business acquaintances from far and wide, making it one of the largest funerals ever held in this part of the world. The service was led by the Bishop of Richmond, the Right Rev Dr John J Pulleine of Stanhope who six years earlier had officiated at the funeral of Joseph's father, Francis Vickers of Belle Vue.

In his Will, each of his nephews and nieces received cash and shares in the Tow Law Auction Mart Company Limited.[303] In addition, Lawrence William Vickers of Belle Vue was given Joseph's house and land at Park House, Stanhope. And true to a promise he had made several years earlier, Joseph declared:-

> I give devise and bequeath unto my said nephew Thomas Herbert Vickers my farm known as Thornley Hall and Thornley Grange Tow Law aforesaid together with all the implements live and dead agricultural stock thereon and all the articles upon the said farm for his own use and benefit absolutely.

The only proviso was that his wife Jane should be allowed to live rent free at Thornley Hall if she wished. The greatest part of the complex Will is devoted to ensuring that Jane has sufficient funds for "maintaining, educating and bringing up in a manner suitable to her station in life my adopted daughter Jennie Hamilton Vickers".

Tom Vickers was the natural successor to his uncle at Tow Law Auction Mart which remained in the Vickers family until it closed in September 2005. At the time of the 1911 Census, Tom, an Auctioneer and Valuer, was living at Thornley Hall with his brother Francis Edwin, a joiner, and sister Mary Edith, a dairy maid. Shortly afterwards, Tom married policeman's daughter Florence May (Florrie) Snowdon in 1911 at Stanhope. Thereafter, he steadfastly maintained the public version of the events concerning his first marriage, that after his wife's death, he had given up his daughter to his uncle for adoption, and that Jennie Hamilton Vickers was a half-sister to the children of his second marriage. In legal terms and in the eyes of the Church, Tom's position was the correct one, but in reality, Jennie was his first cousin, and first cousin once removed to his children.

Jane Vickers was still at Elm Park in 1911, looking after 5 year-old "niece" Jennie Hamilton Vickers with the assistance of two servant girls. By the end of the First World War, she had moved to Hexham to be near to her brothers, Frank and Tom Sanderson. Frank's son John Thomas Sanderson and his daughter Jennie once went to stay with Jane Vickers at Broomley Villa, Hexham in about 1920. Jennie was getting ready to go to a dance when her father said, "Your Auntie wants you." Jennie went to her great aunt's room and was stunned to receive a cheque for £100[304]. That was a lot of money in those days, but Joseph Vickers had left what was a considerable fortune of £22,000[305] to Jane.

---

[303] Tow Law Auction Mart became a limited company on November 3, 1904.
[304] £100 in 1909 would have the purchasing power of over £8,000 in 2010

# END OF AN ERA

Jane died in Hexham on August 11 1933, aged 82 years. In her Will, drawn up on April 1 1926, her adopted daughter Jennie Hamilton Vickers was bequeathed her furniture and household effects, linen, jewellery and other personal effects, with the residue of the estate, after expenses, being divided equally between brothers Frank and Thomas Sanderson. Significantly, in a Codicil to the Will drawn up 4 months before her death, Jane bequeathed Broomley Villa "together with the land and buildings belonging thereto" to her beloved adopted daughter, Jennie Hamilton Vickers.

Jane's brother-in-law William Vickers junior of Pease Myers died of a stroke and exhaustion in 1920, the death being reported by daughter-in-law Annie Vickers, the wife of Lawrie Vickers of Belle Vue.

## *Concluding Remarks*

From the moment I saw the letters of Francis Vickers about six years ago, they have held a fascination which I know is shared by others who have had the good fortune to see them. They have been the inspiration behind this book, the research for which has provided many insights into this remarkable period in the history of Weardale.

The second half of the nineteenth century, from the time that George and Thomas Vickers migrated to Ontario, Canada, to 1901 when Queen Victoria died and Francis wrote his final letter to cousin Thomas, was a time of great change in England. The number of people working on the land declined from nearly 1.4 million in 1851 to less than 0.8 million by the turn of the century. Many had migrated to the colonies in search of a better life, and many others had moved to the towns and cities where wages were higher. For farmers, the loss of labour was partly offset by the increasing use of machinery, but they faced hardship from the late 1870s because of a succession of poor seasons. Furthermore, by the 1870s, the United States of America and the flourishing British Empire were a source of cheap produce and stock to feed a growing population, and this also contributed to hardship for farmers, not least in Weardale. The industrial workers of the dale also experienced periodic distress not only as a result of decline in lead and ironstone production but also because of on-going disputes between the extraction companies and the Ecclesiastical Commissioners. As a consequence there was a steady migration from Weardale of farmers (including members of the Vickers family), miners, and quarrymen, many of them seeking opportunities far from home in Australasia, America and Canada. The Weardale Museum at Ireshopeburn has records of correspondence between Victorian migrants and their kin back in Weardale, including copies of the letters of Francis Vickers to his Canadian cousins.

It is noteworthy that County Durham in general and Weardale in particular was staunchly Liberal, i.e., radical and progressive, and led by enlightened politicians like Sir Joseph Whitwell Pease and Major Frederick Beaumont. Dissent predominated in the dale and encompassed not only the miners, quarrymen and agricultural labourers, but also many establishment figures and successful tenant farmers like Francis Vickers of Belle Vue. This dissent together with progressive political ideas meant that there was a great appetite in the dale for change, for extending the suffrage (but not just yet for women) and attaining true representation in Parliament, for trade unionism, for reforming the House of Lords, for reducing the power of the landlords and the clergy, and there were

---

[305] £22,000 in 1909 would be worth £7.34M in 2010 in terms of average earnings

even strong calls for disestablishment of the Anglican Church. One surprise was the passionate support for Irish Home Rule, although not so surprising on closer examination when it became clear that there was a strong identification of Weardale folk - who at various times suffered at the hands of the Church, absentee landlords, and mine owners - with the oppressed rural Irish working class. Many of the issues of political reform promoted by these radical Victorians were implemented, but over 100 years later, some remain unresolved. The Irish Question is now being addressed through the Peace Process, but the course of Anglo-Irish relations might have been quite different and perhaps less "troublesome" if Gladstone's efforts to establish Irish Home Rule had been successful.

I had long known that my farming kin from Weardale were successful tenant farmers, but I had not appreciated just how influential many of them had been in the dale. Joseph Vickers of Howl John and his sons were noted for their expertise in stockbreeding and brought great prestige to the dale when the white shorthorn bull, *Duke of Howl John* was Champion Bull at the 1880 Royal Show at Carlisle. Joseph's son William of Howl John and his grandson William of Pease Myers, were progressive in their politics, providing leadership to farmers and quarrymen through their radical speeches. To the undoubted annoyance of many of the establishment figures in the dale, they advocated representation of farmers by farmers in the House of Commons, campaigned for more land to be brought into cultivation rather than be kept for game, for rent reductions, and for farmers to work in combination. It was not least through their efforts that The Wear Valley Farmers' Club was established in 1882. William of Pease Myers' brother, Joseph Vickers of Tow Law, was also instrumental in establishing the Farmers' Club, and the same year established Tow Law Auction Mart which brought a new lease of life to Tow Law and made Joseph a wealthy man.

Today, there are few members of the family bearing the surname "Vickers" left in the dale, but their presence there from at least the seventeenth century means that the numerous descendants will have left an enduring imprint on Weardale. And migration of family members in the Victorian period, even if only those mentioned in these pages are considered, means that there are now thousands of descendants in the United States, Canada and Australasia. There are many stories still to be told.

11-4 Jane Vickers nee Sanderson (1851-1933). Jane left the bulk of her substantial estate to her adopted daughter, Jennie Hamilton Vickers.

# INDEX

## A

Abraham, William MP for Limerick · 96
Allison, Joseph (champion wrestler) · 25, 97
Ambler, William Hammond · 113
Arnison, Dr Charles · 75, 76, 106, 110, 142
Atkinson, James of Mordon · 74
Atkinson, Margaret (Sanderson) · 56
Attwood, Charles of Wolsingham · 26

## B

Backhouse, Charles J · 59, 110
Backhouse, Edmund (MP) · 32
Bainbridge, Cuthbert jnr · 16
Baty, Margaret (Vickers) · 127, 132
Baty, Thomas · 127
Baty, William Thomas · 127, 166
Beaumont, Major Frederick MP for South Durham · 25, 28, 32, 173
Beaumont, Walter · 47, 48, 49, 50, 140
Beaumont, Wentworth Blacket · 31, 47, 48, 134
Bell, John (Music Teacher) · 117, 165
Bell, Mary Anne (Vickers) · 51
Bell, Willy of Heathery Cleugh · 110, 111
Belle Vue Farm · v, 8, 10, 16, 17, 21, 40, 45, 51, 68, 143, 155, 159, 164
Benson, John (Registrar) · 160, 162
Bents Show · 140
Bere, Mary Ann (Vickers) · 15, 21, 166
Bird, William of West Hartlepool · 132
Blacklaw, Elizabeth (Reed) · 41, 51, 64, 65
Blenkiron, James (Chief Agent of Weardale Mining Co) · 75
Booth, General William · 148
Bowles, Thomas Gibson · 29
Bowman, Mary (Vickers) · 3, 4, 16, 21, 100, 116, 169
Bowman, William · 16, 39
Bray, Peter · 26
Brennan, Bridget (Vickers) · 88
Briens, Sergeant William · 121
Bright, Richard Jnr · 141
Bright, Richard of Cowshill · 65, 141
Brough Hill Fair · 106
Brown, Francis of Greenhead · 41, 64, 127
Brown, Hannah (Heads) · 126
Brown, Joseph of Greenhead · 12, 64
Brown, Peter · 66
Buchannan, Arthur of Guisborough · 71

Burdett, Sir Francis · 60
Burdus, Mary (Heads) · 126, 129
Burke, Patrick of Wolsingham · 153
Burt, Thomas MP for Morpeth · 24
Butcher, Horace · 75, 76
Butler, Joseph (Rector of Stanhope) · 61
Butler, Samuel (1613-1680) · 60

## C

Cain, Joseph Cowper, Mining Agent · 25, 31, 40, 47
Canney, Dr George of Bishop Auckland · 22
Carr, John T of Cowshill · 148
Cat Castle Bridge · 42, 43
Chamberlain, Joseph (Liberal Statesman) · 7
Charlton, William (Stanhope Stationmaster) · 138
Clarkson, Thomas (Anti-slavery campaigner) · 132
Clayton, Annie (Vickers) · 130, 159
Cleveland, Duke of · 58
Cobbold, Rev Richard of Wortham · 11
Collingwood, Elizabeth (Vickers) · 3, 10, 37, 92, 103
Collingwood, Featherstone · 92
Collingwood, Francis · 92
Collingwood, John · 92
Collingwood, John Jnr · 131
Cooke, William of Hexham · 53
Copeland, Robert · 74
Cotton, Mary Ann (Poisoner) · 21
Coulthard, John (Black Jack of Bedlington) · 57
Coulthard, Samuel of Middlesbrough · 57
Craig, Sheila (Hogarth) · 12
Crawhall, Charles Edward · 87, 104
Crawhall, John · 56, 77, 87, 104, 117, 132
Crawhall, Judith Maud · 87, 118
Crawhall, Mary · 87, 118
Crawhall, Thomas · 63, 75, 77, 87, 162
Crawhall, Thomas Currah · 87
Crosby, June · v, 1, 20, 94, 156
Currah, Annie (Crawhall) · 87, 148
Currah, Emerson of Woodcroft · 147
Currah, Joseph Stephenson · 87
Curry, George of Wolsingham · 75, 76, 107, 124, 158

## D

Dalkin, John Myers of Westgate · 121, 139

175

Darlington Hiring Fair · 33, 34
Davison, Jane (Vickers) · 161
Dawson, Isabella (Bowman) · 16
Dawson, Joseph of Ireshopeburn · 110, 111
Dawson, Thomas · 122
Dent, Rev William (PM Minister) · 19
Devey, Dr Thomas of Wolsingham · 122
Disraeli, Benjamin · 30, 31, 50
Dix, Charles (Solicitor) · 109, 110, 111
Dixon, Alice (Vickers) · 15, 126
Dodson, John George (Liberal MP) · 60
Dowson, John of Newlands · 160
Dun, Finlay (Journalist) · 58
Dunn, Edward of Shildon · 34, 103

## E

Easton, Dr John of St John's Chapel · 148
Eddowes, Rev John of Eastgate · 117, 125
Education Act, 1870 · 23
Edward VII, King · 159
Egglestone, William Morley · 40, 67, 97, 129, 135, 136, 140
Elliot, George William, (MP for Northallerton) · 22
Elm Park, Tow Law · 160, 169, 170
Emerson, Frances Priscilla (Currah) · 87
Emerson, Richard of Frosterley · 96
Errington, Roger of Sunderland · 54
Espin, Reverend Thomas · 122, 123, 124, 151
Eusemere, Ullswater · 132, 133, 138, 160

## F

Featherston, Jacob Ralph of Black Dean · 19, 78, 96
Featherston, Sarah · 39
Ferguson, John of West Cornforth · 153
Fish, Gertrude (Pearson) · 103
Flood, The Great Weardale · 68
Fry, Theodore (MP for Darlington) · 23
Furby, Jane (Vickers) · 34, 101, 103
Furby, John · 34

## G

General Election of 1874 · 27, 28
**Gilmore, Rev Hugh** · 20, 23, 24, 40
Gladstone, William Ewart · 7, 30, 31, 50, 69, 70, 84, 96, 108, 121, 122, 149
Glendinning, James, The Flying Tailor of Allendale Town · 57

Greenhead · v, 7, 8, 9, 12, 13, 35, 64, 65, 127, 128, 161

## H

Hackworth, Timothy · 113
Hamilton, Joseph of Wolsingham · 166
Hamilton, Mary Elizabeth (Vickers) · 166, 167, 168, 169
Hamsterley · 1, 4
Harrison, Sheila (Potter) · 5, 7, 53
Heads, Joseph of Greenfoot · 125, 126
Heatherington, David (Weardale Museum) · v, 106
Heatherington, Ken (Weardale Museum) · vi
Heslop, George · 103
Hildyard, John Arundel · 125, 130
Hildyard, JRW of Horsley Hall · 40, 53, 55, 89, 92, 99, 100
Hodgson, Brown of Heatherycleugh · 57
Hodgson, John R of Crook · 150
Hodgson, Jonathan (Master, Stanhope Workhouse · 76
Howl John Farm · 3, 7, 8, 16, 37, 53, 55, 88, 114, 128, 130, 131, 132, 168, 172
Howl John, Duke of · 38, 53, 55, 88, 132, 171, 172
Howl John, Prince of · 55
Hurricanes in America · 102, 105
Hutchinson, Richard of Howl John · 16

## I

Influenza Epidemic of 1889-90 · 118
Irish Home Rule · 70, 95, 121, 149, 174

## J

Jaynes, Thomas (Solicitor) · 121
Job's Hill Farm · 92
Johnson, Jane (Benson) · 162
Johnson, William of Catton · 57

## K

Kandahar, Battle of, 1880 · 55
Kelly, Ned · 55
Knight, Rev JGB of Eastgate · 131

# INDEX

## L

Lattimer, Andrew  PM Minister · 83
Lazenby, George · 19
Little Jimmy · 106, 140, 141, Wilkinson, James
Little, George of Eastgate · 53, 125, 129
Livingstone, Dr Thomas · 83, 87, 100, 113, 114, 122, 124, 158
Lloyd-George, David · 108
Longstaffe, Joseph · 128
Love, William of Wolsingham · 59
Lyall, Edward (Civil Engineer) · 135, 136

## M

Maddison, Joseph of Hill End · 76, 80, 95, 96
March Monday · See Darlington Hiring Fair
Marshall, Mildred Dorothea of Darlington · 148, 149
Maw, George (Solicitor) · 62
McLean, Lemuel Booth of North Dakota · 117, 155
McLean, Thomas A · 155
McNaughton, Prof David · 61
Methodism · 1
Mewburn, Robert · 122
Mews, Richard · 40, 139, 140, 141, 142
Milbank, Sir Frederick of Teesdale · 90
Moore, Annie Dixon (Crawhall) · 117, 118, 132
Moore, Hannah (Morley) · 118
Moore, John · 117
Moore, Thomas · 117
Morgan, Jane (Vickers) · 5, 12, 161
Morley, Annie · 118
Morley, Henry · 76, 129
Morley, William Jnr · 40, 74, 75, 76, 80, 83, 117, 118, 129
Morley, William Snr · 27, 40, 53
Morris, Sydney  Home Rule Advocate · 95
Moses, Thomas of Tow Law · 158
Muschamp, John Dover · 19

## N

Neave, Mary Blanche (Hildyard) · 100
Nicholson, John Edward of Lanchester · 129

## P

Parker, William of Haydon Bridge · 97
Parnell, Charles Irish Nationalist · 70, 96
Patrick, Ralph of Stewart Shield Meadows · 91
Patrick, Thomas of Steward Shield Meadows · 77, 91
Pearson, George · 27, 34, 42, 43
Pearson, Joseph Vickers · 35, 42, 103
Pease Myers · v, 8, 9, 10, 13, 39, 55, 128, 129, 143, 172
Pease, Arthur · 71, 72, 73, 91
Pease, Henry Fell · 19, 23
Pease, Henry of Stanhope Castle · 20, 134
Pease, Joseph (1799-1872) · 32
Pease, Sir Joseph Whitwell · 25, 28, 32, 72, 122, 131, 135, 137, 138, 148, 149, 173
Pentland, Thomas of Ireshopeburn · 132, 141, 148, 155
Petty, Sarah (Vickers) · 55, 117, 134, 159
Philipson, Featherston · 165
Philipson, John · 96
Philipson, Margaret (Patrick) · 91
Philipson, Mary Jane (Stephenson) · 128
Philipson, Ralph · 96
Philipson, Rev Emmerson · 101
Philipson, Thomas of Eastgate · 76, 128
Pickering, Henry of East Newlands · 160
Primitive Methodism · 18, 19, 20, 23, 24, 102, 116, 155, 165
Prince of Howl John · 88
Proud, John Thomas (Solicitor) · 109, 111
Pulleine, Dr John J.  Bishop of Richmond · 124, 130, 158, 165, 172

## Q

Queen's Jubilee · 69, 71, 73, 74, 148

## R

Race, Councillor George of Westgate · 148, 149
Railway, Opening of Weardale Extension · 137
Railways · 4, 11
Raine, Esther (Crawhall) · 87
**Raine, Mary (Vickers)** · 4, 11
Red Rosette · 53
Reed, George · 42, 89
Reed, Jane (Vickers) · 37, 42
Reed, John · 27, 41
Reed, Joseph Henry · 77
Reed, Lizzie Jane · 77
Reed, Margaret (Sanderson) · 42, 56
Reed, Mary (Brown) · 41, 64, 126
Reed, Matthew Jnr · 42, 129
Reed, Matthew of Shield Ash · 64
Reed, Thomas Matthew · 77
Rent Reductions · 79, 90, 130
Ridley, John · 76
Ridley, Margaret (Crawhall) · 87

177

Ridley, Matthew of Peakfield · 80
Ridley, William of Tow Law · 75
Rippon, William · 63, 92
Robinson, Ann of Elm Park · 107
Robinson, Joseph of Huntshieldford · 48
Robinson, Robert (Land Agent) · 107
Robinson, Thomas of Shield Ash · 79
Robson, John of Ireshopeburn · 57
Robson, William · 121
Roddam, John Joseph of Newtown · 40
Roddam, John of Steward Shield Meadows · 91
Roddam, John Watson · 68, 125, 141, 158, 164
Rosebury, Lord · 122
Ross, John of Tow Law · 111
Rowland, Robert · 83, 84
Rowlandson, Samuel of Newton Morrell · 59, 60, 90, 92
Rudd, William of Middlesbrough · 57
Ruddick, Young of Staindrop · 57
Rumney, Thomas · 47, 48

## S

Salisbury, Lord · 70, 122
Sanderson, Elizabeth (Vickers) · 55, 129, 159
Sanderson, Francis of Hamsterley · 1
Sanderson, Francis of Harperley · 39
Sanderson, Frank of Nafferton · 4, 168, 169, 173
Sanderson, Jane (Reed) · 42
Sanderson, Jane (Vickers) · 55, 65, 74, 168, 169, 171
Sanderson, Jennie (Thompson) · 172
Sanderson, John of Broomley · 39
Sanderson, John of Harperley · 2, 4, 127
Sanderson, John Thomas · 172
Sanderson, Margaret (Hall) · 39
Sanderson, Mary (Stephenson) · 39
Sanderson, Ruth Kipling (Watson) · 74, 111, 169
Sanderson, Sarah Ann (Baty) · 127, 166
Sanderson, Thomas Jnr of Thimbleby Hill · 8, 51, 56, 59, 64, 68, 76, 92, 114
**Sanderson, Thomas of Broomley Farm** · 169, 173
Sanderson, Thomas Snr of Thimbleby Hill · 56
Sandow, Eugen · 111, 112, 113
Schofield, Rev James · 117, 131, 132
Scott, Mary (Vickers) · 34, 161
Seaham Colliery Disaster, 1880 · 55
Siddle, Ada Florence of Victoria · 36
Siddle, Annie (Vickers) · 168
Siddle, Frank Jardine of Victoria · 36
Siddle, George Henry · 27, 35
Siddle, Joseph Herbert Vickers of Victoria · 36
Siddle, Mary Jane of Victoria · 36
Siddle, Robyn Dianne (Roper) · 5, 7, 36
Siddle, William · 35, 36

Sim, George Robert (Dramatist and Poet) · 26
Sinclair, James · 55
**Sisson, Robert (Blacksmith)** · 156
Slater, Richard of Earnwell · 65
Snowball, Hannah (Morley) · 40
Snowball, William of Wolsingham · 124
Snowdon, Florrie (Vickers) · 172
Stanhope School Board · 23, 24
Stanhope Town Hall · 24, 110, 160, 162, 163
Stanhope Workhouse · 26, 74, 76, 113
Starforth, Thomas of Spennymoor · 133
Stead, William Thomas, Editor of *Northern Echo* · 6, 45, 50, 151
Stephenson, George (Railway Pioneer) · 4
Stephenson, Henry of Billingshield · 40, 128
Stephenson, John Henry of Billingshield · 74, 125, 128
Sterling, David · 64
Steward Shield Meadows · 91, 92
Stobart JP, William Culley · 21, 22, 23
Stobart, Henry Smith. · 22
Stotsfield Burn · 16
Sweet Wells Farm · 40, 53, 74

## T

Taft, William Howard, US President · 7
Taylor-Smith JP, George of Colepike Hall · 86, 151
Taylor-Smith, John D of Colepike Hall · 133
Teale, John (Solicitor) · 121
Temperley, Harriet · 100
Thompson, Flora · 108
Thompson, Isaac · 109
Thompson, James of Hurworth-on-Tees · 23
Thompson, John (Solicitor) · 63, 163
Thompson, Robert of Ferryfield · 76
Tinkler, Francis (1824-1896) · 127
Titanic · 7
Tom Tidler's Ground · 107
Toronto, near Bishop Auckland · 22
Tow Law Mart · 74, 84, 86, 111, 133, 149, 151, 152, 171
Toyn, Joseph of Cleveland · 83
Trotter, William of South Acomb · 59
Trustlove, Thomas · 21, 22

## V

Vickers, Alice Maria (McLean) · 117, 155
Vickers, Archibald of Dean Head · 34
Vickers, Arthur · 166
Vickers, Charles Jnr of Snowsfield · 7, 8, 40, 56, 57
Vickers, Charles of Ontario · 117

# INDEX

Vickers, Charles Snr of Snowsfield · 56
Vickers, Elizabeth (1860-62) · 17
Vickers, Elizabeth (Walton) · 37, 53, 103
Vickers, Elizabeth (Watson) · 12
Vickers, Elizabeth Eleanor · 55, 118, 159
Vickers, Elizabeth of Mown Meadows (Naisby) · 37, 46
Vickers, Emily · 118
Vickers, Ethel · 118
Vickers, Frances of Dean Head · 64
Vickers, Francis Edwin · 86, 169, 172
Vickers, Francis of Belle Vue · 3, 4, 5, 9, 10, 20, 21, 40, 42, 126, 169, 171, 173
Vickers, Francis of Dean Head · 34
Vickers, Francis of Pease Myers and Stotsfield Burn · 39, 40
Vickers, Frank (1749-1822) · 11
Vickers, Frank of Dean Head · 27, 34, 51, 103, 154, 155, 160, 161
Vickers, Frank of Ox Close Farm · 17, 40, 50, 55, 77, 86, 128
Vickers, George (1865-66) · 17
Vickers, George William of Ontario · 5, 9, 13, 47, 65, 88, 96, 166
Vickers, Hannah of Great Aycliffe · 34
Vickers, Isaac of Victoria, Australia · 35
Vickers, Isabella (Crawhall) · 17, 40, 56, 77, 86, 104
Vickers, Jane (Scott) · 35
Vickers, Jane (Siddle) · 27, 35
Vickers, Jane Ann (Pearson) · 27, 34, 61, 101, 103
Vickers, Jennie Hamilton · 169, 170, 172, 173
Vickers, John of Great Aycliffe · 103
Vickers, John of Greenhead · 5, 35, 64, 161
Vickers, John of Mown Meadows · 7, 37, 42, 53, 55, 88, 160
Vickers, Joseph of East Thickley · 27, 34, 51, 61, 62, 103
Vickers, Joseph of Howl John · 3, 4, 7, 11, 37, 47, 88, 154, 174
Vickers, Joseph of Mown Meadows · 37, 46
Vickers, Joseph of Snowsfield · 57
Vickers, Joseph of Tow Law · 16, 40, 50, 55, 59, 74, 77, 84, 85, 86, 115, 118, 121, 131, 133, 148, 151, 154, 160, 166, 171, 172, 174
Vickers, Joseph of Victoria, Australia · 27, 35, 103
Vickers, Ken of Greenfoot · 7
Vickers, Lawrence William of Belle Vue · 128, 159, 164, 168, 172
Vickers, Margaret (Heslop) · 34, 103
Vickers, Margaret (Reed) · 42, 77, 89
Vickers, Margaret (Sanderson) · 3, 4, 127
Vickers, Margaret of Snowsfield · 57
Vickers, Margaret of Stotsfield Burn · 39
Vickers, Mary (Dunn) · 103
Vickers, Mary (McLean) · 155
Vickers, Mary Annie (1884-97) · 78, 118, 134
Vickers, Mary Edith · 86, 172
Vickers, Mary of Greenhead · 35
Vickers, Mary of Mown Meadows · 38, 53, 160
Vickers, Mary of Snowsfield · 57
Vickers, Matthew of Mown Meadows · 37, 46
Vickers, Minnie (Farrage) · 2, 37
Vickers, Thomas Herbert of Thornley Hall · 86, 129, 164, 168, 169, 171, 172
Vickers, Thomas of Ontario · 5, 9, 13, 15, 96, 126, 155
Vickers, Thomas of Stotsfield Burn · 39
Vickers, William (1853-53) · 17
Vickers, William of Howl John · 37, 53, 74, 76, 80, 83, 84, 88, 91, 107, 114, 124, 127, 130, 131, 132, 138, 174
Vickers, William of Pease Myers · 17, 40, 50, 53, 55, 78, 79, 80, 81, 97, 111, 117, 129, 133, 141, 143, 159, 173, 174
Vickers, William of Snowsfield · 57, 59
Victoria, Queen · 10, 69, 73, 159

## W

Waistell, William (Teesdale Guardian) · 76
Walton, Joseph · 53, 103, 162
Waskerley · 23, 55, 143, 166
Watson, John of Earnwell · 65
Watson, John of Greenhead · 12
Watson, John Walton · 74, 110, 111, 121, 153
Watson, Ralph · 132
Watson, William of Short Thorns · 109, 110
Watson, William of White House · 40, 81, 92, 107, 132
Wearmouth, Mary Jane (Tinkler) · 127
Weeks, Henry of Victoria · 36
Wheatley, Robert of Tow Law · 133
White Duke · 53
Whitfield, Jane (Vickers) of Pease Myers · 39
Whitfield, Thomas · 97
Wilkinson, James · *Little Jimmy*
Wilkinson, Rev George Pearson · 107
Wilson, John of Newlandside · 51, 53
Women's Suffrage · 24, 71
Wood, Constable John · 121
Wooler, Arthur of Wolsingham · 171
Wren, John of Wolsingham · 76
Wyld, James (Liberal MP) · 60

## ABOUT THE AUTHOR

Frank Sanderson was born in 1946 in Barnard Castle and was brought up in St Helens Auckland. He attended King James 1 Grammar School, Bishop Auckland before graduating as a teacher in the 1960s. After a brief school-teaching career, Frank returned to the University of Leeds to complete a Masters degree, followed by a Doctorate in 1974. In 1975, he and colleagues at Liverpool Polytechnic launched the first Sports Science degree in Western Europe. He was awarded a professorship in Health Sciences at Liverpool John Moores University in 1992.

A former county squash player, Frank is an experienced skier, an optimistic golfer and an enthusiastic gardener. He has been an active family and local history researcher since the 1970s and, after recently retiring, relishes the opportunity to spend more time on this absorbing interest.

fhsand35@yahoo.co.uk

Made in the USA
Charleston, SC
29 October 2012